Grace Will
Lead Me Home

ROBIN GIVENS

—⚬⚬⚬—

Grace Will Lead Me Home

miramax books

HYPERION

NEW YORK

ISBN 1-4013-5246-4
ISBN-13: 978-1-4013-5246-2
First Edition
10 9 8 7 6 5 4 3 2 1

Dedication

This book is dedicated to my Lord and my Savior.

And . . . I would like to dedicate this book to all of the fatherless daughters who grow up feeling abandoned and unworthy of "good" love. I always felt that if I weren't good enough, pretty enough, perfect enough, worthy enough for the first man in my life to be with me, stay with me, stick with me, and simply love me . . . then how would and why would any other man do what my father could not or would not do? How could any man love me? I never said the words and it was a very long time before I recognized the feelings. But now that I have I recognized the pain and realized my behavior I have also come to know I am not alone. What you may not know is that neither are you alone, in spite of the emptiness our fathers have left in our hearts. Soon you will be searching (though unawares) for a man with whom you can repeat the very same scenario. For all of the abandoned little girls searching to fill the emptiness, all of the lonely little girls desperate to be made worthy, I want you to know the fault does not rest with you. But unless and until we make the choice to be whole, to be healthy, to be healed, the ache grows over time and the longing gets louder. This book is for you. You have a Father who will always be there for you . . . embrace him . . . I know . . . He has made an unworthy little girl feel the most special little girl grown up in the whole world

. . . And finally I would like to dedicate this book to my sons Buddy and Billy, whom I love with all of my heart and all of my soul . . . one day you too will become fathers. I only hope that by the grace of God I have given you an abundance of love so that the little girls who one day call you Daddy can be showered in that love. Humbly it was my intent that this book should serve to remind you the importance of your role as fathers . . . you see, the greatest legacy I can leave you children is my walk with God.

Chapter One

I have known of God all of my life. I was raised Catholic, going to mass every Sunday. When we had a special request of God we said the Rosary, and if we were even more concerned we resorted to novenas. I believed in God and, from every indication, God believed in me. Of course I wanted God to be pleased with me, but most of all I wanted God to make me happy . . . and indeed the relationship was quite rewarding. But ritual and even religion do not ensure a relationship with God. It is by experiencing God that we get to know him . . . and it is in knowing God, truly knowing God, that we get to know ourselves. After years of ritual and religion, I was finally introduced to God by Michael. I can say that surely I know God by name. God has a way of getting your attention and making sure you never forget. For me this relationship is . . . home.

I awakened at my usual time, though it had been a late night, especially for the boys. I had let them stay up until just after we blew our horns, threw our confetti, and kissed one another—Happy New Year! They were in the deep and peaceful sleep that childhood permits, the kind of restful sleep that grown-ups envy, since it brings such great comfort and renewal. On my way to the kitchen, I stopped to close Buddy's bedroom door. I lingered for a moment. He practically looked like a man now at twelve years old, sprawled out in a bed that until recently had swallowed him up. *We really need to have some more shelves built,* I thought, before continuing down the hall. *Buddy is running out of room for his tennis trophies.* I reached Billy's room next. Before I closed that door, I took a moment and smiled, as I breathed in the fragrance of yet another blessing—my golden-haired six-year-old boy. *Life has been good to me,* I thought.

I headed through the living room and toward the kitchen. Draped in a big, shaggy throw, my sister Stephanie was asleep on the sofa. We had stayed up late sipping a little champagne and sharing some reso-lutions, but mostly reminiscing about Christmas holidays as kids. She decided to spend the night and was sleeping as peacefully as the boys.

I stood at the doorway to the kitchen and realized the boys would be much more excited about chocolate croissants than with my mak-ing eggs. I turned and tiptoed back to my bedroom, not wanting to disturb anybody. I grabbed my down coat and a pair of boots from the closet. I felt eager now. The time alone would be as much a treat for me as the croissants would be for the boys. I stuffed the flannel pajama pants I was wearing into my boots.

"Where are you going?" Stephanie asked, pushing her long dreadlocks to one side as she lifted her head from the pillow.

"Sorry, I was trying not to wake you," I apologized. "I'm going to get some breakfast for the boys. I was thinking about chocolate croissants. Do you want something?"

"Chocolate?" She thought for a moment, fluffed the pillow, and lay her head back down. "Too sweet for me . . . make mine plain."

"I won't be gone long," I assured her, as I eased out of the apart-ment. And she simply answered, "We're fine. Take your time."

———ఎఒఒ———

I stepped out into a bright day that felt more like the anticipation of spring than the dead of winter. Not knowing quite where I was headed, I walked. Alone for a rare moment, enjoying the silence, able to hear my own thoughts—I kept walking. I took deep breaths along the way, refreshed by the crispness of the cool air.

I replayed every moment of this holiday in my mind as I walked across Fifty-fourth Street and headed north. I passed Petrossian's where, on Christmas Eve, Mom and Stephanie had surprised me with a belated birthday celebration. "Rob, can we take a break now?" Stephanie had asked, pretending to be tired of shopping for toys. They indulged me with champagne and caviar, and we laughed for what seemed like hours. It was like old times.

I walked up Seventh Avenue, where only the night before the ball had dropped into a new year. It appeared the city had already moved on. The streets were swept clean. Only bits of confetti that had resisted the brooms remained, and I spotted a black top hat made of paper, with a bold fuchsia feather and silvery, sparkling numbers that reminded me of the year I had just entered, anticipating it with love, hope, and forgiveness—2006. Forgiveness, in particular, had been a long time coming.

I reached Columbus Circle. "Hey, Robin. How's it goin'?" yelled a policeman standing with two other cops. I was delighted to answer him: "Great!" "Happy New Year," they all said. I closed my eyes for a moment and repeated to myself, "It *is* going great." I was as excited to be in New York as the tourists who were out first thing this New Year's morning. I hadn't lived in New York for quite some time. I had called several places home in an attempt to find one that would be truly home—a place where I'd find warmth on the coldest days, light on the darkest nights, and solace in times of suffering. But with my family and so many friends here, the fact is that New York has always been my home.

Yet there had been a time when this home did not provide the comfort that it should, when being in New York meant living with a bit of anxiety and fear. A memory from that time surfaced, a young woman telling me, "He should have kicked your ass . . . he should have killed you." I looked away from my friend—we had been engaged in a conversation. She had coaxed me from my apartment, away from feeling sorry for myself and out for a movie. Now I gazed into this stranger's face distorted with anger. Through the venom I could still see the innocent beauty of a girl who had to be in her early twenties, about the same age I was then. And I marveled at a campaign of hate that led this young woman to believe that another young woman deserved to be brutalized. So when Michael threatened casually and with conviction, "I don't have to kill you . . . I'll make it so bad you'll want to kill yourself. You'll have to leave home, you won't feel safe anywhere," I believed him wholeheartedly, and his words proved prophetic. There was really no need for his warnings. And with every display of his power, I lost more and more confidence. When I objected that a newspaper story wasn't true, he simply responded, "I have the power to make the truth what I want it to be." The lies seemed to sell papers, and they certainly manipulated public opinion and fueled ill will. But most painful of all, most frightening of all, they confirmed my husband's power. "If you sling enough mud," I once heard Phil Donahue say, "some of it is bound to stick."

Headed north on Broadway, I stared up at the street sign—Sixty-fifth Street. I hadn't planned to walk that far, but certainly I was enjoying it, despite the memories that at one time would have been quite painful. I could now recall them with greater understanding, and I could focus on happier, more recent events.

The boys and I had arrived in New York about a week before Christmas. We spent the week shopping and just reveling in the city and each other. The kids had been looking forward to snow but the weather was more like spring. Now, I looked up again to see where I was . . . Seventy-fourth Street. Just a few more blocks to Zabar's. Stephanie and I did a lot of our growing up just a block away from here. Mom always made sure we had something special from Zabar's on holiday mornings, and I found myself making my way there now. Perhaps that memory of childhood rituals, the desire to give my children similar memories, had been leading me uptown all along. I felt happy and hopeful and free. But above all else, I was thankful that my present moment, my here and now, was beyond anything I could have imagined.

Eightieth Street, finally. There was a short line, so I took a number and waited at the counter. After a few moments, the counterman yelled, "Number 64!" I waved my ticket and said, "That's me." He smiled in recognition and said, "Hey, Robin, what can I getcha?"

"I'll take a dozen chocolate croissants," I answered.

"What, no pumpernickel? No rugelach?" he prompted, remembering the specifics of my mother's usual order. I smiled back, tickled by just how familiar I was to him and how familiar he was to me.

"No, I'm just here to get chocolate croissants for my boys." Suddenly I was bursting with pride, feeling I was continuing a family tradition in, literally, my own special flavor.

"I bet they're getting big, huh? I haven't seen 'em in a long time," he went on.

"Really big," I answered, now smiling from ear to ear.

"Well, you're in luck, Robin—I have some chocolate croissants right out of the oven."

Oops! I'd almost forgotten about Stephanie. "Make that ten chocolate and two plain."

"You got it." He handed me the bag of chocolate croissants first—"Careful, they're hot"—and then the bag of plain ones.

"You take care and say hi to your mom. And Robin—Happy New Year!"

Once again, I was pleased to say "Happy New Year!" in return.

———— ∞ ————

I left the store carrying both bags and a cup of coffee I'd gotten for myself and headed down Broadway. I wondered if the boys might be awake and asking for me. It was too warm for gloves so I pulled them off and stuffed them into the pocket of my big down coat. This walk had reminded me just how much I love New York, but it was also difficult to put out of my mind the reasons why I felt I'd had to leave my home, the events that had shaken my family loose from its core, but not from each other. My mom added extra locks and an alarm to an apartment that for years had been kept safe simply by the protective scrutiny of our doormen. The safety and, most of all, the sanctity of home felt violated

I fumbled in my pocket, past the gloves, and pulled out my cell phone. I scrolled down the stored numbers and stopped at one in particular. I felt anxious about making this call. My legs felt a bit weak and my head felt a bit light, but actually I felt a bit lighter too. There was a bench in front of a coffeehouse near Seventy-second Street. My heart was pounding and I took the liberty of sitting there, cell phone in hand, as I sipped my coffee and drifted off in thought . . .

"Rob, come on! Ma told us to hurry up," Michael said, rushing down Broadway. But I wasn't trying to hurry or even keep up. "Michael, the snow is so great!" I yelled as he got farther away. On my hands and knees in the fresh snow, I made a couple of snowballs to catch him by surprise.

"Will you come on?" he called once again.

"No," I answered, as a snowball struck him in the chest.

"Rob, stop it," he said, dusting the snow off his coat, unfazed by my attack. "Do you have the list?"

"No," I answered again, throwing another snowball. This one was even less successful than the first, as he turned away so it never even touched him. I became a little pouty. He wasn't playing and my snowballs were all duds.

"What do you mean, 'no'? Ma gave you the list. I know I saw it." He was taking this shopping far too seriously.

"It doesn't matter. I don't need a list, I already know what to get. I don't know why she bothers to write a list anyway." Maybe now he'd relax and play a bit. "She always gets the same thing," I went on, preparing another snowball. "Everybody in Zabar's knows what she gets. Every holiday breakfast, it's the same thing. Pumpernickel bread, brie, mango chutney, whitefish," I said, walking toward him. "Salmon roe, roasted red peppers, and a loaf of French bre—" Bam! What felt like a boulder of snow covered my face and pushed me back onto my butt. Even before I'd had a chance to throw my latest bullet, he'd gotten me. I screamed, "I can't see! I can't see!"

"You can see, Rob," he said, bending over to wipe the snow off my face. "Open your eyes, silly."

"That hurt," I said.

"It did not," he said, kissing my cold cheek. "You should have seen your face. Pow!" He laughed, pretending to fall back into the snow, mimicking the way I'd looked when his snow-bomb hit. Now I was laughing too. "You were so busy running your mouth, you didn't see it coming." There were times when I just loved his laughter, when it was warm and comforting. Those were the times when he was the very definition of a friend.

He pulled me to my feet, dusted off my coat, and hugged me tight. "You're cold," he said, holding my chilled hands in his to warm them. "I love you," he whispered in my ear. And with a loving pat on the butt, he said, "Let's go, Rob."

"Hello? Hello? Robin, are you there?" The voice jolted me from my memory. I'd nearly forgotten that I had pressed the "send" button on my phone. I hesitated to answer . . . but only for a brief moment.

"Mom, it's me." But of course she knew that already. The pounding of my heart made it hard to hear my own thoughts . . . but there was only one thought that was truly important. I took a breath, a deep cleansing breath, and let it out.

"Please forgive me." I'd already said I was sorry at least a thousand times over the years, and heaven knows I *was* sorry I'd brought him into her life. But there was something different about today. I had let go of the past and I had forgiven. I had forgiven Michael, and nothing is more empowering than the act of forgiving. True forgiveness is simply, purely redemptive. Forgiving had reminded me that my life was a gift from a far greater power than The Baddest Man on the Planet. Michael truly did not hold any power over my life, and he could not take away my living—unless I allowed him to do that. The things I intended to do, the living I was intended to do, all I was intended to be could never truly be taken away. That's true for all of us. I had forgiven Michael and I needed my mother to forgive me. She had been a fierce protector of the gate, and it was as if I had opened it and all hell had broken loose.

"Please forgive me," I said again, and added, "I wish I had listened."

As I pressed the "end" button and slid the phone back in my pocket, I realized that she had already forgiven me, and she had just been waiting for me to reach the place where I could forgive myself. A long chapter of our lives had come to an end. There was nothing left to be fixed, to be changed. I could live in the promise of today and in the hope of tomorrow.

I am going to do something that would've been impossible not so long ago. I am going to reflect on my life honestly, clearly, without blinking or looking away. No matter how sordid the details or how painful the remembering, it's important for me to honor and even celebrate the path that led me here. I'm doing it for myself, to document my journey. I'm doing it for my children because, of all that I have and all that I wish for them, our greatest gift to our children is our walk with God. And I'm sharing it with you because when we look back at the chapters of our lives, there's at least one that was so horrible that we were afraid it would be the *last* chapter. I call this chapter "Michael"—maybe you've named yours after a husband or wife, a parent, an addiction or some other dis-ease. Maybe you're going through that chapter right now.

Despite the superficial differences, all these chapters share a rock-bottom sense of despair and hopelessness. In my Michael chapter, I feared for my family and for my life. There were so many days I was sure I couldn't go on, and almost as many days when I didn't want to. But things change when we change—and not a moment before. We forgive, we are forgiven, we grow, and we go on.

Sometimes change is hard to see. I suppose it's like Buddy in his bed, on the morning of New Year's Day. One day the bed swallows him up and then, before you know it, you wonder how the bed can hold him. That's how life is. One day it may seem it is too much to handle; that all of our efforts to change have gone in vain—then oh, so suddenly, we find ourselves transformed and we are bursting at the seams, with joy.

Chapter Two

My story begins with grace, which is a gift we neither earn nor merit, and I've had a constant reminder of its presence in my life. I've been comforted by Grace, disciplined by Grace, kept by Grace. You see, my grandmother, the woman who gave birth to my mother, the woman who became my beloved Nan . . . her name was Grace, and my story begins with her.

One October night in Lexington, Kentucky, in a little shotgun house on Short Street in the colored part of town, there was a gathering of family to welcome a new one of their own. They ranged in color from "could pass" to bittersweet chocolate. From "May I help you, ma'am?" to "You can't try on clothes in this store." From "Let me show you to a table" to "We don't serve Negroes in this restaurant." It was 1946, and this beautiful little town in central Kentucky was segregated by law but secretly united at its very heart. With high, rugged mountains to the east and gentle hills rolling to the west, Kentucky is as beautifully complicated in its landscape as it is in its history, and my family exemplifies these complexities and contradictions.

"Push, Grace, push." Lucinda stood at the head of the bed, grasping her sister Grace's hand tighter and tighter, as if she could help push. "You've got to push!"

"I *am* pushing!" Grace yelled back. Dr. Beauford sat at the foot of the bed, his patience a complete contrast to Lucinda's urgency.

"Lucinda, give me some of those soda crackers," he said. She reached for the box of saltines on the nightstand, next to a bottle of Coca-Cola. (In telling the story, Nanny always said, "Ruth was so hard to birth into the world! With Peggy, I drank Coca-Cola and ate soda crackers the whole time. But with Ruth, there was no time and no relief!")

"Push, Grace!" Lucinda said once more.

In the other room, Liza, the feistiest one of the family, had grown bored. "Why doesn't Grace stop all of that noise and just push?" she asked.

"You never had a baby in your life, Liza. Why don't you hush your mouth!" scolded Ella. It was a big family—five boys and ten girls. Grace, the baby of the family, and then Ella, and Liza, in that order, made up the younger trio of sisters. Elizabeth, Georgia Mae, and Edna were the oldest, and Lucinda, Ruth, and Alice considered themselves the middle girls. (Another girl, Sunshine, died as a child, in a tragic accident.)

Liza eased a flask of Kentucky bourbon from her purse. "All this screaming and crying is making me a wreck," she said. Ella, the only one who seemed to notice, shook her head in disapproval. Ruth stood by the fireplace rubbing her hands. There was no real chill on this fall night but she too wanted a bit of comfort and, as a reserved and religious woman, Liza's method didn't suit her.

The father-to-be was bound to be anxious for the son he thought was now being born. He and Grace already had a four-year-old girl named Peggy, and everyone looked forward to this little boy. In 1946, the foolproof determination for gender was the baby's position in the mama's belly. Carrying high meant a girl and low meant a boy. Grace had carried so low that everyone was confident that this was indeed a boy. His name would be Louis Newby, III, after his father, Louis Newby, Junior.

"Grace, stop making all that racket and push!" Liza yelled. Moments later, they heard the baby's wail. Lucinda came into the room, smiling. Newby's chest expanded several inches with pride and anticipation as Lucinda stepped into the room.

"Grace is fine," she said. Everyone breathed a sigh of relief. Then, almost as an afterthought, she added, "And it's a girl." Liza's protest came quickly: "Not another darn girl!" Newby was, to say the least, a bit let down and said nothing. After a long, uncomfortable, loud silence, Ruth spoke in a whisper that seemed to go unheard: "Well, maybe you'll name her after me." This brought up an important point: No one had even bothered to choose a girl's name.

Lucinda turned back into the bedroom. "I think Ruth wants you to name the baby after her—and I don't think Newby much cares." Seeing her sister's face fall, Lucinda tried to make up for her uncharacteristically blunt statement. "Oh, honey, I'm sorry . . . I just mean . . . I don't think he'll mind if you name the baby after Ruth. That's all."

"I know he's disappointed," Grace whispered. "I can never quite find a way to make Newby happy." Then she looked up at Lucinda. "Why would I name her Ruth when you're my favorite sister?" Grace never lost an opportunity to show her appreciation to the woman who had always loved her and had in fact raised her after their mother died. Of course, she looked to Lucinda for comfort now.

"He's disappointed, isn't he?"

Lucinda wrapped the baby girl in the blue blanket they'd assumed they'd need. "Grace, sometimes God doesn't give us what we want; He gives us what He wants us to have." She smoothed a bit of baby oil on the newborn's hair and lay my mother in my grandmother's arms. "And who wants more for us than God?"

It was a question intended to put Grace at peace. Lucinda kissed her sister on the forehead. "Ruth doesn't have any children. I think it would be very nice to name the baby after her."

My grandmother smiled down at her new daughter. "Then we'll call her Little Ruth."

Edward Turner was a carpenter, a tall fair-skinned man who could have passed for white. Instead, just before the turn of the twentieth century, he married a petite, dark-brown woman named Mary Beauchamp, and together they raised fifteen children, five boys and ten girls. All the children were born in the house Edward built on Dakota Street in Brucetown, in the East End of Lexington, Kentucky. It was a fine house with a wraparound porch, set back on a large lot marked with a picket fence. Edward's workshop was tucked away behind the house, along with the smokehouse where they cured ham and bacon.

A lot of living went on in that house in Brucetown, along with some dying. Their oldest daughter, Sunshine, was the first loss experienced in that house, when she was eight years old. After Mary Beauchamp Turner died, Lucinda, or Cindy, moved back into the house to take care of her father and the younger children, including my grandmother, Grace. Cindy was the darkest of the girls and always their father's favorite. He—and only he—called her Brownie. By the time Grace Turner was fourteen, Edward Turner was dead, and her sister Lucinda was in charge of the family. Once everyone was grown and on their own, Lucinda took charge of her own life and seized new opportunities. In 1948, she and her new husband moved to New York, part of the great migration of colored people from

South to North. Aunt Cindy never expected that her beloved Grace, with two little girls of her own in tow, would follow her before long.

The fate of Grace and Newby was determined at another family gathering, this time to mark the death of one of the oldest girls, Elizabeth. She'd been laid out in the living room, in a white dress, her rose-colored casket draped with white carnations. Everyone remarked on how beautiful and peaceful she looked, which is exactly the right thing to say at such a time, between bites of chicken and sips of bourbon. Of course all the Turners were there, as well as various in-laws and outlaws, including Grace's husband's parents, Mama Mack and Duck Mack. Duck got his nickname from his short, squat build and turned-out feet. His stepson, Louis Newby—known simply as "Newby"—was a good-looking man, with smooth copper skin. His work enhanced his handsome physique. Newby proudly considered himself an artist, not simply a bricklayer. My grandmother Grace wasn't the only woman who found Newby attractive, and even after their marriage, he indulged his roving eye.

While most of the family gossiped and traded stories, the Turner girls were hard at work in the kitchen, preparing the food that would honor their sister, and soothe and comfort those who mourned her. They made fried chicken, of course, but also country ham from Edward's smokehouse and wild greens gathered from the yard; corn pudding and baked macaroni and cheese; and that special blend of mashed potatoes and rutabagas with plenty of butter. Aunt Ruth was finishing up a cake with the extraordinary caramel icing that only the Turner girls made. Between sips of bourbon, Liza had been kneading the dough for dinner rolls, and now she put it in a bowl and covered it with a damp dishcloth so it could rise. Cindy, who was down from New York, had run the scrubbed linen tablecloth and napkins through the wringer and, her mouth full of clothespins, was hanging them out to dry. Grace was ironing the special tablecloth their mother had embroidered so many years ago. It lay over the linen cloth on these special occasions. One iron heated on the stove while she smoothed the fancy cloth with the other.

Ella wasn't busying herself. She just sat, apparently lost in thought, taking long drags from her cigarette. Ella and Grace were not only sisters; they were best friends. Ella was just barely a year older and the sisters could almost have passed for identical twins, except that Ella's freckled face was just a bit more brown, while Grace's freckles sat on a palette of pale yellow skin. Both had long, wavy, black hair, tiny waists, and rounded hips. They both liked to show off their gorgeous legs with high-heeled pumps and seamed stockings.

Finally Ella spoke up, as if she and her sister were alone in the room.

"Grace, what are you going to do about Newby? You know you're going to have to do something."

Grace put down her iron and walked over to an old wooden highchair. She bent down and picked up the toy Little Ruth had thrown down. She caressed the baby's cheek and returned to her ironing. It was as if her sister hadn't spoken at all.

Ella took one more deep drag on her cigarette.

"Everybody knows that's Newby's baby," she said. "He can't deny that boy—he looks just like him."

Ruth dropped the knife she was using to ice the cake, glared at her outspoken sister, and turned to Grace. "You know that in His time and in His way, God will deal with Newby. You have to trust Him to handle what we can't do much about, and He will make all the wrong in our lives more than all right. He's got a way of working it out."

Now Liza jumped in. "What's that expression—God helps those who don't take no stuff from a no-count man." She laughed teasingly. "I'd put some saltpeter in that nigga's food, 'cause it's gonna be hard to keep the women away from a man that looks that good." She enjoyed both offering advice to Grace and ruffling Ruth's feathers. "In due time, Ruth? Newby's time is long *over*due."

Liza took a quick sip from her glass and when she spoke again, she was no longer laughing. She looked around at all her sisters, including Cindy, who had returned from the backyard and was standing in the doorway. "Grace oughta be more bothered 'bout that nigga whopping her ass when he finally does come home at night, never mind about him sleeping around. The way he whips her ass, she oughta pray that he stays gone." The two older sisters looked stunned, and for once Ella was pleased to hear Liza speak out of turn. "Baby, you can't let no man raise his hand to you," she said softly.

Ruth looked stricken, as it dawned on her just what her baby sister was going though. "Oh, Lord, Grace! Why didn't you ever say anything?" And tears began streaming down her face.

Grace just lowered her head, humiliated. Liza picked up a knife from the counter and held it for all to see. She waved the knife back and forth as she spoke. "Let that nigga have all the babies he wants—but you gotta let him know that the next time he tries putting his hand on you, he gonna lose his thing right along with his hand."

"Liza, please," said Ella, while Ruth continued to quietly sob.

Grace did not acknowledge her sisters, but she heard every painful word.

Lucinda moved toward the sister she'd helped raise and, standing on the other side of the ironing board, said in her calm, gentle voice, "Grace, Mama would roll over in her grave if she knew that Newby was hitting you." Tears began to stream down Grace's face, but she never lifted her head. Lucinda went on, "And Papa would never forgive me for letting it happen."

Just then Mama Mack entered the kitchen. She'd obviously overheard the sisters' conversation. Mama Mack was a beautiful woman, regal in stature, with very fair skin and high cheekbones. She'd been raised by her unmarried mother because—it was long rumored—her white father already had a wife. From the time she was a girl, she'd spent her life in the midst of Lexington's finest families and had been a cook for the biggest horse breeders in town. She was always impeccably groomed and her sharp nose was always pointed up a bit as she walked . . . and now she slowly walked toward Grace, still at the ironing board. No one else moved a muscle.

Newby was Mama Mack's only son, the apple of her eye, and as far as she was concerned, he could do no wrong. Her voice was icy as she told Grace, "You shouldn't go around spreading lies like that. You know my son never laid a hand on you. And you can't blame a man if he has to go outside the home to find some love and appreciation." Grace kept her head bowed, tears dripping onto the beautifully embroidered tablecloth. Of course, she'd known the truth about Newby's running around, even as she permitted his denials and accepted his excuses. Some of his women had been bold enough to call the house, and she'd managed to overlook that too. But now there was a baby boy, and that was much harder to ignore. And now, here was her mother-in-law looking down her nose at her, blaming her, accusing her of lying. Grace's tears dried and she allowed herself to feel the anger that had been simmering for so long.

"Hell fire," she said quietly. This had been her mother's way of expressing the deepest rage. "Hell fire!" she said again, just a little louder, as she picked up the hot heavy iron off the stove. Raising it high, she took a step toward Mama Mack, stared at her with absolute contempt, drew in a deep breath. No one else moved. Finally, Grace hollered, "Hell fire!" and Mama Mack took off running, with Grace and her iron right behind. Liza whooped and hollered. "Oh, shit, the devil's got her! Ruth, you better do something!" Ella started after Grace and Mama Mack, just as Mama Mack ran right through the table linen hanging on the clothesline. "Grace! Grace! Come back here!" Cindy called. Mama Mack kept running, and Grace kept chasing her, past the smokehouse now. "Run, Grace, run!" yelled Liza. "Get that heifer!"

"Oh, my Lord! Oh, my Lord! Lucinda, do something!" Ruth cried. "Oh, what would Mama and Papa say if they could see this?"

Liza took another sip from her glass, wiped the tears of laughter off her cheeks, and began putting the cut-up pieces of dough on the baking sheet. "Lucinda," she said, slowly and clearly, "leave that girl alone. It's about time she took charge of her life. And, Ruth, you want to know what Mama and Papa would say? They'd say: Yes, Grace, it's about time—about *damn* time."

In the end, Grace did not clobber Mama Mack with the flatiron, and everything got smoothed over long enough to get the cooking done and have a nice wake for Elizabeth. And that night, Newby hit Grace for the very last time.

By the time Lucinda returned to New York, plans were already in place for Grace and her daughters, Little Ruth and Peggy, to follow soon after.

Chapter Three

The porter, a tall handsome man, had just stowed away Grace's new Samsonite luggage—a going-away present from her sisters—when the conductor called out, "All aboard! Aaaaall aboard!"

Grace grabbed Little Ruth's hand, then Peggy's. "We'd better go," she said. The Turner sisters, teary-eyed, gathered around to kiss them good-bye. Big Ruth was the last. She kissed Peggy, then Grace, and then reached down to pick up Little Ruth. "You're God's special little girl!" she whispered, kissing her gently on the cheek, hugging her so tightly the girl could hardly breathe. "You won't forget that, will you?" Little Ruth shook her head, her cheek damp with her aunt's tears. Big Ruth put her down and guided her as she walked up the steps to her mother.

"Grace, I can't believe you're really leaving!" Ella called out, happy for her sister but sad to lose her best friend.

As the train started to pull away, Ruth offered her sister advice and reassurance one last time. "Grace, I am so proud of you, but God is *most* proud of you. Can't you just feel the thunder of God's pleasure?" Ruth said, looking up at Grace and walking alongside the train. "Oh, praise the Lord! See the light of his smile!" The train picked up speed, and so did Ruth. "Grace, you keep praying. Pray without ceasing. That's what those knees are for, not just scrubbing floors. And, baby, you can rest assured that I will be praying right with you." By now Ruth was no long running but practically floating in the air, her voice carrying over the sound of the chugging engine.

Liza decided to join Ruth and, though she was a bit more plump than her sisters with a lot more bosom, she managed to keep up. "I'll be praying," Ruth hollered over the train whistle. "I'll be praying that God sends you a good man who will love and honor you, a man to help you take care of those children, a man who'll take care of you too." Liza trotted alongside, her ample bosom bouncing up and down with each stride. "I'll be praying too!" she yelled. "God might be tired of listening to Ruth, but He ain't heard from me in a while. I'll tell Him to make sure the man He sends you ain't some no-count nigga!" Liza was laughing too hard to keep going, so she stopped running, but she kept laughing and her bosom kept right on bouncing. Ruth continued running. "Every morning before my feet hit the floor, I make sure my knees touch the ground! You do the same, Grace!"

Finally she reached the end of the platform and stood still, watching the train disappear from sight. She drew a breath, relieved and satisfied. She'd said everything she believed God wanted her to tell her baby sister.

The conductor had seated Grace and the girls in the car with the sign reading "Colored People Only." Peggy read the sign to Little Ruth, whispering the words in her ear. Peggy made even these words sound magical.

They were the only colored people boarding the train in Lexington. "We must be awful special to have a car of our own," Little Ruth said. Peggy rolled her eyes and told her sister, "You're so silly." Ruth didn't mind. She knew Peggy didn't really mean it. "Ears are the way we taste words . . . just like your mouth tastes food," Peggy once told her and Little Ruth never forgot it. She got to sample all of Peggy's words, because she was the only one Peggy trusted enough . . . except for the times Peggy was sure she had just the right recipe of words. Then, and only then, she'd read them to their daddy and let him taste the words too.

The sisters had on matching plaid dresses—red, blue, yellow, and green—with crisp white collars and a bow in the back. And though they hadn't been allowed to try on the dresses in the store, their mother had a good eye and so the dresses fit perfectly. Peggy and Little Ruth wore gloves, just like their mother, but Grace also wore a hat with a veil that dipped down to just below her eyes.

After the porter showed them to their seats, Grace unpinned her hat and placed it on the rack next to their overnight bags. She lifted Little Ruth onto the seat next to Peggy and smoothed their dresses before she sat down herself. The train had moved so far from the station that they could not see Aunt Ruth or Aunt Liza or anyone anymore. Then the porter announced, "Supper is being served in the dining car. Are you ladies ready for supper?"

By the time they'd finished eating, the girls were exhausted. Grace unpacked their pink flannel nightgowns and helped them change, draping their dresses carefully across the back of an unoccupied seat. The porter handed out blankets and pillows; Peggy went to sleep right away, but Little Ruth seemed restless. "Stretch out a little more, baby," Grace whispered, stroking her back. Cradling Little Ruth's head in her lap, Grace stared out the window and gave up on sleep, until the smell of bacon and eggs awoke her the next morning.

Grace took a look around the car. *Now this is how life is meant to be lived*, she thought. They were no longer alone in the car, and colored folks and whites alike shared the compartment. They must be out of the South by now. It was time to wake the girls for breakfast.

————— ∞∞ —————

After the girls had scrubbed their faces and put on their dresses, the porter came around to gather their blankets and pillows.

"You visiting kinfolks in New York?" he asked Grace.

Still feeling unsure of herself, Grace hesitated. "Well . . . actually, New York will be our new home."

The man nodded. "That takes a lot of courage. But you seem like a mighty strong woman to me, and I'm a good judge of character. You don't have nothing to worry about, ma'am. All you got to do is look forward to a good life. And you've got just enough time for breakfast before you get there."

Grace tied the bows at the backs of the girls' dresses and straightened her skirt. As she led them to the dining car, her heart felt just a little bit lighter.

————— ∞∞ —————

After breakfast—eggs, grits, and bacon, "Just like you make, Mama," Peggy said—Grace started gathering up their things.

"We will be arriving in New York Penn Station in ten minutes," the conductor announced. The porter placed their bags near the door, where the redcaps could reach them when they got off the train. "Thank you so much," Grace told him. "You've been so kind."

He smiled. "Ma'am, it's been my pleasure. You just keep looking forward and remember—however things used to be don't have nothing to do with how they're gonna be."

And he moved off into the next car.

————— ∞∞ —————

Grace sat back in her seat and pulled on her gloves, then helped the girls with theirs. The train got slower and the buildings got bigger the closer they got to their new home.

"Now arriving at New York Penn Station," the conductor announced.

She thought about the porter's words. *Courage . . . But I'm so afraid*, she thought. She stood, picked up her pocketbook, and took her daughters' hands.

"Come on, girls," she said, in a clear, strong voice. "We're here."

Chapter Four

Lucinda and her husband, Billy, met them at the station, relieved and thrilled to see them. Cindy squeezed her baby sister so hard she nearly knocked Grace's hat off, hatpin and all.

They climbed into a brand-new 1952 Chevy, Grace and the girls in the backseat. In the front seat, Lucinda reached over and adjusted the collar of Billy's crisp white shirt, smoothed the lapel of his suit jacket. *This marriage is no longer new*, she thought, *but it somehow gets just a little better every day*. Billy took off his hat and handed it to her, smiling, and Lucinda held it in her lap.

Grace felt the smooth leather of the seats. "This is beautiful," she said.

"Billy hit the numbers," Lucinda said, with a mixture of pride and disapproval. Peggy opened her mouth to ask a question, but Billy quickly asked, "How was your trip?" She answered for all of them. "It was so much fun! We ate dinner and then breakfast." She held up her writing tablet. "I wrote about the whole thing. I'm saving everything to read to my Daddy." Grace looked at her, a bit startled. "Well, next time I see him," Peggy said, easing back into the seat.

Harlem was like no place Grace had ever seen. Both sides of the street were lined with four-story buildings, all attached. Lucinda called them "brownstones." No front yards, just a patch of grass and maybe a single tree dotting the sidewalk. *Where in the world will the children play?* she thought. But then she noticed three girls jumping Double Dutch right out on the sidewalk. Ruth noticed too, watching the girl jumping and the two girls chanting and turning, fascinated with their rhythm and their perfect timing.

Billy unloaded the suitcases and a woman called out to Lucinda from a first-floor window. "Is this your baby sister?"

Lucinda stopped to introduce Grace and the girls to Miss Lila before ushering them upstairs.

Home was the three-bedroom apartment directly above Miss Lila's. There was a fireplace in almost every room and heavy mahogany detailing everywhere—atop the squeaky oak floors, around every giant doorway, crowning the elaborate tin ceilings. The girls and their mother shared a bedroom since Aunt Cindy and Uncle Billy's son, Hardell, lived there too. It was a beautiful apartment, and Lucinda made sure the wood sparkled like glass, but if you were from Kentucky, you couldn't help but miss the sweet little frame houses set in their lawns of the bluest bluegrass. And you'd miss the bright sunlight that poured down, even on chilly spring days.

Peggy frowned at the thought of having to share the room, much less the big four-poster bed, and she certainly didn't want her dolls mixed up with Ruth's. "But it's a pretty room, isn't it, Mama?" Ruth asked. Her mother answered, "Yes, baby, it is a very pretty room."

Not long after they arrived, one especially nippy morning Grace slid her foot into a fluffy slipper to discover a mouse. After she stopped screaming, she almost started crying, she yearned so desperately for her own home. And she wondered how she could possibly set a positive example for Peggy during this trying time.

But then, she remembered what her sister Ruth had told her about how her mornings should start. And she began a daily ritual that would last a lifetime and would pull her family through many difficulties. Every morning, before her feet hit the floor or slid into any slippers, her knees would always touch the ground.

———— ✸ ————

Work hadn't been as easy to find up North as many had hoped it would be, but Billy could fix anything and he'd turned his gift into a business. Televisions were just becoming popular, and his radio and television repair shop was thriving. Robinson's Repairs was also a gathering place for neighbors, including children, and one of the daily stops for the numbers man—Mr. Neil, Miss Lila's husband, a perfectly groomed man who was, Billy said, "the picture of wealth."

In the back room, Peggy taught Little Ruth to weave potholders on a metal frame but Ruth lacked her sister's patience and never learned to crochet doilies or knit doll clothes like Peggy did. However, Ruth also lacked Peggy's reserve, a quiet, pensive manner that oftentimes led her to find comfort with paper and pen rather than people. Ruth needed little prodding to start selling her own colorful potholders and her sister's other creations to the neighborhood ladies, even the men gathered in the shop. Nothing made Ruth happier than spending time with her big sister, soaking up her attention.

At home, Ruth liked to imitate the grown-up ladies, who spent much of their time in the kitchen. She had a wonderful little table for two, where she served dinner to her uncle after he came in from the shop. Right after he told Lucinda how beautiful she looked, swatted her on the bottom and kissed her on the cheek, he would turn his full attention to Ruth. "I am absolutely starving! Whatcha got cookin', good-lookin'?" he'd ask her. That always made Ruth laugh. He would sit at the little table with his knees high above the table-top and she'd pretend to serve him all of his favorites. He would praise

Ruth's cooking and wink at Lucinda, who was cooking the family's supper. Ruth always noticed the way Aunt Cindy looked over her shoulder at him, ever so proud of this man she loved.

———

The night of the Joe Louis–Ezzard Charles fight, the whole neighborhood packed into the shop. Ruth had a front-row seat at the television, right at Uncle Billy's feet. Some of the men in the shop that day had been bragging about having tickets to Madison Square Garden, but Ruth couldn't imagine that anything could be more exciting than Uncle Billy's shop. The women laid out the food in the back room. Lucinda had cooked spareribs, dripping with hot, smoky sauce. Grace made potato salad full of eggs and sweet pickle, and Miss Lila brought her collard greens made her secret way. Aunt Cindy made cornbread too, not the kind you bake in the oven, but hot-water cornbread fried on the stove. For dessert, there was Grace's lemon meringue pie that absolutely no one could rival.

When Lucinda made up a plate for Billy, she didn't use paper plates and plastic utensils. No, she brought out a freshly ironed linen napkin and matching placemat, a sparkling china plate, and real silverware.

Watching her, Grace smiled. "Lucinda, you wait on Billy hand and foot. You act like you're lucky to have him or something," she teased.

Lucinda stopped and looked over at her sister. "Grace, you know what I used to ask God? At the lowest times in my life, I used to say, 'Lord, send me a man that loves You as much as I do. If You send me a man that loves You as much as I do, I know I can serve You better.' I didn't ask for anything else. Bill came to me straight from God. I call that kind of luck a blessing." Lucinda kissed her sister and carried the plate piled high over to her husband. Later, Ruth would remember how Aunt Cindy bragged, "God comes first in Billy's life; that's why coming in second is so special." Billy held the very same position in Lucinda's life—second only to God. And it was a good thing that they both ranked so high with each other, because without exception, they always put themselves last.

The night of the fight, Ruth was firmly in the Joe Louis camp because that's where her uncle was. Mr. Neil the numbers man teased him about it—"Mmm, mmm, mmm. Just won't give up on Joe Louis, will you? Billy, you mark my words. Ezzard Charles may not knock him out, but he will never give Louis back the title." Ruth fell asleep in Billy's lap long before the fight was over, but the next day she heard Mr. Neil teasing, "Billy, I should have bet you twenty dollars. I'd be twenty dollars richer today."

Uncle Billy just laughed. "Neil, don't you come in here, talking that nonsense."

⸺ ◦◦◦ ⸺

Soon the girls were settled in school, Ruth in kindergarten and Peggy in the fourth grade. Peggy was a brilliant student, intellectually and creatively gifted, mature and always well-behaved. Her feelings remained hers, except for the times she shared them with Ruth, telling her how much she really hated the new school.

One night, the girls were lying in bed while their mother was listening to *The Shadow* on the radio in the living room and Peggy told her another secret. "I'm Daddy's favorite girl," Peggy said. "He likes me better than you and a whole lot better than Mama." An adult would have recognized how much Peggy was hurting, how heartbroken she was. Little Ruth only wanted to tattle. Before she could, Peggy clasped her hand over her sister's mouth and leaned in as if to whisper some of her beautiful words. Instead she shrieked—a piercing, strangled shriek that left Ruth's ears ringing but couldn't be heard from the other room.

Ruth didn't tell. "Anyway," she thought, "it doesn't matter one bit if Daddy likes her better than me because God likes me best of all—

better than any little girl in the whole wide world. Aunt Ruth told me so."

As Christmas approached, Uncle Billy suggested a trip to B. Altman to see the holiday lights and visit Santa Claus. One Saturday, they headed downtown, and while Uncle Billy escorted the girls on their visit, Lucinda and Grace went to look at the women's dresses. As Grace admired a green velvet dress, the saleswoman said, "Would you like to try that on, ma'am?" Grace looked at Lucinda, who nodded. Colored women were indeed allowed to try on dresses in B. Altman's.

"Yes, I would," she said. "Yes, please." The saleswoman escorted her to the dressing room, hung up the garment, and said she'd return shortly. Grace reveled in the fitting room, with its beveled glass mirror in a gilt frame, and a beautiful armchair upholstered in red-and-gold brocade. Slowly, Grace slipped into the green velvet, savoring every moment.

As soon as she stepped out of the dressing room, Lucinda said, "Grace, it couldn't be more perfect for you. Let's have it wrapped—we'll have Santa bring it to you." Grace was worried about the expense, but Lucinda insisted.

When the saleswoman returned, she apologized for keeping them waiting. "We've had a horrible time trying to get holiday help, so we're understaffed," she said. Grace perked up. "Perhaps I can help."

When she left B. Altman's that afternoon, Grace had a new dress and a new job.

"May I help you, sir?" Grace had been eyeing the handsome man as he unfolded scarf after scarf in the B. Altman accessories department. He looked up at her, and his youthful, honey-brown face and dancing brown eyes made a contrast with his gray hair. He fixed his gaze on Grace—elegant, impeccably groomed, wearing a winter-white suit, incredibly beautiful. For a moment he could only stare.

"May I help you?" she repeated.

"I'm looking for a scarf," he finally answered.

"I noticed," she said with a smile, adding to herself, *since you've unfolded most of them.* "Does the lady have a favorite color?"

"I don't really know."

"Does she prefer silk or chiffon?"

"I don't know that either. What do you like?"

"I like yellow, and I prefer silk," Grace said. "But it's purely a matter of taste."

He smiled. "It seems to me you have wonderful taste. I'll take two yellow silk scarves." He still had not taken his eyes off Grace.

"Two? Shall I wrap them together or separately?"

"Separately," he said, and Grace thought, *Finally! A question he can answer.*

⸻

The man showed up the very next day at just about the same time. *What is he doing here?* Grace wondered, as she handed a customer her purchase and wished her a Merry Christmas.

Grace turned to the man, but before she could say a word, he said, "Would you have a cup of coffee with me?"

"Oh, goodness, no," Grace said quickly. "I'm here to sell scarves."

"I know," the man replied. "And you do that beautifully. Please—just a cup of coffee?"

"Absolutely no, sir. I'm here to sell scarves," she repeated, wondering how she'd given him the wrong impression.

The man tried to put her at ease.

"I understand," he said. "You're worried you don't know me. You see . . . it's just that I feel I know you. Some people you know better

in a split second than you will ever get to know others in a lifetime."
As he continued talking, Grace began to feel her nerves settling and
realized that although the man towered over her, he didn't seem in-
timidating. Harry Scott was his name, although he preferred to be
called Scott.

"Well, perhaps another day," Scott said. "By the way, do you like
this blue silk chiffon?"

She nodded. "It's nice—very sweet."

"I'll take it," he said.

Over the next several days, Scott arrived at Grace's department at the
same time every afternoon and chatted with her until she relaxed and
began to enjoy his company and even look forward to his visits. He
bought a total of five scarves: the two yellow ones and the blue one,
plus a floral pattern and one with a paisley print. Finally, one evening
after Grace and Lucinda had washed the dishes and put the girls to
bed, Grace told her sister about Scott.

After she described the situation and her confusion, Grace said,
"I guess I wonder if it's right to have coffee with a man who just
waltzes into the scarf department. . . . I guess what I really wonder is
what you think."

Lucinda smiled at her baby sister. "Maybe he didn't waltz in at all.
Maybe God brought him there, as much for him as for you. But right
now, you don't need to know what I think about a cup of coffee. You
know perfectly well that you just have to learn to trust your senses."

"Maybe one cup of coffee," she told Scott the next day. "Just a quick
cup of coffee. I get off at six, but then I have to get right home to my
daughters."

Scott beamed. "We can meet right across the street at Schrafft's—and Grace, I promise I will get you home early."

When Grace arrived at the restaurant, Scott was already there, sipping a cup of coffee. As they talked, she discovered that he was cultured, mature, and endearingly respectful. He may not have made her pulse race, but he seemed a good, stable man, and her reaction to him was one that was unfamiliar. She eased back in her seat, suddenly feeling less adrift.

Scott sent her home with a box of petit fours for her daughters and insisted on paying for a cab back to Harlem, despite her objections. Settling into the backseat, she smiled and waved good-bye. *I don't think I've ever been treated this well in my life*, she thought. *At least not by a man.* Just as the cab left the curb, she heard Scott calling her name and turned to see him chasing the taxi. Telling the driver to wait, she peered out the car window as he caught up. "I nearly forgot," he said, out of breath. He handed her a B. Altman shopping bag. "Something for you." Then he waved good-bye again and the cab sped off.

Grace settled back in her seat and opened the bag. She laughed as she pulled out a blue chiffon scarf, then a yellow silk scarf, and then another, and another—all the scarves she'd sold him earlier. Except for one yellow scarf he had given old Mrs. Whitney, his dearest client. Smiling, Grace felt blessed, so blessed. She hadn't felt so much of God's love and care in a very long time. She remembered something she'd once heard Liza say: "You can walk into a blessing just as soon as you can walk into some shit."

Grace soon began seeing Scott, and he met her family. He seemed to delight in carrying the girls on his broad shoulders, and certainly Ruth loved being up so high, almost in Heaven. Grace came to appreciate his kindness, his generosity, his steadiness.

"Mama always said if you find a man with character, you've found a man worth his weight in gold," Cindy told Grace shortly after she met Scott. "Now, Scott is a man of character. And, Grace, he's a man who loves the Lord—there's not a finer man than that."

Scott was more than twenty years older than Grace—fifty-two to her twenty-nine. She may not have felt the same passion that she'd had for Newby, but she also loved him in a way she could never have loved Newby—the way a woman learns to love a man who deeply loves and honors her, one she can trust . . . a man who loves and cares for the daughters that she cherishes beyond all else. Scott was simply a good man, and the love Grace had for him ripened with time and matured with her own maturity . . . and it was the kind of love that makes a woman glow from the inside out.

Grace and Scott were married at St. Catherine's Catholic church in the spring of 1953, with Scott's best friend officiating. He had never been married before. It was as if he had been waiting for her all his life. "It's about time, Harry," Father Wallace told Scott in his thick Irish brogue. (Only Father Wallace got away with calling Scott by his given name because, as he explained, "Harry is a good Irish name, and because I know things are not always what they appear, I'm certain that you, my dear friend, are a good Irish man.") Grace felt so comfortable and welcomed at the church that she had little trouble settling into her new religion. Father Wallace baptized the girls and made sure they were enrolled in religious instruction, and he soon became such a regular guest at Sunday dinner that a place was always set for him at the table. He always sat next to Ruth, who noticed that he had a very distinct fragrance—not cologne, but a familiar smell that Ruth knew and liked but couldn't quite place. One afternoon, as he kissed Ruth on the cheek, it came to her. Father Wallace smelled just like Aunt Liza! Ruth loved to be reminded of her aunt, and so she would always love the fragrance of bourbon that Father Wallace carried with him. It made her happy.

So many things about her new life made her happy. She had a new father and a new home, and in a way a new mother too—a happy mother Ruth couldn't remember seeing before.

However, Peggy seemed to resist the changes that were taking place in her life, as if to show loyalty to her father, a quite natural response. She may have kept her sorrow private, but whether we mask our grief or show it for all to see, no loss goes un-experienced.

———∞———

Scott bought a home in the suburbs for his new family—well, not quite the suburbs but for colored people in the 1950s, the northeast Bronx was practically like Scarsdale.

They were the first colored family on the block. The people they bought the house from had been Italian immigrants who had planted the backyard with fig trees and vines that bore clusters of grapes that seemed to leap out of their skins into the girls' mouths. It seemed the entire neighborhood was Italian. Yet the newest family on the block had a lot in common with their neighbors, since they also had left a very different culture, seeking a better life. And, like most first-generation immigrants, Scott and Grace would work tirelessly, he at his business and she in their meticulously kept home, to provide the best for the second generation. That generation, Peggy and Ruth, had the task of assimilating into the new culture and making their parents proud.

———∞———

As the young Italians in the neighborhood were learning to speak English, Ruth and Peggy were learning to be comfortable in their own skins—brown skins, in a place where that was a rarity. For Peggy it was a constant struggle, while Ruth made friends with ease. In fact, she became an honorary Italian. A skinny little girl with a great big appetite, she loved being invited to eat pasta at Ann Marie's house on Sunday after mass. "Let me put a little more gravy on your macaroni," Mrs. Pasalaqua would tell her, which always made Ruth smile—the red marinara sauce was nothing like the pan gravy her mother made.

On Saturdays, Ruth would have her friends over to make pull candy. It was like magic—one moment they were pouring sugar into a heavy pot and the next they were pulling out the sticky goo, the best candy they'd ever tasted . . . what an awesome transformation. "Mrs. Scott, can I use blue food coloring?" Ann Marie would ask. "I've never seen blue candy." Grace would smile and say, "Honey, you can make your candy whatever color you want," and Ruth would beam with pride. Then the doorbell would ring, and they'd know that Gilda, who needed a little extra time to convince her Puerto Rican father to let her join in, had finally arrived.

———— ✖️ ————

They became a threesome, three daughters of vastly different cultures. Ann Marie's parents grew up in Italy, but she had been born in the United States. Gilda's parents were from Puerto Rico and though she'd been born there, she spoke perfect English, with only a faint trace of an accent. Gilda, especially, seemed to love knowing Ruth. She'd press her own arm against Ruth's and say proudly, "Look, I'm colored too!" Ruth sensed that Gilda's parents were much less pleased about their friendship. When Ruth visited, Gilda's father would say, "Gilda, your friend has to go home now—*has tu tarea*."

"Papi says I have to do my homework," Gilda would tell Ruth, then take up the fight with her father. "Papi, does she have to go now? We're playing! Just a little while longer?"

"*Ahora*, Gilda," he answered. "*Has tu tarea*." Before Gilda had time to translate, Ruth would say, "I know, I know. He said you have to do your homework."

They'd laugh, and Gilda would say, "You have me to thank for speaking such good Spanish."

Even if Gilda's father wasn't all that enthusiastic about Ruth, she loved Gilda's name for him. It sounded so special, so loving. And so Ruth's anglicized version became her name for Scott. On the short walk home from Gilda's she practiced aloud. "Poppy, can you take me out-side to ride my bike? Poppy, can you buy me a new doll?" She was de-lighted. She skipped all the way home and saw Scott reading the newspaper. He peered at her over the paper and through his bifocals, and she beamed at him. "Hi, Poppy!" she said, and skipped away.

One afternoon, Grace welcomed Scott home from work with some especially good news.

"We're expecting," she said.

"Expecting what?" he asked cautiously.

She smiled. "Well, I'm not sure. I'd love to have a boy, but it might be a girl . . . but I know it's a baby."

He reached out the big hands she loved, scooped her up in the strong arms that comforted her, and spun her around the room. He had never been happier.

Hearing the commotion, the girls ran into the room and he hugged them tight, one in each arm. "What is it, Poppy?" Ruth asked. They'd never seen him so excited, hadn't even dreamed he could be so excited.

"Do you want a baby brother or sister?" he asked them. "A baby brother," Ruth quickly answered, thinking that a baby boy sounded like so much fun. Peggy didn't answer, but in her quiet, thoughtful way, she was just as excited as her giddy younger sister. And anyway, she knew that you got the baby God wanted you to have.

They were thrilled to welcome little Harry, Jr., always called Pep, in 1952, and their new family seemed perfect.

Ruth was delighted with her new life, her new family, her new father, and even her new religion. She felt every bit as special as Aunt Ruth told her she was. She could barely remember what it had been like back in Lexington. The only thing that made her unhappy was the nightmare that woke her up frightened and disturbed. She seemed to have it so often. "Children have nightmares," her mother told her. "But they're not real, and they're nothing to be afraid of. They're just part of growing up."

But Peggy wasn't feeling the same excitement that Ruth was feeling, and she sure wasn't filled with the joy of this new family. She'd always been more introspective than Ruth, and now she seemed to retreat almost entirely into her writing . . . it was through her writing that she could best describe her feelings. And reading was an ideal complement to her writing . . . it provoked thought and helped order her thinking. More and more, reading and writing provided the safety and sanctity that a new and unfamiliar world could not offer a young girl . . . especially if that new world felt like a betrayal of the one she had left.

Ruth thought her mother didn't quite understand how much Peggy loved words; whether reading them or writing them, she had a kinship, a friendship with words. "Daddy loves words too," Peggy would tell Ruth. But they hadn't seen Daddy in years, and Peggy desperately missed him. And the little bit of poetry she read to Ruth from her diary was all about him.

> *You were taken from me,*
> *I'll never stop trying to understand why.*
> *A brokenhearted little girl is left only able to cry.*
> *But only inside where the world does not see . . .*
> *Only inside where I can truly be me.*

"But we have a new father now, Peggy," Ruth said. "One that God sent us." She was trying to ease Peggy's pain, but she could see it wasn't helping.

—❧—

Ruth knew her mother and Aunt Cindy were worried about Peggy too. She overheard them whispering about what a sensitive child Peggy was, how delicate. While Ruth agreed that Peggy was sensitive, she thought her sister was more dramatic than delicate. She seemed as strong as an ox to Ruth, especially when she'd hold Ruth down and scream in her ear, which was becoming much too often. But what troubled Ruth more was her own nightmare, which came night after night now. In her dream, she was in a crib, watching a mean, violent man hit her mother, over and over. Ruth reassured herself with her mother's words: *It's not real, it's nothing to be frightened of.*

Then Peggy began having fainting spells. The doctors all told her they could find no physical cause for them, and Grace felt a twinge of guilt over having left the father Peggy yearned for, despite her devoted new father. Finally, one of the most severe of these fainting spells landed Peggy in the hospital, and the father she missed so terribly was summoned to New York.

The day Newby and his new wife were to arrive, Grace and Scott were called to the hospital. "Mrs. Scott," Peggy's doctor asked, "has your daughter recently suffered any severe trauma in her life?"

"No!" Grace answered quickly, shocked by the question. It was only then that she began to realize how traumatic it is for a little girl to lose her father. Everyone had assured her, "Children adapt and adjust so easily." But as the doctor explained, losing a beloved parent is never easy for a child to deal with. Losing the first man she loves can be one of the most traumatic events that a girl can face.

Peggy remained at the hospital one more night before being sent home with some medication and a referral to a doctor who helps heal the pain of the brokenhearted. Both Scott and Grace were devastated, feeling they had failed her.

When the doorbell rang, Grace was cleaning a spotless room, wanting it to be absolutely perfect. "That must be Daddy!" Ruth called out. She wondered how she was supposed to behave. Should she run up to him, as if she were happy and excited to see him? She couldn't even remember what he looked like. Should she ask him why he hadn't bothered to come visit before, or why he'd let them go in the first place? Or maybe she should say nothing because she had a new father, one that God had given them, one who loved them and made their mother so happy.

Grace began the long walk to the door with Ruth at her side. Slowly, she opened the door and there he stood. The man looked down at Ruth and gave her the biggest smile. "Come and give your daddy a hug," he said. Confused, Ruth clung to Grace, hid her face in the soft cloth of her mother's apron. The thoughts tumbled through her head: *You're the man in my dream, the angry mean man . . . the man that hurts my mother, over and over . . . you can't be my daddy, I have a daddy, and he's a wonderful father . . . you're the man in my dream.*

Chapter Five

Ruth tiptoed into the room she shared with Peggy to peek in on her sister. Even for a Saturday morning, it was awfully late for Peggy to still be sleeping. Ruth had slept a little late herself; the family had stayed up late the night before. Mama had prepared a wonderful, festive dinner—a combination of a welcome-home celebration for Peggy and a good-bye dinner for Newby and his wife. Now their father was on his way back to Lexington, and Peggy would go back to school on Monday. Ruth was ready for things to go back to normal.

Peggy's beautiful brown face seemed so peaceful, resting on the sparkling white pillowcase. Ruth crept back into the room and gently pulled up the white eyelet comforter to cover Peggy's shoulders, then left her sister to sleep.

When she looked in later, Peggy hadn't moved. This disturbed Ruth . . . but just a bit. She gently shook her sister. "Peggy?" When she got no response, she shook the girl harder, called her name louder. "Peggy, wake up!" The shaking grew fearful, almost violent, and finally Ruth called out, now panic-stricken—"Mama!"

It didn't take long for the ambulance to arrive, and it didn't take long for them to get her to the hospital. It didn't take long to pump the pills from her stomach—certainly not as long as it would take to ease the pain in Peggy's heart.

While their mother and Poppy made the trip to the hospital, Ruth went back into the bedroom. She knew where Peggy kept her diary, and she took it over to the window, where the morning sun shone the brightest. She leafed through the journal and stopped at a page that read: *I love my room and sometimes I love my life but I miss the way my life used to be. I miss my friends but most of all I miss my Daddy so much.*

Ruth turned to another page. *When I write to Daddy, sometimes it takes him so long to answer . . . sometimes I have to write him two times before I get an answer and last time I didn't get an answer until my third letter.* Ruth knew that Peggy missed their father; so did she. But Ruth was so grateful for the father God had given them in Poppy that she made an effort to move on from the loss. Sometimes it seemed that Peggy really didn't try.

> *Daddy didn't tell me he was getting married. I think he should have just made sure we liked her. I don't think she's very pretty at all. Mama is much prettier . . . but I do understand how Mama could get on his nerves sometimes . . . She really gets on my nerves when I'm trying to write. Mama never says, "Peggy, read me what you're writing." Daddy always wanted to hear what I was writing. But Mama is still much prettier. Why did he have to go and get married anyway?*

Poppy was a good man, a very good man. Ruth was convinced that Peggy knew that. But as far as Peggy was concerned, she already had a father, one who was as irreplaceable as he was unattainable.

Ruth turned to the last entry in Peggy's diary.

> *Like food . . . like water*
> *Like air . . . like breath*
> *No one can live without a father*

No matter how strong you are
Or how often you are told to be
Like my breath . . . I cannot survive with him taken from me
I gasp and struggle and try to survive
But it is far too painful to be alive

———— ⚬∞⚬ ————

That summer, Aunt Ruth came to New York to pick up Little Ruth—
seventeen hours each way on the train. For some time, the plan had
been for both Ruth and Peggy to spend some time with Aunt Ruth in
Lexington that summer, but it did not seem like the right time for
Peggy to be so far from home. So the two Ruths made the journey together. The faintly familiar memory of the aroma of bacon and eggs,
and the chugging of the train, made Little Ruth realize it had been a
long time since she'd left Kentucky.

Ruth had a wonderful time those two weeks. She'd always remembered Aunt Ruth as a beautiful woman with an ageless face and
figure, who paid careful attention to her appearance, and now Ruth
got a chance to know her better. The house smelled of furniture polish and fresh coffee, and it was every bit as neat and polished as the
woman herself, full of lovely antiques that she had gotten locally and
fascinating collectibles that came with the stories that Aunt Ruth had
also collected during her proud service as a WAC in World War II.
She had the most beautiful vases and porcelain dishes and pillows
she'd had made from the fine fabrics she'd brought back from France.

Little Ruth discovered the changes in the family since she'd been
to New York. Ella had moved to Greensboro, North Carolina, married a preacher, and never picked up another cigarette. Now she had
three daughters of her own. Georgia Mae had gone to be with the
Lord. But some things never change . . . Liza was still lovin' to sip her
bourbon.

Ruth noticed that both the formal dining room table and the

table in the bright yellow kitchen were always set for two, just as they had been when her aunt's beloved husband, Jimmy, had been alive. According to Grace, Aunt Ruth liked living alone—fewer fingerprints to polish away, less mess tracked into the house. Even so, it was clear to Ruth that her aunt loved having someone else to sit down with at those tables.

The two of them had a routine. Each morning, Aunt Ruth brought the newspaper in off the porch and poured herself a cup of just perked, piping hot coffee before she started breakfast for Little Ruth. "Let's see if we can find something to do today," she'd say as she opened up the *Lexington Leader* and turned to the "Colored Notes." The "something to do" was always in the obituaries column. "Oh, my goodness, I had no idea that Miss Eula Mae's funeral is to-day!" Or maybe it was Cousin Ernest or Missus Johnson from down the road. Whoever it was, Aunt Ruth would say, "I'd better hurry up and make breakfast so we can get dressed!" Aunt Ruth would scan the column for details while she gathered up potatoes and onions for home fries. Hot link sausage for her and mild for Little Ruth and, of course, homemade biscuits. And she always made fried apples for those biscuits with nutmeg, cinnamon, and loads of butter. There was always time for a good hot breakfast, even—or especially—before a tearful funeral. Monday through Saturday, there was a funeral to go to, at Shiloh Baptist or Pleasant Green Baptist or Main Street Baptist, and of course on Sunday there was the regular church service at First Baptist. That's how Little Ruth learned the gospel songs she'd love and sing all her life. She knew a few already, because when she and her own mother were alone in the house, Grace (the Catholic convert who became a closet Baptist) would blast the Victrola and sing along to the songs she'd grown up with. "His Eye Is on the Spar-row" was always a funeral standard: "I know He watches me . . ." An-other was Grace's favorite song, "Amazing Grace," and Ruth loved the song that seemed to touch everyone's heart, stir everyone's soul, and bring a tear to everyone's eye: "Amazing grace, how sweet the sound

that saved a wretch like me . . ." Ruth could hear her mother's voice
even as she listened to the choir sing at the funeral now.

> *I once was lost but now I'm found,*
> *Was blind but now I see.*
> *T'was grace that taught my heart to fear,*
> *And grace my fears relieved.*
> *How precious did that grace appear the hour I first believed.*
> *Thro' many dangers, toils, and snares, I have already come.*
> *'Tis grace has brought me safe thus far*
> *And grace will lead me home.*

Watching the mourners weep, Ruth remembered her mother's
own tears whenever she sang this song. Despite the joyful cries of
"Thank you, Lord!" each time at the song's end, Ruth could sense
there was just a bit of sorrow among those tears of joy, or perhaps it
was the lasting memory of what she had to go through to get here
"safe thus far." But as Grace always said, "The cross is what keeps you
close to the crown."

About midway through Little Ruth's visit, she found herself amongst
the women who gathered in the shop at the back of the house. After
all, it was the place to be for women of unimpeachable taste and flawless grooming. Ruth was the only beautician in the shop, because she
would not have trusted anyone else to do her signature waves. There
were often long waits, but nobody seemed to mind. This was time to
catch up on what was happening in the lives of other women, time
to offer support and encouragement, or just get some good old
mother-wit on just about any subject, from a wayward child to a wan-
dering man.

There were women there as usual, and one of them asked, "Ruth, is that Grace's child? That child is the spittin' image of her mama. I'll bet Grace is as pretty as she's ever been."

"Mmm-hmm! Grace is more beautiful than ever," Ruth answered the woman resolutely. "She's got a good man now."

Her aunt mentioned, almost casually, that Ruth's father might stop by that afternoon. Little Ruth wasn't sure if she was excited; she was definitely confused. "Should I put on the new dress you bought me?"

"Oh, no," Aunt Ruth said, waving away the suggestion. "We'll just see if he shows up."

He didn't show up. However, he did call the day they were leaving for New York. He spoke to his daughter almost formally. "I'm sorry I haven't had the opportunity to see you while you were here. But I will see you soon."

He didn't sound so scary, Ruth thought. *But why* couldn't *he come see me? I wish I knew why Peggy loves him so much. Maybe because he looks so much like her. Maybe because he always listens to her beautiful words. I just wish I knew . . .*

In New York in the early sixties, things were changing but not nearly enough. The mind is a hard thing to change—yet it is out of the heart that flow the issues of life and the heart that is the most challenging change of all. Ruth was a student at a Catholic high school, and still faced subtle signs of racism that can make a young girl feel blatantly unwanted and deeply hurt. Ruth was on the student council, the debate team, and the basketball team too. It's hard to be so much a part of something but feel so set apart. Ruth was very social by nature, but her social life was much constrained by her color. Imagine the struggle when one's nature is in conflict with one's environment. I suppose it is a struggle that only serves to make you stronger.

Ruth and the only other colored girl, Emelda, found themselves very much on the sidelines at the few dances they attended. Finally at these social gatherings, they started leaving early and heading to Vinnie's for pizza—fifteen cents a slice, smothered in mozzarella, the best in the Bronx. They were always welcome at Vinnie's. They'd watch him toss the dough in the air, again and again and again, until the round ball was a thin circle, perfectly prepared for his amazing sauce. Ruth loved to cook and she really wanted that recipe, but whenever she asked, he'd say, "It's a family secret." To which she always responded, "But Vinnie, I'm family!" That made all of them laugh. They always finished the night with zeppoles, licking the powdered sugar off their fingers as they ran back to school in time for Uncle Billy to pick them up.

"How was the dance, girls?" he'd ask as they climbed in the car. "Did you have a good time?"

"We sure did!" Refusing to give in to the pain of rejection caused by ignorance and injustice, they really did have fun. Occasionally, for a brief moment, the thought might cross their minds—*What is wrong with me?* But in a split second, they knew the answer. Nothing. Absolutely nothing.

If Ruth's social life didn't thrive at school, her spiritual and academic life certainly did. Throughout high school, she believed she might have a calling to become a Sister of Charity, just like Sister Rose Frederick, her beloved French teacher. Quite progressive for her time, Sister Rose was, to Ruth, a feminine expression of God. She glided through the halls in her ankle-length habit, skirt swaying one way while the rosary at her waist swung the other, her shining brown face framed by her snowy bonnet—more nobility than nun. She was a figure of respect and inspiration for all the girls. Sister Rose counseled Ruth not to rush into a vocation.

"Take your time," she said. "This is not a decision you need to make now, and it is certainly not one to be made in haste."

Ruth didn't feel she was being at all hasty. She had always felt a closeness to God, a commitment to Him, just as her mother, Grace, did . . . their lives were full of miracles large and small. And they both considered Poppy one of God's greatest miracles.

She took the girl's hands in her own. "A relationship with God can take on many forms and many faces—a religious vocation is just one of those. Take your time—the most important thing is that you not stray too far from God because just how far we walk away from God determines the challenges of the road back home. What is God's will for your life? That is the question you need to ask yourself and pray for Him to reveal. Until you have His answer, anything you do will be hasty."

Yet, as graduation approached, Ruth felt more and more pressure to sort out her future. Even more troubling, Ruth was feeling a restlessness, a discontentment that she could scarcely describe. She never wanted for anything, including love; her mother, Poppy, Aunt Cindy, and Uncle Billy all made sure of that. But she suddenly and increasingly felt a need for something none of them could give her. She needed to know her father, perhaps because she was struggling to know herself. She wanted to understand this man who had frightened her so and who still mystified her. Ruth always wanted everyone around her to be happy, and she knew this growing need would not make her parents happy, so she had never mentioned it. But it was important enough to her that she decided on a plan, regardless of how little others might understand: During her visit this summer, she would stay with her father instead of Aunt Ruth, at least for part of her stay.

Peggy seemed to have finally discovered something that pleased her; she was in nursing school. Perhaps she thought that helping to ease the pain of others might just help her ease her own. And now she had also found a young man that she cared about. But Ruth knew Peggy still carried much of her old pain. And maybe Ruth thought that she could carry the mantle for both of them.

Ruth broached the subject carefully, but, as she expected, her parents were not pleased. "You've never shown any interest in getting to know him before—why now?" her mother said. And, "All of a sudden, it's not enough that Poppy has been the best father you could have?" Though she never said so, Ruth knew it was less "all of a sudden" and more like "all the while"—despite how much she truly loved and appreciated Poppy. Finally, seeing how much it meant to her, Ruth's parents gave their blessing and she flew to Lexington. Finally, she would get to know the man who haunted her dreams and increasingly clouded her days.

———⦷———

But the visit did not turn out according to plan. Instead of spending time with her father, Ruth ended up spending most of her visit with her very likable stepmother. Betty seemed more interested in her than her own father did. Ruth soon realized that the marriage had serious problems, the kind her own mother would easily recognize, and that her mother had experienced.

History, Grace used to tell her daughter, has a way of repeating itself. Some of us repeat one aspect, some repeat another, and we need to be careful—truly careful, she always said—about what we carry on. My mother wouldn't get to know her father any better that summer, but she would get to know my father. Longing for Louis Newby, she met Reuben Givens. Far away from the solid, steady love of Poppy and Uncle Billy, she was swept up in the excitement and romance Reuben offered.

One thing is certain—my mother never again mentioned entering a convent.

Chapter Six

Music blaring, pins clanging, friends laughing—that was the sound-track for Ruth and Reuben's courtship.

Ruth was keeping score while her new friend Connie was bowling. Connie was a tall, curvy, "high yellow" redhead. Though the girls had just met, their families were old friends. It was rumored that Newby had had a crush on Connie's mother. "With just a twist of fate," Connie told Ruth, laughing, "we could have been sisters." Ruth thought she was beautiful and admired her sexy confidence. Connie was going with a guy named Joe, Jr., and they wanted her to meet his friend Reuben. Reuben was one of the biggest basketball stars in their high school, although it turned out he was good at just about all sports.

Connie ran her finger down Ruth's scorecard—"Now with my last two gutterballs . . ." and they both laughed. Just then, Connie felt a hand on her shoulder. It was a tall, milk-chocolate young man with just a hint of swagger. He leaned in to whisper, "Introduce me to your friend." Which she did: "Reuben Givens, this is my friend from New York City, Ruth Newby."

Reuben's smile could light up a room, and when he turned it on Ruth, she melted. "Would you like to dance?" he asked. Ruth looked at Connie, who smiled and waved them off to the area the young men and women had claimed as a dance floor.

Ruth wanted to impress this young man. She was so afraid that her evenings at Vinnie's would betray her and she'd embarrass herself on the dance floor. It was a huge relief when Reuben wrapped his arms around her and took the lead as they danced to The Drifters crooning "There Goes My Baby."

⸻

That summer, Ruth fell in love to the music of Otis Redding, Wilson Pickett, and Sam Cook. And she fell in love with Reuben Givens. Maybe her father didn't pay much attention to her, but Reuben Givens sure did. He was so exciting. All the boys liked him because he was such a fine athlete, and all the girls liked him because he was so fine. Everyone wanted his attention, and Ruth had it. He went wherever she wanted to go, including to visit her Aunt Ruth.

Ruth was shocked and saddened to see her aunt looking so frail. *Mama said she was under the weather*, Ruth thought, *but this seems much more serious than simply being under the weather.* It was impossible to believe that someone so dear to her, the woman she was named for, who had become such a pillar of strength for her, might ever weaken.

Aunt Ruth gave her niece a big hug and kiss. Proudly, Ruth said, "Aunt Ruth, this is Reuben Givens." Aunt Ruth took a moment to look him up and down.

"Hello, Reuben," she said. "You kin to those people in the South End?"

Reuben gave her a big smile. "Yes, ma'am. But I was raised by my grandmama and granddaddy in West End."

Big Ruth looked at her precious namesake for a long, long moment and then said simply, "Baby, you need your hair touched up." Leading her by the hand back to the beauty salon, she called out, "You have a seat in the parlor, young man. We'll be right back."

Aunt Ruth set her niece down in the swivel chair and pumped the footpedal to raise it to the right height. She plugged in a little oven and placed a hot comb and a curling iron inside. She didn't say a word, and Ruth felt the tension heating up as fast as that oven.

"Hold your head down, baby," she said, and pushed down with a bit of force so that she could reach the hair on the nape of Ruth's neck. The quiet was deafening and Ruth could hear the sizzling of the hot comb when it met the pomade. She winced, not because it hurt, but because the situation seemed so uncomfortable. Her aunt spoke up at last.

"You know, baby, you have to be careful with some men, because some men will take your looks."

Her head still lowered, Ruth lifted her gaze to get a glimpse of her aunt's face in the mirror, searching for the meaning of this bit of wisdom. She recalled that day in the beauty shop when Aunt Ruth had said her mama was more beautiful than ever because of her good man. Now she spoke quietly, with intensity.

"Some men have a way of just sucking the life right out of you . . . take your heart and suck the love out of it too. 'Cause, baby, truth be told, that's where a woman's beauty comes from. Comes right from her heart."

Ruth lifted her head and the women stared at each other in the mirror. Even in her frailty her aunt had such a glow. On the walk back toward the parlor, Aunt Ruth continued sharing her wisdom with Little Ruth.

"Now, that young man wears some sweet-smelling cologne," Aunt Ruth said, "but that can't cover up the trouble I smell. I know some of his people, and the apple doesn't fall far from the tree."

She's being too hard on Reuben, Ruth thought. *But she'd never think any man is good enough for me.* Not wanting to argue, she said nothing.

"I don't know what it is about some women hellbent on loving the wrong man, on trying to fix something that only God can fix."

Before they reached the parlor, the older woman gave her niece a hug and kiss. "You say good-bye to that young man for me." Looking straight into Ruth's eyes, she said, "And, honey, mark my words, you hear?"

If youth is wasted on the young, so too is wisdom.

———

That night at the bowling alley, an Otis Redding song was playing when Ruth noticed a pretty girl smiling at Reuben. Looking up, she saw that Reuben was smiling right back.

She pulled away from his arm draped around her waist, while Otis sang about a love that had become a habit. Furious, Ruth stalked out of the bowling alley and Reuben followed.

Out in the parking lot, she protested. "How could you flirt with her like that, right in front of me? It's a disgrace!"

"Oh, Ruth, come on," he said, with a bit of a chuckle.

"Well, it's disrespectful."

He laughed. "You're imagining things."

As he walked away, she ran after him. "I *saw* you!"

He turned and she saw anger rising in his face. "You're out of your mind," he said. She grabbed his arm but before she could say anything else, he picked her up and threw her against the hood of a car.

"Don't you *ever* grab me like that again."

She'd never experienced such rage, at least not directed at her, yet at the same time, it was oddly familiar. For a split second, one brief moment, she wondered, *Is this the loving man of my dreams or the frightening man of my nightmares?*

But Ruth agreed with Otis. Though it hadn't been long, "I can't stop now."

———

Reuben Givens and Ruth Newby, the two people who would become my parents, were soon married and shortly after that, they were in

New York. Reuben's cousin Lou "Slick" Johnson, a professional baseball player, had set up a tryout for Reuben with his team, the Brooklyn Dodgers. Naïve and hopeful, the couple was sure he'd make the team and they'd be able to build a life and raise a family beginning with the baby they were now expecting.

But Reuben didn't make the cut, and he had no backup plan. They lay in bed one Saturday morning shortly after tryouts, sorely disappointed. Ruth longed to be comforted, but while he held her in his arms, he had no real comfort to offer. Softly, the radio played Sam Cook's velvet voice singing "A Change is Gonna Come."

Reuben kissed her on the forehead. "I'm just worried that I can never be the man you deserve to have—and I think I'm even more worried I'll never be the man I deserve to be." Now Reuben kissed her lips. "If I leave now, I can still get a few weeks picking tobacco and make us some money for Little Reuben. I don't really know what else to do."

So he returned to Lexington, and once again, Ruth found herself living with her mother and Poppy.

"We are on the cusp of change. For many it seems too long coming . . . lives have been lost." Heads nodded, the church filled with murmurs of "Amen" and "That's right." Every member of the congregation had seen the peaceful demonstrations disbanded by fire hoses and police dogs, and though there seemed no way to control the increasingly violent reaction to the civil rights movement, neither was there a way to hold back the swelling momentum of this movement.

It was Thanksgiving service. They were at the church that had been Aunt Cindy and Uncle Billy's. Miss Lila had also recently become a member. Afterward everyone would sit down for dinner at Grace and Scott's. Ruth thought of the last time she'd been sitting in this church, when Uncle Billy had gone to be with the Lord. She could still see Aunt Cindy throwing herself onto Uncle Billy's casket as it was being closed, wailing, "Take me with you, Billy, take me with you." Everyone wondered how one could live without the other. And Ruth remembered Miss Lila saying, "The Lord sure knew what He was doing when He took Billy first." Miss Lila was born again now, and Mr. Neil had joined her today, after some gentle prodding. After all, he had not completely given up his numbers business. "The Lord says come filthy and guilty, and I can sure do that," he would laugh.

Now the preacher's words caught Ruth's attention again.

"People have been lynched, beaten, and burned—broken bodies for a just cause inspire determination. But it's the broken spirits I'm talking about—broken spirits left to roam the earth aimlessly and hopelessly." Again, the congregation murmured agreement. "You can punish someone for killing the body, but there is no punishment for killing the spirit. No earthly punishment, that is. But I am here today to tell you that we serve a just God. He is a merciful God—but He is indeed a just God." Some people rose to their feet now, and the "amens" and "mm-hmms" were louder. "His time is not our time. But in time, justice is served. God has His say. Yes, I serve a merciful but a mighty God . . . and I am here to thank this mighty God I serve because I know that praise and thanksgiving open the floodgates of His blessings." His voice swelled—"Thank you, Father! Thank you, Father!"—and the church echoed with thanksgiving. "And all we need to bring about change is His blessing. *Thank* you, Father!" Then the choir's voices rose in song: "How great Thou art . . . how great Thou art."

There wasn't a dry eye in the church—or an ungrateful heart.

As people filed out of the church, Ruth, still seated, reached down to rub her swollen ankles. Her mother took her elbow and helped lift her from the pew. "Come on, let's get you home so you can put your feet up." Grace was pleased by how beautiful Ruth looked in her blue maternity dress. She smoothed the white collar, stroked her daughter's hair. "It won't be much longer now."

"I hope not, Mama," Ruth said. "Just long enough for Reuben to get here."

As they walked into the house, the phone was ringing. It was

Reuben, with disappointing news. Ruth tried to keep her voice steady. "I was really hoping you'd be here for Thanksgiving—you told me you would."

"I'm just trying to make as much money as I can for you and Little Reuben."

"Are you sure it's a boy?"

He laughed. "I only know how to make boys."

Is that a joke? she wondered. Reuben went on. "I'll be there for the baby, though. We've still got three weeks."

"You won't take that long, will you? Mama said that sometimes first babies come early."

"I'll be there, I promise."

Despite all his efforts to reassure her, Ruth hung up the phone not feeling the least bit reassured. Physically exhausted and emotionally let down, she laid her head on her mother's shoulder and cried. Grace held her daughter and stroked her back.

"That feels so good, Mama. My back hurts so bad. It's been hurting since I got up and it's just not getting any better."

Grace held Ruth at arm's length and looked at her closely. Then she turned to her sister. "Lucinda, we better hurry and get dinner on the table. I think Ruth might be going into labor."

"No, Mama," Ruth said, a bit of panic in her voice. "I've still got three weeks."

"We'll see what God has to say about that," Aunt Cindy answered.

Ruth smiled. "Well, I hope he says I can eat Thanksgiving dinner, because I am starving, and I'm not leaving without something to eat."

They all laughed—the whole family had long wondered how tiny Ruth could put away so much food—but then Ruth clutched her belly in sudden pain. "Oh, my God!" she said. "Mama, hurry up with the food."

It was the traditional Thanksgiving dinner—turkey with cornbread dressing and, just for variety, a little oyster dressing on the side. Glazed ham with cloves, pineapple slices, and cherries. Baked macaroni and cheese, the mashed rutabagas Ruth loved, fresh green salad, candied sweet potatoes, and sweet potato pie. Homemade rolls and home-made cranberry sauce.

The family gathered around the table: Poppy at the head, with Aunt Cindy on his right. With Uncle Billy gone, their son, Hardell, sat on Lucinda's right with his wife, Mae. Peggy was seated to the right of Mae and her husband, Stormy, across from her. Ruth was next to Peggy and across from her was Pep, the older of her two brothers, who was now twelve. Four-year-old Mike, who had been quite the happy surprise, was on Ruth's right, with Tina, the Neils' daughter, across from him. Miss Lila and Mr. Neil sat across from each other, next to Grace, at the foot of the table.

Poppy reached toward Cindy, and everyone linked hands in a cir-cle. Poppy began to pray, sharing the words he had written and com-mitted to memory for this occasion.

> *Heavenly Father, on this Thanksgiving Day,*
> *We bow our hearts to you and pray.*
> *We give you thanks for all you've done,*
> *I especially thank you for my daughters and sons.*
> *For the beauty in my wife—Your glory I see;*
> *For the joy of my health, my friends and family;*
> *For each day's blessings, your mercy and care.*
> *I have so many blessings that you have graciously shared*
> *So today I offer my devotion and praise*
> *And a commitment to follow you for the rest of my days.*

Ruth grimaced in pain. The contractions were coming nine minutes apart now. Turning to his sister-in-law, Poppy continued.

Now I'll turn to Cindy to whom I just want to say:
Without you, I would not be nearly so grateful today.

Applause erupted from everyone at the table—they were all touched by the earnest emotion from a man so controlled. But no one smiled more brightly than Peggy, who more than anyone else appreciated his words, so painstakingly chosen to express such beautiful feelings. Now she had grown to treasure the love he offered as well. She was finally at peace with herself, at peace with the family that had been created for her, and as a nurse, she poured all of her passion into helping other people who were experiencing pain. Lucinda offered her own words of thanksgiving, and everyone at the table followed. Each expression of gratitude was heartfelt; some were eloquent, others were funny. Mr. Neil said, "I'm gonna speak some words on my friend Billy's behalf. 'Cause I know what he'd be sayin'. He'd say, 'I'm grateful Lila's got your behind in church today. I don't know how she did it, but I sure am grateful.'" Mr. Neil held up his glass, as if to raise a toast to his dear friend. "And I'd say, 'Billy, there just might be a place for me up in heaven after all!'"

Then it was Ruth's turn. "Lord, thank You for all You've given me," she said. "Thank You for my father"—she smiled at Poppy—"and my mother. If You will answer this prayer, I will ask for nothing else . . . I beg You to please let me be as loving, as self-sacrificing, as giving as the mother You have given me." Grace's eyes filled with tears, and Ruth grabbed her belly—another contraction.

───※───

Ruth piled her plate with a little bit of everything and a whole lot of some things. She looked at her watch and realized her contractions were getting closer, so she began to eat a little more quickly. She had one more contraction, and then the strangest sensation. She stood up and walked through the dining room, then through the kitchen, and had almost made it to the bathroom when her water broke. "Mama!" she called.

Grace rushed to her and began issuing orders. "Lucinda, call Dr. Suriano—his number is in my book—and tell him we're sorry to disturb his holiday, but we're on our way to the hospital." Poppy called a taxi—Uncle Billy was the only one in the family who drove—then he grabbed the bag Ruth had packed and followed them out to the car that had arrived promptly, thank God.

Dr. Suriano burst through the delivery room door barely in time to catch the baby. "How are you doing, kiddo?" he asked Ruth as he pulled up a stool right between the stirrups. "Can you push for me? Give me a big push. You're almost a mother now . . . just one more push. There you go . . . there you go . . . and you've got . . ." He handed the infant to the nurse. "A daughter!"

Smiling, the nurse held out the baby to Ruth. "Here's your little girl—life will never be the same." Ruth gazed at the newborn with disbelief. "Hello, baby!" she said. "I'm your mother—and I promise I will always be there for you."

"Good job!" the nurse said. "Now let me get her cleaned up."

Ruth awoke in her room with her own mother next to the bed, smiling at her.

"Ruth, she's absolutely beautiful," Grace said.

"Oh, Mama, you've seen her? She *is* beautiful, isn't she?"

Just then the nurse came in carrying a bundle wrapped in pink and laid it in Ruth's arms.

Grace was bursting with joy at the sight of her daughter holding her own little girl. She kissed Ruth's head, looked down at the tiny baby, and breathed in the fragrance of pure love.

"Ruth, I will always be there for you," she said.

Ruth looked up and smiled.

"Mama, you must be reading my mind."

I was born on November 27, 1964—I missed being born on Thanksgiving Day by just half an hour. My father missed the entire event. He never made it back to New York at all.

From the beginning, we've always thought of Thanksgiving as my birthday. In fact, my mother considered naming me "Thanks"—as in "Thanks Givens." My father overruled her. He thought it would be cool if we all had the same initials: Reuben Givens, Ruth Givens, and now Robin Givens. Robin Simone Givens.

Chapter Seven

That holiday, the Thanksgiving I was born, set the pattern for my father's role in my mother's life and in mine. With her own mother's help, she surrounded me with love and joy and celebration, working so hard to make up for what, and who, was missing. Yet, despite all her efforts and good intentions, there was a crack in the foundation, though it seemed to go unnoticed at the time. Although she was the glue that would hold our family together there was a hollow at the base of the structure that she could not fill or fix. I know she loved me then, loves me now, and always did her very best for my sister and me. I think my father loved us too, as much as he could. Still, as so many of us discover, sometimes the only legacy one has to give is their pain and hurt.

———— ∞ ————

Not long after my birth, my mother moved back to Lexington in a futile attempt to save her marriage. She wouldn't stay long . . . just long enough to witness his womanizing, experience his brutalizing, and become pregnant with my sister.

It was a winter day, and my mother was making the bed with me, just over a year old, standing in my crib. She stopped—*was that a noise in the kitchen?* My father was at work and she and I were alone in the house. She listened but heard nothing and started tucking in the sheets. Then she heard it again—this time she was certain.

Mom lifted me onto her hip and headed for the kitchen. She held me tight as she peeked through the doorway. *Was someone there?* Yes—a man, standing near the refrigerator. As she drew in a breath to scream, the man turned and she recognized my father.

"Oh, my God! You frightened the heck out of me. What are you doing here?"

"I live here," he said, his tone cold and nasty.

"Are you all right?" No answer. "Is something wrong?" No answer. She continued to quiz him until he interrupted her with a question of his own: "Why are you such a nervous wreck all of the time?"

Startled, she asked, "Am I nervous?"

My father laughed, an ugly sound. "Yes, you are. You're losing it." He kept laughing at her as he took a beer from the refrigerator, shaking his head as if her question, and she herself, were hopelessly ridiculous.

"It's too early to be drinking," she said.

His eyes began to fill with rage, and, holding me with one arm, she reached for the coffee can. "Honey, why don't you save the beer for later and I'll make you some coffee?"

Watching his face, she knew she had made a mistake. Questions and doubts swirled in her head. She tried to change her tone, smooth things over. Putting the coffee can down, she walked over to my father.

"Is everything all right?" she asked, and began to stroke his back.

"No, everything is not all right—I lost my f——in' job!"

As he spoke—*pow!*—he smacked her hard, a backhand across her cheek. She spun across the floor and fell against the refrigerator, and I fell with her, screaming and crying.

"Why are you always looking for a problem?" he roared at her. Then he stormed out of the kitchen and into the bedroom.

Stunned, still pressed up against the refrigerator, my mother held me close and tried to comfort me. I kept crying and screaming, and my father yelled, "Now look what you've started!"

My mother kept patting me, kissing my cheeks. "Shhh, baby, please don't cry."

"Shut that baby up!" my father yelled.

"Hush, baby," she whispered in my ear. "Mommy's got you, it's okay, baby, it's okay." Gradually I stopped crying. She tried a smile to soothe me but her mouth hurt. She felt a lump inside her lip and then noticed a few drops of her blood on my yellow lace dress.

She carried me into the bathroom and stared into the mirror. There was a tiny split on her lip and the swelling inside her mouth was becoming visible outside as well. Blood still trickled from her mouth. But nothing was more alarming, more upsetting, than her blood on my dress.

"Oh, baby, I love you so much." She hugged me close to her and the tears poured down her face and onto mine. *I'll keep my mouth shut. I'll never say it again*, she thought. *Whatever it is.*

She ran cool water and washed her face. She put the stopper in the sink and let it fill, took off my dress, and put it in to soak. She talked to me cheerfully, but the whole time, her mind was busy going over and over what she had said, trying to figure out what it was she should never say again.

"Let's get you something else to put on," she said, carrying me toward the bedroom. At the door, she hesitated. My father sat at the foot of the bed, his face in his hands, his body shaking with sobs. For a long moment she watched him, then he lifted his face.

"Ruth, I am so sorry. I don't know what got into me."

I don't either, she thought.

"It will never happen again. I promise." He reached out for her, and after a moment she walked over to the bed and sat down.

"I want to do so much for you, baby," he told her, "but I just can't seem to do anything right."

He buried his head in her lap, and she consoled him just as she'd consoled me. But now her thoughts were even more confused, chaotic: *Can I trust him? Is it all over now? Do we just go back to normal? Why am I comforting him? What is it that I'm not supposed to say?*

"Please forgive me," he begged. "I'll never do it again."

He kept his promise, remained contrite and controlled long enough that she thought this might be the way things would stay. They were home one Saturday night, my father watching the Celtics play Philly and my mother drying dishes in the kitchen. The doorbell rang. My mother wasn't expecting company, but Reuben jumped up and ran to the door. He threw it open wide, as if to make his friends welcome immediately, and then there were three big men in the living room, slapping Ruben on the back—"Reu-*ben*, my man!"—and high-fiving.

The tallest man's hands were so large, he could easily palm a six-pack of beer, and he held one six-pack in each hand. As he bopped through the door, he handed the beer to my father. "Keep 'em chilled, my man," he said, laughing. Another man carried a brown paper bag twisted at the top, and from it he pulled out a bottle of bourbon. "We would have been here sooner but somebody came in the liquor store with a deadly weapon. She had a rear end that could kill a nigga." He licked his lips and slapped my father five and they all laughed. The last man, short compared to the others but still tall, was empty-handed. "What's the score, man?" he asked.

"You haven't really missed anything," my father said. "The game just got started." Carrying the beer toward the kitchen, he told the others, "Make yourself at home."

My mother, still at the sink, watched as he crossed the room and opened the cupboard to get some glasses. She smiled at him.

"Reuben, I didn't know you were having guests."

"They're not 'guests.' They're my friends," he said, his tone disgusted. He grabbed four glasses, took a bottle opener from the drawer, and tucked a bag of chips under his arm.

"Wait," my mother said, slipping the bag from under his arm. "Let me put these in a bowl for you."

He snatched the bag out of her hands.

"It's fine just like this, Ruth. You just love to put me down, don't you?"

What did I say this time? she asked herself. Aloud, she said, "I'm not putting you down, honey, I just thought it would be nice to serve them in a bowl."

He left the kitchen angry and she looked down at me, sitting on the floor. "Oh, baby, Mommy's got such a big mouth."

My mother lifted me up and stood me on my feet. She held out two fingers for me to wrap my plump hands around while I steadied myself. One chubby little leg moved forward, as I began to take a step, confident she was there for me.

"Look at you," she said. "You're the best little walker in the whole wide world." She made sure I was balanced and she took my hands from her fingers. I took one step, then another, and then a third before I realized what I was doing. Losing a little confidence, I stood a moment, unsure I could take another.

"Look at you, look at you!" my mother applauded. "Come on, you can do it." But I was not quite convinced. I carefully eased myself back down to my butt. She scooped me up and smothered my dimpled cheeks with kisses—dimples that I had inherited from her. "I love you. I just love you so much. You must be so tired from all that walking. It's time for you to have a bath and go to bed." Mom kissed me once more and put me on her hip.

She greeted the three men sitting in front of the television, drinking bourbon and beer. "Hey, beautiful!" the tallest one, the big bopper, hollered—what was his name? Charlie, she thought. Charlie turned to my father. "I don't know what a woman like that sees in you, Reuben. Good thing she didn't see me first." Everyone laughed. She'd seen these men on the basketball court but she didn't know them well. They seemed to her like the type of men trouble just might follow.

Reuben walked over and lifted me from my mother's arms, smiling down at her.

"Leave Robin down here with me for a while."

She was happy the rage had subsided. But still, she hesitated. She didn't want to say the wrong thing again. "Okay. I'll run a bath and get her pajamas." She cupped my cheeks in her hands and kissed me once again. "I'll be right back, baby," she whispered.

She hurried upstairs, feeling oddly nervous. *She's fine—she's with her father.* The hot water wouldn't run, the right pajamas were nowhere to be found. *Why do they have the TV so loud?* she wondered. *Why are* they *so loud?* Finally, the bath drawn and my pink pajamas in hand, she ran back downstairs.

Just as she entered the living room, she heard Charlie say, "Yo, man, you teach her how to drink like that?" Then she saw my father adjusting the picture on the television, his back to the others. Three feet behind him, I was leaning against the coffee table, both chubby hands clutching his beer can, draining it dry. Charlie and his friends got a big kick out of it, but my father swooped down, embarrassed, I suppose, shouted in my face—"What are you doing?"—and snatched the can away with one hand. He pulled back the other, as if to summon all the strength that he could, and swung at my behind. Knocked off my feet, I landed on the floor and, startled and frightened, I began wailing.

My mother ran the few last steps to me and scooped me up. She stood on her toes, and lifted her face as close to my father's as she could. She wanted to emphasize her point. "Don't you *ever* lay another hand on her as long as you live." The joking and laughing stopped; there was just the blare of the basketball game on TV. Everyone was still, including my father. My mother went on, her voice strong and firm. "Before you try to reprimand Robin, somebody needs to reprimand you."

As she carried me upstairs, she was shaking but she had no regrets. *Let him beat me to a pulp, but he'll never lay another hand on my daughter.*

Later that evening when she looked in the mirror at a bruised eye already turning black, she consoled herself, promising *It won't be much longer.*

⸺◦◈◦⸺

When my mother realized she was pregnant again, she knew leaving her abusive husband would be more difficult—but her resolve never wavered. Folding clothes, lying awake and alone in bed, walking with me, she tried to encourage herself. "I can take care of myself," she'd say. "I can take care of myself and my children. I *can* do this. I *have to* do this."

She hated to tell her mother what was going on and she kept putting off the phone call. Finally, bathing me in the kitchen one evening, she reached for the phone. There were voices already on the line. "I can't wait to see you again," a woman was saying. Confused for an instant, my mother thought there was a problem with the line. Then, she heard my father's voice: "What about Saturday night? I'm going to be with some buddies of mine watching the game. I really want to see you. I miss you, baby."

My mother began to ease the receiver back onto the cradle, then heard my father say, "Hello? Hello? Ruth? You on the line?" *Oh, God, what will he do if he thinks I'm eavesdropping on him?* Fear rose up in her throat like bile. It was the dead of winter, an icy January rain pouring down. She grabbed me from the sink and put a bath towel around me. She snatched up her coat and quickly wrapped it around both of us. Carrying one child in her arms and another in her belly, my mother ran from my father.

She crossed the street to a neighbor's house, running toward the soft light of the doorbell. Hiding in the shadows on the porch, she pressed the bell and listened to the gentle chimes. No other sounds, no footsteps, no calls from inside. She pressed again. "Oh, please come to the door," she whispered. "What if he finds me? Please, please, let somebody answer." Finally, she ran around to the back of the house and hid in the bushes. She tucked me deeper inside her coat and pulled the collar over my head.

After what seemed like ages, headlights shone in the driveway, then turned off. "Oh, thank God! They're home, baby!" She listened to the Lee family enter the house, then peeked out to make sure my father was nowhere in sight. Her heart pounded as she rang the bell again, but she willed herself not to show fear or desperation.

When the door swung open, she gave her neighbor a charming smile. "Hello, Mr. Lee! Would you mind if I use your phone?"

"Of course, come in, Ruth. What are you doing out in this weather?"

She shook her head in mock exasperation. "Oh, I feel so silly, I got locked out with the baby. I was giving her a bath, and I stepped outside to get a clean towel off the porch, and it all happened so quickly."

Mr. Lee smiled. "These things happen. Of course you can use the phone." And then we were both swept up into the Lees' kindness. Mr. Lee fetched a blanket for me, and Mrs. Lee fixed a toddy—"Just a mild one, sweetheart. It'll do you good." Once they'd settled her down, Mrs. Lee said, "Now I'll hold the baby, and you go on in there and make your phone call. And you just take your time now, you hear."

Ruth dialed the familiar New York number and her mother answered.

"Mama, come get me," Ruth said.

Grace said she'd be on the earliest flight out the next morning. Mom gave her the Lees' number to call, thinking, *I can't go home. I'll just have to figure out an excuse to ask them if I can stay here.*

The last thing Grace asked was, "Is Robin all right?"

"Yes, Mama, she's fine. Don't worry."

"Baby, I'll be too busy praying to worry."

Ruth hung up the phone and went back into the living room. Mr.

Lee smiled at her. "Mrs. Lee is making up a bed for you and the baby in the den. It's too cold and wet to be bothered with getting back in the house tonight."

Ruth was so grateful that Mr. Lee saved her the embarrassment of asking if she could stay. And early the next morning, a woman who was terrified of flying boarded a plane to bring her daughter home.

Chapter Eight

"Ruth, when are you coming back?"

"I'm not."

My parents had this conversation several times after my mom returned to New York. She couldn't say that she never considered going back to Reuben. Of course she wanted her family intact. In the life she'd plotted out for herself, she had a husband, a loving and caring husband, and her children had a father who would slay all their dragons, drive away all their monsters. But there comes a time to face the truth, to admit that what you want is not what you've got.

Sometimes Reuben called sobbing with remorse and regret. Sometimes his declarations of love were thickened from drinking. Again and again, she tried to explain why she was not coming back.

"Reuben, my very first memory of my father is him hitting my mother. It's actually my very first memory of anything at all. For so long, I thought that memory was just a nightmare, a frighteningly painful nightmare, because I was told I was much too young to remember—I must have dreamed it. But I found out later that it wasn't a dream at all. I don't know how I became that woman, but I'll do anything to keep my children from waking up in this dream too."

He didn't seem to understand or certainly he would never admit it if he did. He'd try different approaches to produce the outcome that he wanted. "You're just too nervous." Or, "You're making too much of a big deal about things." When he realized she was serious, he'd become venomous. "Stop this shit and come home," he'd say. Or, "If you think anybody wants a woman with two children you are sadly mistaken." Finally, he'd pull out all the stops. "I hope you're ready to walk the streets, since that's what you'll have to do to take care of two kids."

That was when she felt not only betrayed but guilty—after all, she had chosen this man to be her husband, the father of her children. All she could do now was push away his words, refuse to let them contaminate the rest of her life. Hanging up the phone, she would pick me up and settle me against her belly, drawing the strength she needed from her children, for her children.

———— ❧ ————

My sister Stephanie arrived three months after we returned to New York. Three months after that, Nanny kept the baby while my mother and I flew to Juarez, Mexico, so she could divorce my father. The plane was full of women, and a few men, all with the same destination and the same agenda. It was like a specialized package tour: a three-day visit and you were free of—well, whatever a divorce could free you from.

My mother gazed around the plane. Some of the women were crying, but not her. She knew the woman across the aisle, Karen, because they had the same divorce attorney. Karen was crying, so my mother leaned across the aisle.

"I'm having a glass of champagne. Why don't you have one?"

"You're taking this whole thing very well," Karen said as she dabbed at her eyes with a tissue.

"It's the beginning of a whole new life for me," my mother said.

"Me and my two children. And it is for you too, a wonderful new life. It's like having a baby, painful for sure, but it's a whole new life."

The woman smiled just as the stewardess was returning.

"I'll have a glass of champagne too," she said. Once Karen had her glass, she and my mother toasted to their new lives. I raised my glass of apple juice, already enjoying my very first vacation.

My mother had wanted nothing more than a chance to raise her family in a traditional way. Instead, with two young daughters, she was among some of the first women to take on a new role as the head of a family. Today, single working mothers are not at all unusual but in the mid-1960s, she said it was so unusual that it was often a source of embarrassment for this pioneer.

My father didn't do much to help ease her burden. The family court ordered him to pay child support, which he did—for about two weeks. She never insisted that he fulfill his obligations. Maybe it was fear that made her choose the path of least resistance . . . fear of his reaction to her demands. And maybe it was hope . . . hope that fewer demands just might keep the door open for him to have some kind of emotional relationship with his daughters. But regardless of her financial decisions and difficulties, she never let my sister or me feel that we wanted or needed a thing.

She'd buy one Popsicle from the Mister Softee truck and brag to the driver, "My daughters are the best sharers in the world!" Well, of course we had to prove her right. Or, if the budget didn't allow even one Popsicle, she would tell us, "Oh, you don't want to get stains all over that outfit Nanny bought you. You know how she is. She'll want you to look just so when she takes you out. Let's wait until tomorrow." If ever there were something we didn't have, we certainly were not aware. On the contrary, we were just two very special little girls.

But, looking back, I realize that she must have felt the pressure of raising two little girls alone, especially in those earlier days. One of the things I enjoyed most was setting the table for lunch. It made me feel like such a big girl. I remember one day when my baby sister kept interrupting me, tossing her toys out of her playpen. "Mom, make Sissy stop!" I complained. At the ironing board, Mom barely paid attention to me or the clothes, because she was completely focused on the radio. "Hush a minute, baby," she said, and turned it up. The man's voice, rich and smooth, filled the kitchen.

"There is no problem too big or too small that I cannot help you to fix. Do you long to bring a lost lover back, do you need to pay your bills, or do you want to fix somebody who has wronged you? I can help you fix it all. I guarantee it! I am the spiritualist T. J. Degora. You pick up the phone and call me today, and your troubles will be gone tomorrow." Mom scribbled down the phone number, then turned the radio down again, and gave me a radiant smile. "The table looks beautiful, baby!"

We heard T. J. Degora a few more times at lunch before my mother finally called the man and made an appointment. She didn't want a lost lover back, she said, she wanted a very neglectful father to start paying child support. T. J. Degora nodded; apparently he'd heard this one before. He reached into his cabinet of potions and pulled out a small bottle.

"This is the one you'll brew. Make sure you open all of the windows before you start, then bring to a boil every bit of it in a quart of water, every bit of it. And when you see the rising vapors"—he lifted his hands, fingers wiggling to mimic the vapors—"turn down the flame and just let it simmer until there is nothing left." He leveled a stern finger at my mother. "But you've got to make sure the windows are open." Then he eased back in his chair and smiled.

"You'll get your child support. I guarantee it!"

He sounded quite convincing, and my mother wanted to be convinced. He handed her the potion, but before he let go of the bottle he reminded her once more: "Just make sure the windows are open."

When she got home, she opened every window in the house and then went back to make sure. She chose what seemed to be the ideal pot, measured a quart of water, and poured in the potion. She turned up the heat and watched. *Oh, it's bubbling—I'm not supposed to let it boil, just bring it to a boil!* She lowered the flame. *I better check the windows just once more.* Returning to the kitchen, she pulled up a chair and watched the vapors rise. Suddenly, she experienced a twinge of guilt or fear, she was not quite sure what the feeling was or what it was she was doing. She blessed herself with the sign of the cross—but she still let the liquid simmer until there was nothing left. "Oh, God, please forgive me," she said.

The next morning, she asked for forgiveness again when she woke up, and yet again as she opened the front door to walk out to the mailbox. It was a large stack of mail and she went through it slowly. No check. The same thing happened the next day, and the next, and the next. On the fifth day, she finally said to herself, "What an absolutely ridiculous thing to do, going to that man. Lord, please forgive me." She reached in and found an unusually small stack of mail. My mother resisted looking through the envelopes until she'd put the coffee on to percolate. Yet still she looked through the mail with some anticipation. The very last envelope was the one she had been waiting for . . . the one the spiritualist had guaranteed would come . . . an envelope with my father's return address in the upper left corner. She looked up to the heavens and asked once more, "I hope You'll forgive me . . . please?" For a while my mother just held on to the envelope, hardly daring to open it.

Inside was a card with pretty pink flowers, and a message in his writing: "I can't get you off of my mind. I will do better. I guarantee it." And several crisp bills, which my mother quickly placed in her Bible. She bent her head. "Lord, I don't know if it is Your doing, some strange coincidence, or the power of the potion, but I promise You,

I will never do that again." And she slowly put the Bible back where she always kept it.

"Some things," my mother always said, "are just too dangerous to play with."

∽∾∽

My mother never went back to the spiritualist, and she took the admonition "The Lord helps those who help themselves" to heart by going back to school to study computer technology.

But that didn't stop my mother from taking us to Reverend Ike's church in The Bronx. Mom's cousin, Hardell, and his wife, Mae, were members of the congregation and they swore by Reverend Ike's miracles—a troubled girl straightened out and in college, Hardell's painful back cured without the operation the doctors said he'd need. So one Sunday, as my mother neared the end of her program and began looking for a job, we went with Mae to one of Reverend Ike's services.

For mass, we were well-scrubbed and pressed to perfection, but no one got particularly dressed up. Mae had told Mom that things were different at her church, and all the women dressed to the hilt. That Sunday, Mom made sure we all had on our best outfits. She borrowed a mink stole from my grandmother, and wore one of Nanny's dresses too, a really pretty blue one, with a beautiful rhinestone brooch Mae loaned her. She dressed Stephanie and me in our very best, very fanciest outfits.

We got seats very close to the altar, which was really more like a stage. Actually it *was* a stage, because Reverend Ike held services in a theater on 181st Street in The Bronx. From the moment we walked in, it was an absolute extravaganza, more like a Broadway production than a church service. Music filled the theater that had been transformed into a tabernacle and the lights were low, except for floodlights illuminating the altar. The voices like angels filled the huge room, though we couldn't see who was singing.

We were ushered down the aisle and very close to the front. We would not miss a thing.

Just as we took our seats, the lights dimmed on the stage, the voices grew louder—"Pre-cious L-o-r-d! Take—my—hand! Lead me on, Let me stand." To my surprise, my mother was singing along. Then figures in white began gathering around the altar, with a spotlight gleaming down on the biggest angel of all, his white suit aglow and his conked hair shining like a halo.

"Mom, is that God?" Stephanie asked.

But Mom didn't answer; she was fixed on the man.

"That's not God, Sissy—I think it's Reverend Ike," I answered for her.

Soon Reverend Ike led the song and the angel voices drifted into the background. He sang in a strong deep voice, one that made the entire tabernacle vibrate, and made my heart quiver. He stretched out his long arms just a little more and reached his massive hands out toward the audience. "Precious Lord, take my hand, lead me on, let me stand. I am tired, I am weak, I am worn."

Just then Mom leaped out of her seat, her arms flailing, tears streaming down her face. "Thank you, Jesus, Thank you, Jesus," she repeated over and over, and she would not stop. This never happened during mass. I thought, *Mom's been possessed.* Stephanie stared at me, as if she were wondering if I would do the same, and I have to admit that for a moment I wondered myself if it would happen to me. We watched our mother, who was indeed possessed . . . possessed by the Holy Spirit.

Finally, Mom settled back in her seat, tears still flowing down her cheeks. She didn't seem at all embarrassed, and Mae was absolutely undisturbed, even pleased. But *I* was embarrassed, and I looked around to see if anyone else had noticed our mother's strange behavior. "Oh my gosh!" I blurted out, when I spotted at least a dozen other women who had been possessed too. This Reverend Ike was really something.

My mother was still and quiet until the collection plate came around. "Give generously so that God can bless you!" Reverend Ike told us. My mother reached into her boot and pulled out a crisp twenty dollar bill—her very last bill.

The very next day, the placement office at the school told her that she had an interview with Electronic Data Systems, EDS, Ross Perot's company. After a series of interviews, which included her being flown to Dallas for a group interview, Mom got the job—a very well-paying job at that.

I think quietly we all gave Reverend Ike full credit for this miracle, but even so, that was our first and last visit to his church, and I wondered if Mom thought this was one of those things "just too dangerous to play with."

But even so for years, neither Stephanie nor I left the house before Mom had pinned one of Reverend Ike's prayer cloths to our panties.

Chapter Nine

Not long after Mom got her new job, we moved to Westchester. Our neighborhood was just a stone's throw from The Bronx, and perhaps it was a little less affluent and a little more diverse than much of the rest of the county, but to my mother, still—it was *Westchester*. Affluent, respectable Westchester.

Each morning, rising before the sun, Mom conducted her own worship service. Her schedule didn't allow her to attend daily mass but she seemed determined not to let the sun rise on a day for which she had not clearly expressed her gratitude. Between my grandmother's novenas to Saint Jude, the patron saint of the impossible, Reverend Ike's prayer cloths on our underpants, and the praise and thanksgiving that went on in our home, we were immersed in blessings.

Our fourth-floor apartment was, like the building, new and modern, and my mother took great pride in it. Our bedroom in particular left a warm, vivid imprint on my memory and on my heart. Plush white throw rugs over beige carpet made the floor as comfortable as our beds. Colorful finger paintings and drawings of lopsided houses, proudly framed as if they were Picassos, hung on pale yellow walls. A tea set, given to my mother by her favorite uncle, was always on display in the middle of the room, atop our very own little wooden table with matching chairs. Mom loved to sit at that table, because it was just like the one she had when she was little, where she'd served imaginary meals to her beloved Uncle Billy. When we were at school or out playing, our favorite dolls occupied the chairs. But when we had tea parties, the dolls sat in our rocking chairs, pulled up to the table from their usual places in opposite corners of the room. That way, everyone could join the fun. Dolls came to life and imaginations became reality in that room.

The building boasted tennis courts and a swimming pool, and it was full of interesting and welcoming people. It was like living in a tall hometown, full of immediate and extended family, populated by characters of all kinds, from the bon vivant bachelor with the revolving door to his bedroom, to the odd but harmless eccentric that (I'm sorry to say) we kids often teased. There were kids on every floor, so Sissy and I made lots of friends. I had my first crush on one of the boys in the building. I was crazy about Rusty for years, but he played it cool; the only thing he would permit himself to say was, "Stop bothering me."

Best of all, Nanny and Poppy moved into the building not long after we did. Nothing could have been more marvelous for a woman with a demanding career than to have her mother there, forever ready, constantly willing, and immensely able to relieve her of the pressures and preoccupations of motherhood so that she could concentrate on making a living and creating the life she dreamed of for us. Nanny did everything for us. She pressed our clothes and she pressed our hair. And of course she made the best meals imaginable. With both of them there, this wonderful home became a haven, a sanctuary of a sort. And within a year, my aunt Peggy moved into another apartment upstairs, so that the whole family was literally under one roof.

It was the early seventies, and among the upwardly mobile families who called the building home were many young black professionals, finally on the right side of history, reaping the benefits of the civil rights movement and sharing in the American dream. Bankers, lawyers, corporate executives . . . they were seizing these opportunities with both hands, determined to secure good, happy, and prosperous futures for their families and their community. Hard work, growth, and achievement were the mantra and this was a time like none other, when hope abounded and expectations were high—but within reach. My mother, always the overachiever and the perfectionist, seemed to share the responsibilities of both the men and the women. Mostly full-time homemakers, the women raised polite, well-groomed, college-bound children and created a comfortable refuge for the family. The men, the breadwinners, went out to face the stresses and competition of the workplace. Mom would accept nothing less than the best for her family on every front, and with Nanny's help, she succeeded.

<hr />

By now, I was five years old and Stephanie was three, and Mom enrolled us both at St. Joseph's Montessori. Among the students, every shade in the rainbow was on display, a rich spectrum produced by the storm of the sixties. Our families had made it through that turbulent period with a newfound pride and the determination to build a better America, to forge strong families, and to equip their children for the roles they would play in a new and diverse society. No family was greater evidence than the Shabazz family. Ms. Betty, the beautiful widow of Malcom X Shabazz, entrusted Ms. Ellis, the headmistress of St. Joseph's, with the early education of her five daughters. The seventies seemed a loving time . . . though, really, I had nothing to compare it to. No history, no experience . . . I only knew the love Stephanie and I felt in school, at home, and in our neighborhood—which completed our world.

St. Joseph's offered an excellent education, and I was very well-prepared for elementary school. I spent little time in the second grade, at Lincoln School, and was soon moved to the third. At the end of that year, I was moved up to the fifth grade. Clearly, I was on a fast track, and my mother was eager for me to realize her dream.

"Robin, do you realize that securing your future means choosing a profession you can rely on?" she'd tell me. I'd nod my head in solemn agreement, even though I didn't quite understand what "securing one's future" really meant. "You will always be able to rely on being a doctor," she'd go on. And I would go on nodding, because if it meant that much to her, certainly it was just what I wanted to do—secure my future—be a doctor. "You'll never have to rely on anyone else," she'd say.

Still nodding, I thought, *I think that means I won't need a husband.*

"I'm going to be so proud of you," she'd say and then stare off into the distance with a dreamy smile, as if picturing me in my white coat and stethoscope.

———

Lori Taylor was my very best friend, and we were inseparable at school and at home. Mom liked me having Lori as my friend, especially because Lori planned to be a doctor, too.

Lori was born again, and she made her church seem so exciting. One Sunday, I went with her to services, and I saw so many beautifully dressed women, shouting and praying, filled with the Holy Spirit—just like Mom at Reverend Ike's church. I sat there praying and praying that I too would be filled with the Holy Spirit. I closed my eyes and waited, convinced that any moment the Spirit would descend upon me too. But nothing happened. I left determined that next week I would be filled with the Spirit.

The next Sunday I wore the very best outfit that I could possibly put together. Maybe the especially fine clothes would make a difference. At Lori's church, one person after the other was filled with the

Spirit, and I closed my eyes tight, sure that the Holy Spirit would descend upon me at any moment. "Thank you, Jesus," I threw my head back and with fists clenched, I threw my hands in the air. That was my best imitation of Mom. But nothing was really happening. I tried again. "Halleluiah, halleluiah!" I shouted. My arms were still high in the air, but this time I lowered my head and shook it from side to side, "Halleluiah!" But still nothing. I was running out of things to try.

I parted my eyelids slightly, so I could secretly watch: Women with sweat pouring from their faces were speaking a language that I could not understand, dancing in ecstasy. I wanted that feeling too—I wanted the Holy Spirit. I was determined to make it happen. I closed my eyes tight . . . I clenched my fists . . . I felt sweat rise from my pores and bead on my brow . . . a language that I did not know gripped my tongue and took control . . . words that I did not recognize escaped from me. All of a sudden the spirit roused me from my seat and set my feet dancing and my voice rising with shouts of "Halleluiah—halleluiah—halleluiah." I danced up and down the aisle, my feet shuffled and skipped. My body trembled and finally I collapsed.

After church, as we stood around the buffet table making our plates, I heard Lori tell her sister indignantly, "She was not."

"What did she say?" I asked.

"She said you didn't really get the Holy Spirit," Lori replied. "She said you were acting."

Hmm! Well, maybe I was, just a little.

I suppose part of me hoped that if I acted like the Holy Spirit had come to me, then it really would. But I also wanted to give a good performance, and I was disappointed that I hadn't been more convincing. The truth was, I loved acting. I acted every chance I got. I'd even read the shampoo and conditioner bottles in the bathtub, pretending I was doing a commercial. When Lori and I watched movies, I memorized the lines and said them over and over to myself. Yet, aware of my responsibilities at school and my mother's dreams for my future, I kept my love of acting a secret. Keeping it a secret somehow made it mine and offered me a place I could go for escape.

———— ❦ ————

My mother gave me a choice between studying violin or piano, and I chose violin. That proved to be a mistake. At the first class recital, after three months of lessons, I just let my bow glide above the strings, never playing a note. My mother and Stephanie applauded louder than anyone in the auditorium, and Stephanie beamed at me—she knew how much I'd worried about getting through the performance. Relieved, I unleashed a huge smile in return. Then our teacher, Mrs. Tyner, caught my eye, and I knew that she knew what I was up to.

Fortunately, Mrs. Tyner was not only a perceptive teacher, but also the drama coach. Recognizing something I barely admitted to myself, she cast me as Dorothy in the upcoming production of *The Wizard of Oz*. My mother seemed to realize that this new interest threatened her dream and let me take the role only after I'd promised it wouldn't interfere at all with my academic work.

———— ❦ ————

On the night of the production, everything went smoothly. Everyone knew their lines and so did I; in fact, I knew their lines *and* mine. The audience was laughing and applauding in all the right places. As I linked arms with the Tin Man and the Lion to prepare for our skip down the Yellow Brick Road, we did a double step to get in sync. My ruby-red slipper, apparently in search of a starring role of its own, flew off my foot and into the audience.

I remember the audience's gasp, and watching the shoe float through the air in slow motion before it landed in the grasp of one of the fathers in the audience. Then everything shifted from slo-mo to fast-forward. Without missing a beat, I ran into the audience and grabbed my slipper, telling the man, as if it were part of the production, "Good catch!" before I put it on and dashed back to the stage. There was thunderous applause and the loudest roar of laughter I had ever heard.

At the end of the play, each of us took a bow, and when it was my turn, everyone stood on their feet. They screamed, they yelled, they whooped and they hollered, they applauded and they laughed. I laughed too.

After we'd left the stage, Stephanie beamed at me. "You were so good!" she said. Mrs. Tyner grabbed me around my shoulders and gave me a big kiss and an even bigger hug that squeezed the breath out of me. "Robin was wonderful tonight, wasn't she?" she asked.

My mother smiled and nodded. "She sure was. She worked very hard and put in a lot of time. I have to say, at times I was concerned it might interfere with more important things. But Robin never let it."

My mother could make a nothing moment so exciting. Yet this time, she made my most exciting moment ever feel like . . . nothing.

It was a warm night in late spring, and no one was in much of a rush to get out to their cars. The sidewalk leading away from the auditorium was full of people chatting about the performance.

"Robin, Robin!" I turned and saw Rusty running to catch up with me! His mom and little sister walked behind him. His dad walked with them too—I hadn't seen his dad since he'd left home a year or so before, one of the early divorces in the building. Suddenly I felt sad and embarrassed that my father was not there too.

Rusty caught up with us. "You were good, Robin—really good," he told me. And then he walked on without saying another word. That was the nicest thing he'd ever said to me. But then, I think nearly anything would be nicer than "Stop bothering me." When his family reached us, his mother smiled and said, "Good job, Robin." His dad scooped me up and said, "That wasn't a good job, that was a *great* job." As he put me down, he planted a kiss on my forehead.

I turned and walked toward Mom and Stephanie, who stood waiting for me to catch up. I think that was the first time that I got just the slightest feeling that something might be missing. Already holding Stephanie's hand, Mom reached for mine. I took her hand and the three of us began walking toward the car. All of the excitement of the night was gone—vanished, as if it had never been there at all.

"He would have liked it," Stephanie finally said.

"Who?" I asked, although I knew exactly who she was talking about.

As if she were reading my mind, but of course we could do that. "Dad," she said. "He would have loved it."

Chapter Ten

It was difficult for me not to think of my father over the next few days. I rummaged through my mind in search of some memories that included him. But no matter how hard I tried, I had nothing. No memories of him swooping me up in his arms and planting a kiss on my forehead . . . I had no memories of him hugging me . . . I had no memories of him loving me. I tried, but there was nothing. And not only was my mind adrift in wondering, my heart was lost in longing . . . it was my heart that hurt. The single memory of my father that I could conjure up only made me feel more alone, more longing.

———◦∞◦———

It began as a storybook Christmas. Stephanie and I left milk and cookies for Santa Claus on the kitchen table before running off to our bedroom, dressed in brand-new, pink-and-yellow Cinderella pajamas. Mom followed us into the room to tuck us in. She tucked the crisp Cinderella sheets tightly around Stephanie and pulled up the matching comforter right below her chin. Mom kissed her on the cheek and whispered in her ear, "Who's the best little girl in the whole wide world?"

"Me!" Stephanie answered proudly. Mom came to my bed next and tucked and pulled and gave me a kiss, then whispered, "Who's the best big girl in the whole wide world?"

"I know—I know!" I said, as if I were waiting to be called on to give the answer to a very difficult question . . . just the way I answered every time she asked. "Who?" Mom asked again. "It's me," I answered, right before I got my kiss.

She smiled at us. "I'm afraid Santa won't be able to get through the door with all the gifts he's going to have for two wonderful girls." (Everyone knew Santa came in through the door, since there were no chimneys in the building, and so the families took special care to decorate their doors to welcome Old Saint Nick.) Before Mom left the room, she turned off the lamp sitting on the nightstand between our twin beds. There remained only the glow of the night light, which created a perfect hue for our mind's eye to summon images from the shadows. And the silence permitted our imaginations to conjure up just the right sounds to complete Christmas Eve.

"Listen . . . Can you hear the bells?" I asked Stephanie. After listening for a moment, she announced excitedly, "I can—I can—I can hear the bells! Santa's coming—he's coming!" And she pulled the covers over her head this time, so that Santa wouldn't catch her awake.

———— ✲ ————

The sun had yet to come up when I awakened on Christmas morning. "Wake up! Wake up, Stephanie!" I practically dragged her out of bed and into the living room. There were so many beautifully wrapped gifts under the tree, and each one seemed to be begging us to open it first.

Stephanie and I took turns opening our presents, and soon the floor was covered with crumpled wrapping paper, still glittering and twinkling. Santa brought me everything I'd asked for, including the Baby Alive doll I'd left off the list I'd sent to Santa. I'd resigned myself to a Christmas without Baby Alive—but here she was! That's when I knew Santa could read minds, not just lists.

This Christmas was extra-special because Daddy was coming for dinner. I wanted to look especially pretty, so I dressed in my green velvet dress, the full skirt buoyed up by crinolines my mother had ironed with just the right combination of starch and sugar to make them stand out, white and fluffy as meringue. I fussed with my socks until the lace looked just right against my patent leather shoes. I wanted my father to see instantly how beautiful I looked, that day, just for him. And he'd see all the presents Santa brought me and he'd know I was a good girl.

Stephanie had a matching green velvet dress but she whined about having to wear the scratchy crinoline. They *were* scratchy but, as Mom said, "You want to look pretty for your daddy, don't you?"

So Stephanie and I sat on the sofa in our velvet dresses, and she played with a car from her new racing set while I watched for Daddy out the window, kneeling on the cushion, elbows on the back of the sofa, chin in hands. Time ticked by, and Stephanie grew sleepy—we'd been up so early and we hadn't gotten much sleep the night before. "Don't fall asleep," I warned her. "Daddy's coming and you'll be all wrinkled." I tried to keep myself awake with daydreams about what he would say to me, all the presents he would bring. I gazed down at Stephanie, fast asleep now, curled up with a bunch of her race cars. Stifling a yawn, I told myself, *She's going to be all wrinkled when Daddy gets here.*

⬥

I gazed out of the window for a very long time until, finally too restless to contain myself, I shifted positions. I climbed into the window and sat on the ledge. "This way I'll be able to see Daddy as soon as he pulls up," I thought. I smoothed my dress and tried to get comfortable but soon the ledge became too cold and too uncomfortable to bear. I climbed back down from the window, wanting to lay my sleepy head on the sofa next to Stephanie. But I would not lie down, for fear of wrinkling my dress. Instead, again I knelt on both knees and leaned against the back of the sofa, pressing my cheek against the pillow.

"Please, God, let him come soon," I thought. Time is hard to measure when you're young, but I remember watching daylight turn to dusk. Unable to fight sleep any longer, I drifted off.

I vaguely remember my mother scooping me up in her arms. My eyes felt so heavy. Maybe the heaviness was in my heart . . . disappointment is so weighty at any age, but particularly to a child. I can still see her hanging the pretty green velvet dress back in my closet. She simply said, "We'll save it for next time."

—————∞∞∞—————

"Where's your mind, little girl?" Poppy walked into his den and found me sitting on the floor with my legs crossed and my head in my hands. "You've been awfully quiet these last few days."

"Just thinking," I told him.

"No one in this house is used to you being quiet," he chuckled. "Even when you were a baby and couldn't talk, you ran your mouth. And all I ever said to Grace and Ruth was hush that baby up." His laughter gave way to a cough that lasted for a while. When he got his breath back, he went on, "Now, you want to be quiet and think . . . you have it all backwards, little girl." Poppy meant so very much to me.

He sat in his easy chair and unfolded his newspaper. I loved sitting in the den with Poppy. He read the paper and I read with him; he watched baseball and I learned to love baseball too. Still sitting on the floor, I scooted closer to him, until I sat at the foot of his easy chair.

"Poppy, do you know my father?" I asked.

"I've met him," Poppy said casually, never lifting his eyes from the paper. Then he put the paper down and seemed to think for a moment. "I know this about him: He's got two beautiful daughters."

He began to cough again—he seemed unable to stop it, helpless to control it. When the attack passed, he lifted me onto his knee. I recall noticing that Poppy struggled a bit, that he didn't seem as strong as I always remembered.

"I've got a riddle," he said. "What do you have more of, the more you give it away?"

I thought for a moment, but nothing came to mind.

"What, Poppy?" There was another coughing fit before he answered.

"Love," he said, and he pointed to his heart. "But for you to give love, someone has to give it to you first. That's why it's called 'the gift of love.' Now, what do you think would happen if a little boy didn't have that gift of love? He would never know how to give it to anyone. I think that's what happened with your father. He was never given the gift. And someone simply cannot give what they do not have."

"I have to think about this," I told him. He laughed, and once again coughing overcame him. Finally, he said, "Good, you give that some thought."

⸙

Poppy passed away later that spring. He lost his battle with lung cancer. I was eight years old when I lost the only man who had ever loved me . . . the only man who made me feel I was not only good, I was *good enough*. At his funeral Father Wallace read what he said were words that Poppy thought would give us comfort.

> *As He has been a Father to me—He will be a Father to you.*
> *As He has been a Savior to me—He will be a Savior to you. And*
> *so I leave you in the most capable hands of all.*

I knew that Poppy was talking about God, but I was thinking about my father. I thought about what Poppy told me that afternoon as I sat on his lap, in what was to be our last real conversation. I thought and I thought and I thought some more. And I finally thought I just might have the answer . . .

Chapter Eleven

Once I realized that I needed some connection to my father, I struggled with how to broach the subject with Mom. How do you tell the woman who has cared for you and comforted you all alone, all your life, that you want to know the man who has never cared for you or comforted you at all? How do you tell the woman who has loved you with all her heart that you want to get to know the man who has never shown you any love at all? I didn't know. The last thing I wanted to do was hurt her, but I needed to know something about my father—needed it for myself.

Children of single parents are often very sensitive and attentive to the parent's needs, and I certainly felt that blessing and burden. As I led my baby sister toward this difficult conversation, I was aware that my indomitable mother was still very much alone, that this was one of her few areas of vulnerability. I hoped she could understand my need, separate from hers, and allow me to visit my father that summer.

I don't remember how I brought it up or exactly what I said, but I will never forget the look on her face when she understood: disappointment and hurt, but most of all confusion. She turned to my baby sister and said, "You too, Stephanie?" Stephanie, always eager to please, was caught between the two people she loved most. Flustered, she stammered, "Yes! I mean, I don't know . . ." My mother's eyes welled with tears; she couldn't manage another word, and neither could I. I could not help but feel that I had betrayed the mother I loved so much, watching her leave the room with a heavy heart.

Although my mother did not respond initially, I did hear her talking to Nanny about it the next day. Nan didn't like to meddle; her standard advice was "Do what you think best." But in this case, she didn't hesitate to state her opinion.

We were in her apartment, and though she'd been cooking all day, there was not a hair out of place, and her starched shirt and crisp, pressed jeans were impeccable. She sat at the kitchen table across from my mother, took a long, slow drag off her cigarette, and exhaled.

"Ruth," she said, "Mama always told me, 'Don't trouble trouble 'til trouble troubles you.' Let that boy stay right where he is. He's not studying those children and they don't need to be studying him either." She took another drag. "*Leave that boy alone*," she repeated, emphasizing each word. "Let sleeping dogs lie."

As if she hadn't heard Nan, my mother said, "I just keep thinking about how I always wanted to get to know Daddy." That was the first time I realized that my mother truly did understand my need, even shared it. Mom's response didn't please Nan. She lifted herself from her chair and walked back to the stove. "Well, do what you think best," she said. Her words were weighted with the implication that my mother did not know at all what was best.

Mom called her own father in Lexington to discuss her thoughts. Their relationship had evolved over the years. He seemed to have mellowed—maturity will do that. And he seemed to be happy with his new family, which included five new children. But most of all, he seemed to have grown in his relationship with God and that is when real change occurs. Maybe it was inevitable. Mama Mack had lived a life devoted to the Lord, and she would have wanted her only son to do the same. Now that my mother had daughters longing for the same paternal attention that she had sought, she found it easier to approach her own father. In any event, she explained that we wanted to get to know Reuben and maybe it wasn't such a bad idea. Listening to her side of the conversation, I heard the searching girl she had been all those years ago.

"They—well, Robin, really, wants to get to know him. I guess I can understand that. I know I wanted to know you. But I'm just a little nervous about it. . . . Sure, I know people can change. I've seen the change in you. And if there's any hope of him being a father to them, my conscience wouldn't permit me to stand in the way. Will you please keep an eye on them for me?" I heard her laugh for the first time in days. "No, I see God isn't fussy about who He saves. Thank you, Daddy. I'm glad we can laugh about all this now."

This phone call seemed to ease her mind. With no fanfare and little visible emotion, she told us we'd be flying to Lexington to see Daddy, and that was that. I knew she was conflicted, and she made her anxiety clear, but we were going nonetheless. And she said Daddy was excited about our coming, so that was comforting to me. And I felt so grown up because we were making the plane trip alone. She was trusting me to take good care of Stephanie and myself.

———∞———

Taking the plane alone, in charge of my baby sister, made me feel very responsible. Reassuring Stephanie also helped distract me from my own nervousness. A stewardess walked us from the plane down the corridor, and suddenly a handsome gentleman with smooth copper skin and wavy salt-and-pepper hair swept up both of us in his arms. "Finally, I get to see these two princesses I've heard so much about!"

I had imagined my father strong and dashing, but this man was much older than I'd pictured. But then he showed the stewardess his identification, and it turned out he was Louis Newby—our grandfather, our mother's father.

"Excuse me, sir," I said, as poised and confident as I could be, playing my adult role as best I could. "Where is our father?"

"'Sir,' little lady?" he said. "We'll have to come up with something else for you to call me besides 'sir.'" He was chuckling and sounded like the lead baritone in a barbershop quartet. I stuck to my agenda. "Sir," I would not relent, "is our father coming too?"

He shook his head, smiling. "Your mother told me you were something, and she was right. Sweetheart, I am your Mama's daddy, and that makes me in charge of everything and everybody. You just hold your horses. I'm going to take you to your daddy now." He loaded our bags into a mint green Thunderbird and helped us in.

"After you, Princess." He laughed with Stephanie, who was grinning from ear to ear. "And after *you*, Your Highness." He winked at me. I stifled my delight. Stephanie, the baby, relished the attention, loving every minute of it. I was more reserved. And I was doing my best imitation of my mother.

When the apartment door opened, a tall, lean yet strong man stood there uncomfortably . . . our father. He had perfect features, a chiseled nose, deep-set eyes, and sculpted cheekbones and jaw, all set in chocolate-brown skin. He was handsome, that was obvious, but there was no glow or sparkle in his face, no warmth or humor in his voice. He was nothing like our grandfather, who turned us over to him with great cheer. And I wondered if his cheerfulness might be a hiding place for any concern he might have. He made sure to tell us he'd see us soon. I reassured him, "Thank you. We'll be fine." He kissed us both good-bye and roared with laughter when Stephanie dropped an impromptu curtsey.

Now we were alone with our father. I extended a hand, to break the ice. "I'm Robin and this is Stephanie." It was stilted and awkward, and he just looked at me coolly. "You must be . . ." I trailed off, not really knowing what to call him.

"Your father," he finished quietly. *My father*, I thought to myself, and the thought was pleasing. "We've met before, Robin, and I've known you since before you were born." He sounded both sarcastic and defensive, but then his voice softened. "It's been a long, long while," he said and then, staring at Stephanie: "You're beautiful." I saw now that she was the spitting image of him. He opened his arms to her, and she looked at me to see if I would approve. I nodded. *Why was she so comfortable with this man and I was not? Why was it so easy for her to accept his scant offering of love, and not for me? Why was it that she could offer her love effortlessly and generously, and I could not?* I followed them inside with trepidation.

The apartment was nothing like our home: no pictures, no comforting smell of food, nothing nurturing at all. It was not a place full of love. And in the middle of this emptiness, on a sofa stranded in the center of the room, sat a girl, seemingly not much older than I. She had long, straight pigtails, and her face was fair and sweet and plump, much like a pubescent Gerber Baby. I introduced my sister and myself, and she smiled and said hello. Her name was Robin too. This was my father's new wife, or wife-to-be. I tried not to look as disapproving as I felt. I heard Stephanie giggling and followed the sound into a completely bare bedroom, where she was spinning and dancing excitedly, as if delighted by this empty room. I looked around: no beds, no dressers, another empty room.

"Weren't you expecting us?" I asked my father. "You weren't at the airport, and now . . . where are we supposed to sleep?" Silence, and an emotional vacuum to match the room's emptiness.

"I've got sleeping bags," he said. "It'll be like a camping trip. Haven't you ever gone camping?"

"We love camping!" Stephanie said, always the pleaser. Well, he *was* trying to make it fun, I decided, and gave my best attempt at a smile. I wanted to keep the peace, too, and, after all, I *had* gotten us into this.

He gave us the biggest, broadest smile yet, as if he'd solved all the world's problems. He offered us something to eat, something to drink, but he never said what was so clearly on his mind: *What am I supposed to do with these girls, now that they're here?*

Alone in this empty room he called ours, my baby sister rested her head on my shoulder, and I nestled close to her. "I'm not sure this was such a good idea, Steph," I said.

I felt her shoulder lift in a shrug. "We have to try our best, Robin. We have to try."

∞

We slept on the floor in our sleeping bags, and early the next morning we were awakened by the sun. Its brightness cheered me. Now the room seemed not as bare, and my outlook not as bleak. Maybe things hadn't gone smoothly yesterday, but here we were in our father's home. Once he spent some time with us, once he got to know us, he'd see how special we were. We were his daughters, and this morning was the start of getting to know our father.

Except that our father was already gone and he'd left instructions with his child bride to take care of us: to get us bathed, comb our hair, feed us breakfast. Apparently, he'd forgotten that we weren't babies. In fact, I was ten, Stephanie was eight, and we could do all of these things for ourselves, except perhaps get our own breakfast. I wouldn't let his Robin touch my hair—if your hair isn't right, *nothing* is right, and I had no confidence in little wife-to-be. My refusal seemed to hurt her, so Stephanie said, "You can do mine."

By the time the girl was done, poor Stephanie's long, lustrous hair had been turned into something quite out of this world. With her silky braids somehow standing straight up on her head, she looked like an alien from a cartoon. And so the three of us sat down to breakfast: cardboard toaster waffles swimming in watery syrup. It was apparent that making a real breakfast was something she had not mastered either.

"Where is our father?" I asked the other Robin.

"He had to play basketball this morning."

I bit my tongue. Who *has* to play basketball?

"Could we have something to drink?"

"Well . . . Your father says not until you eat all your breakfast."

"And why is that?"

"He told me it would fill you up and you wouldn't eat."

What a farce. "Well, if we're supposed to fill up, you better give us something to drink because these waffles aren't going to do it. And when will our father be back from his basketball game?" Stephanie pleaded with her eyes for me to go easy, but I bombarded the almost-grown Gerber baby with questions for which she had no answer. Finally I relented; I saw something in her eyes that told me she was as needy as I was.

I led Stephanie to the bathroom and took out the horsehair brush, the fine-toothed comb, and the pomade Mom had packed for us. It was hard to imagine how that girl had managed to do such a terrible job in such a short time. But, with just a few strokes of the brush, Stephanie was transformed into a princess again.

My sister and I took seats on the sofa next to Robin, and there we sat, without saying much at all. In just a day, the lone piece of furniture in this otherwise bereft room had gone from holding one lonely girl to three.

It wasn't long before our grandfather came to pick us up. To this day I don't know how he knew to come, but there he was. This time I was as happy as my sister to see him. He smiled as we piled into his cool, mint green T-bird. "There are a lot of people waiting to meet you two princesses."

We pulled up in front of a grand old house with green shutters and a wraparound porch with wicker furniture and a swing, as elegant as he was. It was the epitome of southern graciousness, and I wondered what he had done to make Nanny leave him. But I decided not to think about that because on this trip, we really needed a hero. He opened the screen door, and we instantly knew we were with family. We were surrounded by the scent of corn pudding and fried chicken, food lovingly prepared for meals full of laughter—an expression of love and family that had forever been part of my experience.

Identical twin girls and a handsome boy came galloping in to meet us, and our grandfather introduced us to his children as "Little Ruth's girls." Soon the woman I assumed was his wife and the mother in this new family came out and grabbed us in a bear hug as if she had been waiting to meet us and could not contain herself.

The twins were as lovely and glamorous as they were welcoming. I felt cool just being related to them. A picture hanging on the wall caught my eye: our grandfather in an army uniform decorated with ribbons. If I thought he was handsome now, when I looked at the picture of him as a young man I could not get over it. He was dashing. "Daddy fought in World War Two," one of the twins said proudly. "He says he brought your mother home from the war in his duffel bag." We all laughed, and I realized that's what I came for: a sense of connection and family stories, even if they were tall tales. There is something about kinship, it's a magical connection like no other.

That night he tucked us into a four-poster bed with big down pillows. "Goodnight, princess," he told each of us, with a kiss on the forehead. I thought about Nan leaving him and decided that whatever he'd done, it was long in the past. Right now, I just chose to accept his love. I lay there in the dark with my sister, and I knew we were both happy to be exactly where we were.

Chapter Twelve

The next morning, it was once more the sun that woke me. But this time, it brought with it the warm, familiar scent of Sunday morning—the aroma of bacon cooking. There was a quiet stirring in the distance, the comforting sound of someone caring. The handsome young man who was our uncle knocked on the door to ask us how we liked our eggs. We raced around to get dressed and go downstairs to join our newly discovered family.

The night before, we'd had supper in the dining room, but now we ate in the kitchen at a long maplewood table piled high with all the Sunday morning standards: a giant platter of bacon, home-fried potatoes, homemade biscuits, grits, fried apples, and eggs. If I had not known better, I would have thought Nanny herself was here cooking.

I assembled the food exactly the way I liked it. I carefully stacked the grits on top of my sunny-side up eggs, then butter that oozed into the grits, followed by four strips of bacon. I cut into this concoction to break the egg yolk so that the bright yellow would spread evenly, and I applied salt and pepper with precision. When this perfect mess was ready, I looked up. Everyone was watching me. "Nanny taught her to do that," Stephanie explained. "It's kind of yucky, isn't it?"

"I wonder where your grandmother got the idea to do such a crazy thing," our grandfather pretended to ponder, with a twinkle in his eye. "Besides, it's not so yucky."

We looked down at his plate and saw a mess to match mine. He laughed, then plowed into his with enthusiasm, and I started on my meal, almost glowing with happiness, pride, and a sense of connection. Such a small thing—liking your breakfast the very same peculiar way—but family connections are made up of small things, and I cherished each one.

———— ⤬ ————

We went to church and listened to the twins sing in the choir, then back home for more food and more fun. I think what we did is referred to as "hanging out," which we never did much of in our more structured life back home. The girls taught us the newest dance steps, we tried on their makeup, and we had a blast. In mid-afternoon, our grandfather loaded some tools in his red pick-up truck and he and his wife drove off to return them to a friend. "You girls be good, hear? We'll be back soon."

We were really not used to being on our own, and it was both exhilarating and a little scary. Of course, all we did was hang out some more. One of the twins asked, "Can you spend the night again?" and I thought, *Why not?* We hadn't heard a thing from Daddy, so I called Mom at home. She was happy to hear we were having fun, and when I asked if we could stay at Grandpa's that night, she said, "Of course you can, honey." Mission accomplished. We all jumped up and down with excitement and continued our silliness, trying on clothes and experimenting with makeup upstairs in the girls' room.

After a while, the phone downstairs rang. One of the twins— since it was so hard to tell them apart, I was not sure which—ran down to get it, thinking it was one of her many admirers. But she returned, disappointed. "Robin, it's your father. He wants to speak to you." I concentrated on walking to the phone, so I would not trip over the dress-up skirt and heels I was wearing, and when I picked up the phone, I tried hard not to smear the makeup we'd caked on.

"Robin, I'll be there to get you in ten minutes," he said.

"Oh, that's okay. We're staying here tonight, but thank you." I was barely paying attention, simultaneously admiring my skirt and trying to keep it from falling off.

Now there was an edge in his voice. "Robin, I am already on my way, and you and Stephanie better get your things together."

I could hear his friends hollering, a basketball bouncing in the background. "You're not on the way," I protested. "You're still at the basketball court. Anyway, we called Mom and she said we could stay here."

"I'll be there in ten minutes."

He hung up and I stared at the phone for a few minutes. Stephanie clanged and clattered down the steps in a long dress and a tiara. She was taking being a princess quite seriously, but with so much makeup on she looked more like a clown. "What's going on, Robin?"

"Change your clothes, Steph, our father says he is coming to get us."

"We're *leaving*? Why?"

Then I changed my mind. "No. We're not leaving. Mom said we could stay, and if she said so, we are staying. She's the boss, not him." And with that, I declared war.

Our two young aunts were fired up for the battle. There was something thrilling about this, like the buzz through a crowd about to witness a fight. "Let's put the couch up against the door," one of them said. "That way he won't be able to break the door down." This was even more dramatic than I'd intended things to be, but this feeling was infectious. We shoved the couch over and changed our clothes to be ready for action.

Stephanie was genuinely scared, but I was resolute. "He's not in charge of us. Why should we listen to him?" She did not agree but as usual went along with me, as always my best friend and staunchest ally. We assumed our positions, hiding. There was silence . . . then finally the doorbell rang. The twins shouted in unison, laughing: "No one's here!"

Stephanie and I were not laughing; we did not know our father, but we had a sense this was serious. My father rang the bell again and again, yelling for us to come out. The twins giggled and shrieked in that combination of fright and pleasure you get from a horror movie. But this was real to Stephanie and me. Nan's words went through my mind, and I felt the terror of rousing those "sleeping dogs." Now he was pounding and kicking the door, yelling at us to let him in. The twins stopped laughing; this was no longer an innocent game.

Stephanie squeezed my hand tightly and whispered, "Let's let him in, Robin. Tell them to let him in." His pounding grew more frenzied; the door shook so hard it jarred the couch pressed against it. Something that had started as a silly prank, with me as ringleader, had turned into a disaster. I insisted to our twin aunts that we needed to open the door. The couch was much heavier than it had been when we'd moved it just minutes before. I guess excitement fuels your strength.

By the time we opened the door, my father was fiery with rage. His child bride was behind him, looking even more frightened, if possible, than Stephanie and I were. But when my eyes met his, it was anger that won out over the fear. *How dare he be angry with me*, I thought. *How dare he not love me all those years . . . how dare he not scoop me up in his arms and hug me . . . how* dare *he.*

"Where have you been?" I snapped. "You have not been around for ten years and now you want to tell me what to do? We come here and you run off and play basketball and now you want to show up and tell us what to do?" And then I took a deep breath, to maintain my ten-year-old version of control. I would not cry; he did not deserve to see my tears. I said simply and coldly, "Mom said we could stay, so we are staying."

My coldness was no match for his. He was ice. "Get your stuff, Robin."

"No, we are staying," I said.

His voice was a low snarl. "Get your stuff, Stephanie."

I stopped her. "Don't listen to him, Stephanie. Mom said we can stay and we don't have to pay attention to him."

Now all of his fury that had been building up for who knows how long erupted. Shame, guilt, regret—I'm sure he experienced them all. But tonight they would present themselves as anger: raw and ravenous rage. He threw me over his shoulder and stormed off to the car. I screamed, with the twins looking on in terror. Stephanie followed behind him, trying to keep up so she could see me. Through my own tears, I could see that she was crying, in perfect silence, and something about that utter quiet enraged me too. Now I hated this man called my father. Flailing my arms and legs, I screamed, "Put me down!"

The oldest of my father's terrified girls—his bride-to-be—hurried to open the car door. "Get in," he ordered Stephanie.

"Don't get in!" I yelled. "We don't have to listen to him!"

But she was good and scared, so she got right in. I kept kicking and kept screaming and even tried holding on to the frame of the door to keep him from shoving me inside, but I was no match for him and he threw me in the car. He took off like a drag racer, with tires squealing. Stephanie shrank into the corner, a contrast to the tornado of rage and resistance I had become. Spotting a police car, I heaved most of my body out the window and yelled for help, crying hysterically. The officer pulled us over with his lights flashing.

"Please call my mother," I begged, sobbing. "Please stop him from taking us!"

My father, suddenly calm, talked to the other man with a charm and warmth I'd heard for the first time. It was almost as if a conspiracy were brewing and this officer was a willing participant. "Officer, my girls were at a party and apparently the older one did not want to leave." He let out the slightest chuckle of exasperation.

The policeman smiled and nodded, turning to me. "You be a good girl and listen to your father," he said, and climbed back into his car.

As he drove off, my father smiled and waved, hissing at me through clenched teeth, "You wait until I get you home." I knew all my hopes for rescue were dashed. Almost resigned, I slumped back in my seat, wiped my tears away, and awaited my fate. Stephanie took my hand, and we rode the rest of the way in scary silence.

When we pulled up to his apartment, he got out and opened the door just for me. As I climbed out, he said, "I'm going to get you."

He let me lead the little parade of agony, following right behind me with an occasional shove, with Stephanie and the cowed girlfriend bringing up the rear. He opened the apartment door and pushed me aside to let the other two enter, and then prodded me inside. I saw that he was almost panting with rage, but at the same time sweating with nerves. Well, I was not about to show him my fear; he'd not have that satisfaction from me. I waited for the next order: I knew something was coming, I could not imagine what.

"Go to your room," he shouted.

"My room?" I asked. "I slept in that empty room one night, but it is *not* my room." He ordered the other two girls to sit on the couch and began pushing me toward the room. Stephanie grabbed me, but I gently eased her away. "Don't be scared," I said and kissed her cheek.

"No, she shouldn't be scared," he yelled, "but you should be!" He had such disdain. "Now get into that room!"

I opened the door to the bare, loveless room. Was it possible that only two days before, we'd begun our reacquaintance? How had it gone so wrong, so fast? He followed me in and we stared at each other, him in one corner, me in another.

I broke the silence. "Okay, now what?"

"Now what? I'll tell you what." He unbuckled his belt and began jerking it through the loops. "Take your pants down."

"No, I won't." He grew more furious, looming over me. "Yes, you will! I am going to give you a beating you will never forget, and it'll teach you not to be such a smart-ass! Take them down NOW!"

Now I was truly terrified. I whispered, "Please close the door. Stephanie is already afraid," and slowly lowered my pants. He kicked the door closed and yanked the belt through the last loop, almost triumphantly. Then he kicked over the lone chair in the room, and I tried to brace myself for what was to come. I was ready to accept the penalty for my actions, for wanting to come here in the first place. I had started this, and I would take my punishment. *Please, please don't let me show him how scared I am*, I told myself.

For a long minute, he stared at me standing there, my pants down around my ankles. *I came such a long way to meet you, to see you, to get to know you. Don't you know how badly I wanted to know you?* In spite of my determination, I started to cry. At the same time I lost control of my emotions, I lost control of my body. Tears erupted from everywhere. My face dripped with tears and the pants that lay around my ankles were soaking wet. "Don't cry now," was all he said as I wiped my face with my hands.

"You have a big mouth, Robin."

"So I've been told," I managed to say.

"And I am going to fix that right now." As I watched him raise the belt as if in slow motion, I closed my eyes and promised myself I would not scream. My heart and soul and tears curled up on themselves, pulling away to someplace safe, and in the distance, I heard the doorbell ring—insistently, again and again, as though someone were urgently trying to get in. My father's swing came to a standstill as he looked in irritation toward the sound.

"Where is she? Where is she?" I heard my grandfather demand, and a second later the bedroom door flew open. He took in the whole scene in a glance, and then, ignoring my father completely, he slowly approached me.

"Hey, Princess, there you are. I've been looking for you." He put his hand out. "Come on, Princess, let's go."

I looked down at my wet underwear and pants. "I can't," I whispered.

"Ah, Princess," he said, pulling my pants up. "Yes, you can."

He held my hand and guided me from the room, without acknowledging my father at all.

"Come on, Stephanie, we are leaving now," he called. As we headed for the door, I saw my father's soon-to-be wife sitting where we'd first seen her, on the couch. I stood there for a second, wanting to beg her to come with us. But even then I knew that she had lessons to learn. I ran to her and wrapped my arms around her in a big hug and then rushed out the door.

Our grandfather drove slowly back to his house, where everyone welcomed us with tenderness and concern. We were safe with my mother's father, but I could not help feeling that I'd been a bad girl, that I'd failed somehow, that all this misery was my fault.

When we called my mother, she insisted that we come home right away, and I was relieved. We said good-bye to our newfound family the next morning, as they still lay in bed half-asleep, and I wondered if I would ever see them again.

The trip to the airport in the green T-bird was very sad. The trip was over, and so were my hopes and dreams about a father who loved us—and I could not get over the feeling that I could have, should have, prevented this disaster. Our grandfather was somber, and I would have given anything for one of his jokes. When we got to the airport, I turned to him and said the only thing I could think of to say: "I am sorry. I am so sorry."

This warm and wonderful man crouched down so he could look me straight in the eyes. "No, *I* am sorry, Princess," he said. "It's taken me a lifetime to learn this, so I don't expect you to understand right away—you just have to trust your old grandpa. There are things people do, mistakes people make—and other people get hurt, even though it's not their fault. You can't blame yourself. I've made mistakes for which I am deeply sorry, and though I have tried to make amends, it has been hard for me to forgive myself. But I could never forgive myself if I thought I had done anything to hurt you."

"I love you, Grandpa," I said as the stewardess came to walk us onboard.

"I love you too," Stephanie chimed in.

"And I love you," he said, lifting Stephanie high off the ground and bringing her huge smile back to her face. "And Your Highness"— he took my hand and gave it a sweet, chivalrous kiss—"promise me you will grant me the privilege of your company again soon."

"I promise," and this time I did not hide my giggles.

Although I did not get what I came for, I left with something I hadn't expected, something very precious.

Chapter Thirteen

Mom picked us up from the airport in New York. Nobody said much on the ride home. We did not rattle on excitedly about what we'd done and who we'd met, the way that I'd imagined that we would. Of course, my mother was not her usual self. Energetic, enthusiastic, determined, and spirited, my mother set the pace. It was up to everyone else to keep up with her, so we girls were usually breathless running alongside her. But not this day. When we returned from Lexington, she was pensive, distracted. While she was affectionate, she seemed distant.

When we got back to the apartment, our adorable dachshund, Eric, provided some distraction—he was overjoyed at our return and covered us with kisses. But we all felt the heavy silence in those first few minutes, until my mother squared her shoulders and asked, almost formally, for us to join her in her room. We sat nervously on the edge of her bed as she paced in front of us. Still she said nothing, but she looked so pained that I could not stand to watch her anymore.

"I know I behaved badly. I am so sorry," I blurted out.

She looked up, clearly surprised. "Oh, no, sweetheart. I don't want you to think that. That's not it at all, not at all. I just want you to know something, both of you." She looked from me to Stephanie, and back to me. Whatever she wanted to say, it was not coming easily to her. "I guess I always knew I'd have to tell you and I suppose the time is here." She stopped again. This was worse than anything, seeing her tentative and fearful.

"I always wanted you to have a relationship with your father, so I thought it was best that you did not know . . ." She dropped to her knees between us and took our faces in her hands. "Your father can get very angry sometimes, uncontrollably angry. I had so hoped that over time he would have changed. And I surely hoped you would never experience his anger."

You don't have to tell me that, I thought. *I figured that one out on my own.*

"When we were married, he would lose control and he would hit."

"Hit who?" I asked, knowing the answer, but needing to make her say it.

She closed her eyes to steady herself again. "Me. He would hit me."

"Hard?" Stephanie asked, with a child's honest curiosity. "With a belt, or not? He was going to hit Robin with a belt. Hard!"

"It doesn't matter, now, honey."

Stephanie pressed her. "Did you bleed?"

My mother looked even sadder, if that were possible. "That doesn't matter now, either, baby." Her eyes were filled with tears. She didn't offer any real details, but she brushed herself off and stood up resolutely. "Forgiveness is the greatest gift we can give people, because I believe in my heart that our forgiveness gives them the power they need to change and it gives us the power to move on. I moved on and I hoped your father had changed."

I frowned. "Well, I don't know that I *can* forgive him," I told her in that precocious way I sometimes had. "Some things are unforgivable."

"I have forgiven him," Mom said quietly, but I was not sure I believed her and I was not at all convinced forgiveness was a good idea anyway. But it takes an awful lot of effort to bear the weight of guilt of carrying the burden of shame. Guilt and shame breeds in families and spreads over generations—the kind of guilt and shame that is never spoken, only hushed. And hush provides the most fertile ground of all. A seemingly strong woman, my mother plotted in secret, whereas I engaged him in the open. She saw this difference between us and it frightened her.

"Did you fight back?" I asked her. She shivered at the very thought of it.

"No, Robin, absolutely not. I just took it and accepted it. I patiently plotted my departure. I'd say nothing, try not to set him off, and finally I saw a way out."

At the time I thought she was embarrassed. A woman—even a very young one—understands the shame of another woman. But now I also wonder if it was hard for her to admit to being a victim because she would never want us, or anyone, to see her as weak. I am sure she wanted to protect us from the knowledge that such things happened, that such violence and ugliness at the hands of people we love could even be possible. But now we knew.

And with that, the conversation was over. She gave us each a hug, and it was never mentioned again. The hush set in.

Chapter Fourteen

I lost my father the summer of 1974—I had never really had a father but that summer I lost all hope of ever having one. Now, almost a year later, sixth-grade graduation was here. I was excited but also a little bit melancholy. Although graduation was still a couple of days away, good-byes had already begun. It was difficult to think I wouldn't be going to school with the kids I had grown up with.

We had one more class event before graduation: Culture Day, designed to show the significance of and respect for the many diverse cultures we were sure to encounter. Each of us was to bring a dish that spoke of our own customs and traditions, and I insisted upon bringing chitlins to school. What better food to represent the southern culture that I was proud to claim as mine?

Soaking and cleaning the chitlins took days. "I think we should buy the prepared kind," Nanny said. "You want to feed an entire class, and that's far too many chitlins to clean. And besides, I'm not sure they're really going to eat them anyway."

On Culture Day, I carried three big containers of chitlins to school—surely enough for everyone in class to enjoy. Ms. Jankowski helped me set them out on the makeshift dining table she'd arranged in the classroom. Everyone gave the background of the dishes they brought and when it was my turn, I proudly told the class about this southern treat, with its origins in the ingenuity of slaves who were able to turn thrown-away scraps into delectable dishes. Of course, I've learned since that many other cultures enjoy their own version of chitlins as a real delicacy. Scraps or delicacy, I couldn't imagine anyone not loving them as much as I did.

"Okay," one boy said, "but what are they exactly, and why do they smell so bad?"

"They don't smell bad," I insisted, thinking to myself, *Oh, what do you know? You just brought in meatballs. Big deal—everybody's had meatballs.*

My friend Charlene wrinkled her little nose. "They're pig intestines," she said. "I don't eat my mama's chitlins and I ain't eatin' yours." Lori laughed, "Only you, Robin, only you." She and I, along with Ms. Jankowski and a very select few, feasted on all those chitlins.

In the days leading up to the graduation ceremony, I started having second thoughts about the dress my mother had chosen. It looked like something a bridesmaid might wear—not a sixth-grade graduate. But Mom loved the dress, so I didn't say anything. On graduation day, I slipped on the long white dress and tied the sash at the back. Long, white, and flowing, with a big fat bow—that I could deal with. But what really pushed the dress over the top was the chiffon overlay, generously sprinkled with yellow daisies.

My mother combed and curled and pinned my hair up in a towering pile of curls. Then she took out a crown of yellow daisies she'd ordered from the local florist and carefully balanced it at the very top of my towering updo. "There," she said proudly, and turned me around to face the mirror so that I could feast my eyes on her handiwork. It was worse than I could have imagined. At that point, I would've been happy to look like a bridesmaid—at least then I'd resemble an actual person. But, no, I looked like a silly ornament on the top of a wedding cake; a stiff, silly doll. I was horrified, but my mother was so happy and so pleased with herself, I couldn't protest out loud.

"Auntie wants you to come upstairs once you get dressed," my mother said, proudly. So I went up to Aunt Peggy's apartment, taking the stairs so I wouldn't run into anyone I knew.

My aunt was a smart and serious woman, I knew that, but I'd never really shared nearly as many intimate moments with her as I would have liked. While she could be warm and funny, she most often seemed a bit distant. But if Stephanie and I never came to her with our heart-breaks and hurt feelings, she was the one we—and all the kids in the building—turned to whenever we had cuts and scrapes, bumps and bruises. I later realized that as a loved and respected nurse, many grown-ups had gone to Aunt Peggy with their own brokenness and pain. I suppose the wounded are drawn to wounded healers.

As my aunt paced in front of me, telling me how proud she was of me, I realized that this was the first time we'd ever spoken, just the two of us, like this. Well, so far she was doing all the talking, but I assumed I'd get a turn at some point. The unexpected attention from my aloof aunt felt a bit awkward, but it also made me feel so very important. I forgot all about how ridiculous I looked and basked in her approval. She'd never before told me how she felt about me.

"Are you listening, Robin?" she asked. "Yes, Auntie," I assured her. I wasn't just listening. I was experiencing the moment, taking it all in . . . feasting on it . . . delighting in it, a moment that meant so much to me. As she paced and spoke, she began to remove the neck-lace from around her neck. For as long as I could remember, she'd worn this gold chain with its perfect diamond. I'd always admired the necklace, the gleaming gold and the sparkle of diamond. Now my aunt walked over to me and placed the necklace around my neck. She stepped back to look at me.

"Robin," she said, "I want you to listen to me very closely. You are a very special little girl, and I always want you to remember one thing." She held my face in her hands and looked deep in my eyes. "Always be careful of what you wish for. Be careful what you set your sights on. You know why?"

"Why, Auntie?"

"Because you just might get it," she said, slowly and deliberately. I blinked. *What in the world is she talking about?* I wondered.

"Okay, Auntie," I said out loud. "I'll remember that."

She nodded and went back to whatever she had been doing before I arrived. I didn't know quite what to do, because I wasn't sure what had just happened. It was something important, I knew: The necklace around my neck was proof of that. So I just sat there, my hand on the diamond.

Auntie returned to the room and looked at me as though she was surprised to see me there. "You better go, Robin," she said. "You'll be late." I leaped to my feet and ran for the door. I'd just reached it when she called out, "Robin! Did your mother put together that silly getup for you?" I turned and saw the biggest smile on her face, and suddenly we shared an intimate knowledge of my mother, her sister. We both loved her, but we knew in her struggle for perfection she could go pretty far over the top sometimes. It was worth looking silly to see that smile. I ran to her and gave her a big hug, and then hurried back to our apartment.

All through elementary school, I'd been teased for being an "egghead." The truth was that I liked studying. Schoolwork wasn't work to me; instead, it could be a whole lot of fun.

Today, I was the last student called up to receive her diploma because I was graduating first in my class. The principal called out my name, and for a moment I hesitated, thinking about this "getup" my mother had put me in. But then I saw my mother beaming with pride and the delight on my sister's face, both of them radiating so much love, and my concerns vanished. I proudly walked up onstage to accept my diploma and award.

⊶∾∾⊷

Ms. Tyner approached us after the ceremony to offer congratulations. "Mrs. Givens," she said, "Robin might enjoy taking classes at the American Academy of Dramatic Arts," and she handed my mother a slip of paper with the school's address and phone number. "Thank you," my mother said, "but Robin will be very busy at New Rochelle Academy. She's going to be—"

"A doctor," Ms. Tyner finished for her. "Yes, I know." I struggled to keep from smiling. My mother and Ms. Tyner had engaged in this exchange in different ways on many occasions and I was truly going to miss it. "Well, the Academy has classes on Saturdays, and I'm sure Robin won't let it interfere with anything." And she turned to me and gave me a hug.

"Good-bye," I said, hugging her tight and trying not to cry.

"Good-bye, Robin! Now, promise me something," she said. "Promise me you'll be happy. Happiness can be a difficult thing to come by, but you do deserve to be happy."

"Okay, Mrs. Tyner," I said. This was the second time that day that someone had told me something very important and completely confusing. She hugged me again, and it felt as if I was being smothered by the best-smelling pillows ever.

Chapter Fifteen

New Rochelle Academy was set on Mt. Tom Road, a lane out of a storybook, lined with old oaks and evergreens shading grand mansions. A long, winding driveway led to the brick mansion that was the school's main building. The campus too was set among the same old oaks and evergreens that adorned the mansions along the road. Every morning our headmaster, Dr. Firestone, stood in front of the building's white pillars, greeting the students. He was a strong, handsome man, his fiery red hair always neatly cropped and combed, his suits beautifully tailored to his broad shoulders.

"Good morning, Miss Givens," he would say, in his aristocratic accent, to Stephanie and then to me. To my mother he would offer a particularly formal "Good morning, Mrs. Givens." Dr. Firestone was perhaps a little pompous, and he had an English accent even though I don't believe he was from Great Britain. But my mother ate it up.

Every morning was like a little victory to her, sending her daughters to such a lovely school, with such an accomplished headmaster. I was sorry that she was deprived of the same ritual in the afternoon, when Stephanie and I boarded the bus to go home.

My mother had the perfect plan for us: a quality education, then the best possible college, and a professional career. I would be a doctor and Stephanie would be a lawyer. We would be independent and self-sufficient, and we would never, ever have to rely on a man. Sometimes when she talked about her plan, she got a faraway look in her eyes, and I knew she was already years in the future, with me saving someone's life or looking on as Stephanie made a brilliant argument in court.

I was in the seventh grade, and Stephanie was in the fourth. Mom had taken her out of Lincoln so she could get a head start on the plan—although Stephanie often seemed oblivious to the plan . . . by choice. Her way was quiet resistance, just not seeing what she didn't want to see. I, on the other hand, was very well aware of my role and responsibilities in the plan. My mother provided the opportunities and it was my role to ignore any fatigue, any doubts, any second thoughts, and to deliver the success she sought. "Every generation is supposed to be better than the one before it," she'd say. Or, "We have to work twice as hard to be half as good."

My mother poured all her ambition, all her energy, into our futures. Like all challenges, she took it head-on, accepted it, embraced it, and loved it. But Stephanie and I were mere mortals, subject to burning out, needing relief, and desperately seeking it.

"Are you chewing gum, Miss Givens?" Dr. Firestone asked me. I was.

"No, Dr. Firestone," I chirped, trying to slip the gum under my tongue.

"A young lady should never chew gum, should she, Miss Givens?"

"No, of course not, Dr. Firestone," I answered.

"Well, just to be reminded of what is acceptable behavior for a lady, perhaps you will copy the fourth chapter of *War and Peace*," he'd say. Why he always picked *War and Peace*, I will never understand. "Good day, Miss Givens. And there will be no need for me to speak with you again in regard to this matter, will there, Miss Givens?

"No, sir," I assured him. He nodded.

"Good. Because I would hate to have to phone Mrs. Givens regarding such nonsense. No doubt she would be as displeased as I."

Now he had taken all of the humor out of this moment. More than anything in the world, my mother hated to be embarrassed. And to be embarrassed because of her own daughter's behavior? I could hear her already: "Are you out of your mind? How dare you! Do you know what it takes for me to send you to that school?" Like all successful headmasters, Dr. Firestone had a gift for discovering the most effective tool for controlling each student, and the threat of calling my mother was definitely the best way of keeping me in line. Anytime he caught me straying off the straight and narrow, even slightly, all he'd have to do was mention a call to Mrs. Givens. "I am relieved that I won't have to speak to your mother," he'd say, confirming his victory. "You and me both," I always said, under my breath.

⸙

At New Rochelle Academy, many of the children were from quite affluent families, but there were a few of us whose parents had to "work their fingers to the bone," my mother liked to say. There was a bit of class diversity, and a slight color diversity. My best friend Monica was a shining example of diversity all on her own. She always described her background as "Out of many, one." She and her sister inherited the beautiful features of their Jamaican mother, with the fair skin and blond hair of their German father. The combination produced two of the most beautiful girls, and freest spirits, in our school.

Whenever I felt like misbehaving, it was Monica who was my partner in crime. She thought I was a bit of a chicken, and she never understood why I was so obsessed with studying. "You need to learn to relax and have some fun, Robin!" she'd say. Monica was warm and funny, and she gave me a much-needed break from all of my duties and suffocating responsibilities.

Then there was my friend Mikki, who in many ways was the exact opposite of Monica. She was also beautiful and warm, but terribly serious. Everything about her seemed perfect, and as much as I loved her, she only increased the pressure I felt. Most of us went to school five days a week, but she went six, attending Japanese school on Saturday. (If my mother could have talked her Japanese school into accepting a lone black girl into this sea of devotees, I would have been right there with Mikki.) If I got ninety-nine percent on a test, Mikki got one hundred percent. If I got one hundred percent, she answered the extra-credit question and got one hundred and three percent. No matter how hard I tried, I always came in second to Mikki.

The one exception was the time she chose the wrong equation on a science quiz. I received one hundred and she—zero. Ms. Zaldo, our science teacher, winked at me as she handed me my paper. She knew how hard I tried, how frustrated I got. I felt a twinge of guilt, being so happy at finally coming in first—and any joy vanished as I watched Mikki staring at her paper, tears of shock and disbelief rolling down her cheeks.

Then there was Marlene, the poster child for the all-American girl next door. She was beautiful, and seemed so uncomplicated. I didn't understand why I was so nervous when she was the only other girl who auditioned for a one-woman play. As we sat with our scripts, listening to our English teacher, my palms moistened with sweat.

"The only thing that I ask of you for your auditions next week is that you know your lines—no reading from the script." Marlene and I nodded, but the knot in my stomach only twisted harder. *What is wrong with me?* I wondered, as we left the room. There was no reason to be so nervous about this audition. I had not only been studying acting, by now I had actually worked as an actress. But somehow this school play took on great meaning, and as its significance grew, so did my fears.

The day of the audition, I was overcome with jitters. I completely ignored the teacher's instructions and read directly from the script. Of course, Marlene got the role. I felt so jealous watching her the night she performed. *I could have done that*, I thought. I promised myself I'd never again let my jitters ruin an audition.

But even with the pressure and the growing pains, things were sort of perfect at my school, with my friends, in my world. It was almost impossible to imagine being any happier anywhere else.

Yet while both Stephanie and I loved the school, did well academically, and dominated the softball and volleyball teams, there was one way in which we were always different. No one else was being raised by a single mother. One time a "nuclear family" was discussed in history class, and I confidently objected to the implication that *not* having both a mother and a father at home was problematic. I brilliantly made the case in favor of single-parent households, defending a position I believed in wholeheartedly—though, truth be told, my heart still had not come to terms with my own need for a father.

Our schoolmates were like family, I said, all of us committed to the happiness and well-being of the others. I argued my point so effectively and my classmates were so supportive that day that nearly everyone agreed with my contention that nuclear families were not necessary.

My mother, however, had other ideas. She had decided that it was time for us to have a traditional family, in a traditional house. Usually Stephanie and I were happy to go along with her plans. We respected her, we admired her, we adored her . . . but we wanted no part of this notion. This dream of a traditional family, a nuclear family, was her idea, not ours. She hadn't consulted us; she hadn't asked us what we thought was best or even what we wanted. She just made the decision. We would leave our apartment and our school, where we had friends and where we felt comfortable, and move to what my mother considered a perfect house in Long Island. Husband and father included, of course, as if he were one of the amenities. Well, we couldn't stop the move, nor the marriage. But that house would never be home, and he would never be our father. Stephanie and I would see to that.

I started the sabotage even before the ceremony began. Monica, my partner in crime, and I drank the punch we knew was spiked with champagne—lots of punch. I stood there swaying, looking at my mother next to this stranger, and *Yuk!* was the only thought I could manage. I closed my eyes and opened them again, hoping I'd see something different. Instead, I was seeing my mother and this man in doubles.

"Are they married yet?" I asked Monica.

"Be still," Monica whispered in my ear. "Stop wobbling!"

The flowers on my mother's floral chiffon dress were dancing themselves into a blur. "I do," I heard her say.

"Well, I *don't*," I whispered in Monica's ear. And sweet little Stephanie said, "I don't either." It was at that point that I bolted out of the room and threw up all over the backyard.

Sick and woozy as I was, I knew my mother would be furious, maybe even hurt. *Well, that's what they both get for making me so miserable*, I thought. Nan escorted me back inside, none too gently. She was chuckling, not with merriment but with something more like rueful resignation. "Girl, nobody hates to be embarrassed more than your mother, and you know how to embarrass her better than anybody." I didn't care.

I felt vindicated in my anger when the sweetest child on the face of the earth went on the attack. "I am the king of the house," he told us every chance he got, so Stephanie rigged every one of his royal thrones with straight pins. "Doggone it," the king said, rubbing at his bottom. "What was that?" He glared at me but I had a clear conscience. Frank soon learned to check carefully before taking a seat.

The poor man tried as hard as he could, but he went about it all wrong. He pushed too hard too fast. He'd already installed himself as the king, and now he was going to be the father. But we already had one father; even if he wasn't one bit concerned about us, even if I wasn't one bit crazy about him, that didn't mean Stephanie and I wanted anything to do with another one.

But he tried. When Mom came in to tuck us in and kiss us good-night, he joined her in this family ritual. Stephanie would wait for him to close in for a kiss, then she'd pull his goatee so hard it brought tears to his eyes. We both showed our displeasure in lots of small ways like this, but my favorite revenge was the Meatball Dinner. Mom, Stephanie, and I all loved eating right-off-the-boat crabs from a Long Island pier. We enjoyed the whole experience: cracking the crabs and searching for bits of sweet, succulent meat, the huge mess of it, the newspapers spread out on the table in place of the usual linen table-cloth. But King Frank found this frustrating, and the crabs couldn't satisfy his royal appetite. On those occasions he would feast on meat-balls my mother cooked specially for him.

Stephanie began preparing early in the day of one of these crab dinners. She spent all morning collecting tiny black ants from the garden and shoved a jar full of the crawly creatures into my face, making me shriek. "Shh!" she hushed me. "They're for Frank's meatballs." Now we both howled with laughter.

As dinnertime approached, I told Mom, "Let us make the meat-balls." She was delighted at this show of interest and generosity. "Don't forget the bread crumbs," she told us as she left the kitchen.

"Mom, we know just what goes in the meatballs," I answered, try-ing to contain my laughter. But as soon as she was gone, we nearly fell down laughing.

We loved watching the king gobble up those meatballs. "The

girls made them just for you, Frank," Mom said proudly, and he was delighted. Then Mom reached for a meatball to judge our culinary skills.

"They're just for Frank!" I said.

"Yeah! We made them for Frank," Stephanie squealed.

Mom slowly drew her hand back from the platter and silently searched our faces. You could almost see her thinking, *Hmmm . . . why are they being so nice to Frank all of a sudden?* After dinner, she finally got the truth out of us, and I think she almost got as big a kick out of it as we did. She never said a word about it to the king.

I made it perhaps a whole month in my new school, but certainly no longer than that, and every moment I was filled with anguish. My mother was constantly bombarding me with questions, asking why I was so miserable, why I'd stopped eating and couldn't sleep, why I'd even lost interest in school. She had been so confident that, given time, I would accept my new friends, accept my new home, and accept my new father. After all, I'd always fallen in line with the plan before. Finally, she sought the counseling of a priest. "Sometimes when you realize a decision is not the best one, it is better to resolve it sooner rather than later," he told her. Nan and Mom discussed it, as well. Mom confessed that she'd had dreams of marrying a man like Poppy, someone who loved her children so much, they couldn't help but give in to loving him back. But Frank was a different kind of man—a very nice man, and in his own way, he was loving and caring and giving. But Mom wondered aloud to her mother if maybe the difference was that Poppy was just so godly.

It wasn't long before Mom was making the long drive from Long Island to New Rochelle each school day, before she went to work. Not long after that, we moved back to Westchester. And very soon Frank was gone from our lives forever. Mom simply chose the happiness of her children over her own and in choosing our happiness, Frank, I am sure, rediscovered his.

⊶∞⊷

Thanks to my mother, Stephanie and I returned to New Rochelle Academy, and I was able to graduate with my friends. I had missed them all terribly, but what surprised me most was how much I had missed Dr. Firestone.

"Nice to have you back, Miss Givens," he told me on my first day back.

"I was gone much too long," I replied.

"You were gone a month, Miss Givens. You are far too dramatic," he said with a smile. That smile made me feel so warm and safe.

Soon the twenty-three of us in the Class of 1980 left our perfect little world. And true to the laws of this world, I wasn't first. I was second. As Mikki walked to the podium to accept her valedictorian award, Monica whispered in my ear, "Whoop-ti-do. So she's first in the class today . . . like it really matters." How many times had she whispered those same words to me? And every time, she made me laugh.

Chapter Sixteen

I was fifteen years old when I entered Sarah Lawrence College. Of course I realized I was much younger than most college freshmen, but I was convinced I was every bit a woman and fully prepared for this experience. I remember my answer to a question from the director of admissions during my interview. I sat in her office feeling nervous but determined, dressed in a blue pleated skirt and a matching blue blazer over a crisp white shirt. I wore argyle kneesocks, and my loafers were so shiny I could see my reflection in them.

"Robin, do you think you're ready for college?" she asked.

"Of course," I said, wondering why on earth she was asking such a question, "I am a woman."

She smiled a forgiving smile that I didn't understand then, but I realize now that she must have thought me very foolish. Yet we only know what we know. And I simply did not know any better.

Sarah Lawrence was founded as a women's college, though by the time I attended, it was a coeducational institution. And for all its prestige, I loved it and chose it because it was just like my beloved New Rochelle Academy. My goal was to be close to home, but some of the schools that I visited in Manhattan seemed big and overwhelming, while Sarah Lawrence felt like an extension of all that I knew; it was simply familiar. And if there were any differences they were ones that I could manage. The street signs were different in this quaint little village of Bronxville. The faces were different too . . . but still there was something familiar about these stately houses set among wise old trees. There's something so comforting about things that have stood the test of time and in the fullness of time celebrate their patience, their perseverance, and their wisdom. But this historical setting contained a progressive liberal arts college. I suppose change sometimes comes easiest within surroundings that offer the comfort of remaining the same. And I'd come to love best the one building that was nothing like the others: our library, designed by Frank Lloyd Wright.

———∞∞———

The outside of my new home, a dignified Tudor mansion, showed no sign that it was actually a dorm for a bunch of young people hardly more than adolescents. My mother's face lit up at the sight of it. She opened the door of the station wagon we'd borrowed from Uncle Stormy and slowly stepped out, wanting to savor this experience and all that it symbolized to her.

Stephanie popped out from among all the suitcases and boxes packed into the car and began unloading them. Each of us grabbed what we could carry and began walking up the cobblestone path toward the house. "Watch your step, Mom," I cautioned, as she gazed at my new home. Though I knew she was proud of me, this was just as much an accomplishment for her, one that she found hard to believe.

We entered the exquisite house slowly, wanting to relish every moment. As we stood on the landing at the top of the stairs, with its mahogany detailing, my eyes were drawn to a portrait of the founder over a massive stone fireplace. Mom put down the two suitcases. "I wish I had bought new luggage," she said aloud, wanting everything to be right and finding it hard to believe that indeed it was.

Stephanie had already unpacked the stereo and was setting up the speakers when we arrived in the room. I chose the bed farthest from the door and closest to the large window that overlooked the beautiful courtyard. I put down my suitcase, unzipped my garment bag, and hung my new pleated skirts one by one in the closet. Mom stopped examining the room and joined me in unpacking. She took cashmere sweaters and argyle socks out of the suitcases she had carried and carefully arranged them in the chest of drawers. As usual, she established an order for everything. "And be sure you find a good place to have your shirts laundered," she said. "Make sure you tell them light starch."

My mother stood at the closet, admiring her choices and their perfect order. Seeing my wardrobe displayed like that, I noticed for the first time that I had different versions of the exact same outfit.

Stephanie bolted out of the room. "I'll get the box with the records," she said.

Moments later, the door opened. "Wow, that was fast," I said, thinking Stephanie had returned. But when I turned toward the door, there stood a dark-haired young girl and a woman who had to be her mother. The girl was dressed in jeans, loafers, and a cashmere sweater much like the ones I'd just unpacked. *Oh, we have a lot in common*, I thought, gazing at my roommate, my new best friend.

"Hi!" I rushed to the door, smiling, with my hand extended to greet her. "I'm Robin Givens."

My new roommate didn't budge from the doorway. She simply stood, with a look of shock on her face. And so I froze too, terribly disappointed and hurt. Mom's eyes were fixed on me, though she never stopped smoothing the sheet on that bed by the window. For a moment everything seemed so still. My roommate was rescued from having to shake hands with me when Stephanie raced through the door and nearly knocked her over.

"Gosh, I'm sorry!" Stephanie said.

Then my roommate's father walked up. He was far better than his wife and daughter at hiding his surprise, and made the introduction for her. "This is my daughter, Heather," he said, shaking my hand and guiding Heather and his wife into the room.

Now my mother was spreading the comforter and fluffing the pillows, never taking her eyes off this unfolding drama. I wasn't sure what was going on, but I sensed that my mother knew precisely. Stephanie had returned with not only a stack of records, but my favorite poster.

"Where do you want Marilyn?" she asked me. I couldn't answer—the tension was so thick. Stephanie ignored my lack of response and began looking through the stack of records. "Do you like the Sugar Hill Gang?" she asked my roommate. And when Stephanie got no response from Heather, she ignored that too and pressed on, seeming not to notice the chill. Stephanie cued up the song she liked most and began singing along with the record, unfazed by the tension in the air.

"Be quiet," I told my little sister, but it was hard not to laugh.

I hoped that Heather would recover from the shock of having me as her roommate and we would become best friends.

"Heather, did you want this bed?" I asked.

"No," she said . . . just, "No."

Well, at least she said something, I thought. *Maybe we've broken the ice.*

I walked my mother and sister back to the car. Now my mother seemed a little deflated.

"Are you going to be okay?" she asked as she kissed me good-bye.

Stephanie answered for me. "Mom, she's going to be great." She hugged me and ran to climb back into the car. I was glad to know they would only be fifteen minutes away.

That night was sleepless for both Heather and me. We did in fact have so much in common. We were each on our own for the very first time, away from the comfort of our families, seeing new faces and meeting new friends. There was one significant difference. Though it was not the first time that one of my friends wore a face like Heather's, it must have been the first time Heather saw a potential friend with a face like mine. I must have fallen asleep in the wee hours, and in the morning, my roommate was not there. As I hurried to get ready for my first meeting with my don, as the advisers were called, I spotted that lovely sweater of hers, so much like the sweaters in my closet, thrown over her chair.

When I returned from my meeting, not only was Heather gone, but all of her things were, as well. And except for the disappointment that I felt as I stood in the room, there was no evidence that she had ever been there at all.

───── ❧ ─────

My don called me to his office later that day. Mr. Clark was a wonderful man and we would become good friends.

"Enjoy your room, Robin," he said. "It looks like you have that great big space all to yourself." His smile looked just a little embarrassed. "You know, Robin," he said, "we are all here to learn. Learning can take us away from what's familiar and to a place that is not very comfortable. It's a pity that some people don't have the courage to take advantage of the opportunities when they are presented. Now, you enjoy your room and try to enjoy your learning."

I turned to head toward the door, sad and stunned. The truth had been confirmed to me. I had looked forward to meeting my roommate, had anticipated sharing so much more than a room with her.

"And, Robin . . ." Ray Clark stopped me at the door. "What she feels has nothing to do with you."

"Thank you," I told him, sincerely meaning it. "Thank you."

I went back to the room and pushed the beds together to make one king-sized bed. The next day I bought sheets and a comforter for my new bed, and two more life-sized posters, a Bogie and a Bacall. After all, Marilyn would need company.

Chapter Seventeen

It was early fall. The temperature was up one day, as if summer simply refused to make a gracious exit, and then down the next, as if it had indeed succumbed to its inevitable end. The stout trees now boasted leaves of radiant red and brilliant yellows, some already drifting into piles on the ground. They cushioned the young men who played on the lawn, as they tackled one another and landed in the crackling piles.

I don't know if being handsome was one of the criteria established for the small population of men at this former women's college, but these were some of the most handsome young men imaginable. Cary Elwes, who looked and sounded like a collegiate James Bond, was the most handsome of the handsome. Cary lived in my dorm and seemed to be the self-appointed captain of the football team that gathered on the lawn to practice. I don't know if they ever competed with another team, and I don't think they actually competed with each other. It was just good fun.

On this particularly brisk autumn morning, I made sure to bundle up before leaving for class. It was my first day out of bed after spending the weekend trying to recover from bronchitis. The guys were having an early practice that day—or at least they were amusing themselves rather early. Even before I opened the door, I heard loud laughter and Cary calling plays in his distinctively charming British accent. Getting a glimpse of this gorgeous man so early in the morning was a good sign for the rest of the day. He always gave me a warm hello, which was typical of his charm, but the warmth was enough to make me melt—even on the coldest of days.

I allowed myself a brief glance in Cary's direction as I walked quickly down the cobblestone path that led away from the house.

"Robin!" I heard that dashing British accent. "How are you feeling?"

I stood still, my legs simply refusing to move. By now he stood on the walkway directly in front of me, still a bit out of breath from playing. "Um . . . uh . . ." I was not a bit out of breath, yet somehow I was breathless, simply too nervous to speak.

"I'm better," I finally answered.

"Well, glad you're feeling better, Robin." Then he ran off and intercepted the football with a laughter that was music to my ears.

Now it seemed too hot for the hat I was wearing. I pulled it off and, a bit dazed, began making my way to class. All the while, I was hounded by my very own guardian angel of the inadequate, which pummeled me with all the brilliant things that I could have and should have said. Over the next few days, I watched Cary laugh and play with such marvelous ease. In acting class I watched him bring a character into being with the same ease; he was magnificent. All the while, I was rehearsing what I would say the next time he spoke to me.

I actually did not have to wait very long. Just a few days later, while I was typing a paper, I heard a knock at the door.

"Robin!" Cary was calling my name again. "Open up."

This time I was ready. *Cool and sexy*, I reminded myself. *Cool and sexy*. I pushed back the chair, slowly took a deep breath and let it go even more slowly, and slowly I began walking toward the door.

"Robin, open up," he said. I couldn't believe how eager he seemed—but I was ready this time. "Cool and sexy," I whispered to myself.

With my heart pounding, I opened the door, smiling the cool and sexy smile I'd practiced.

"Robin, your father is outside," he said, turning to walk away.

I stood practically lifeless—still. My father could not be outside. This must be a practical joke. Cary realized I hadn't moved and beckoned me to follow him. Was he joking? Was he serious?

The panic began to fill my body—rising up from deep inside—and my thoughts were becoming jumbled. I managed to blurt out, "You must have made a mistake."

Now he looked completely baffled. "Your father is downstairs, Robin."

I shook my head. "My father can't be here," I tried to assure him. Actually I was trying to reassure myself.

Cary grabbed my hand and began to pull me downstairs. "Robin, your father is outside waiting for you to come down." His hand felt big and smooth and kind. When we arrived at the front door, he let go of my hand and opened the door. Taking hold of my shoulders, he pointed me in the direction of the man outside.

"See?" he asked.

Yes, I did see.

"Hi, Robin," the man said. The man who reeked of stale beer—the man with crumpled clothes—the man that I hadn't seen in years—this man was indeed my father.

I forced myself to say, "Hello." But I was thinking *Why now? Why here?* Cary stood between us as if he were some kind of referee; I could smell the stench of beer coming from my father and I was certain that Cary could too. I felt Cary's eyes on me, but I did not remove my eyes from my father, as though I could will him to go away, will him to disappear and to vanish from Cary's memory as well as from my own. Does this man enjoy torturing me? It was bad enough that he was here at all but to show up and embarrass me in front of Cary . . . This was my worst nightmare. It was like being caught naked. I stood bare . . . stripped.

As the silence grew, Cary became more and more uneasy. "I'm

Cary, sir," he said, offering his hand. "Excuse me, but I must get back to the books."

My father held on to Cary's hand for a second longer, just to keep him there and spare us both the inevitable tension.

"Thank you, young man," he told Cary.

Uneasy, Cary lingered a moment and then turned and went back upstairs, leaving my father and me alone. When he reached the top of the stairs, it was as if he had second thoughts.

"Are you okay?" he called to me.

Tears forming in my eyes, I answered unconvincingly, "Yes."

He hesitated, and then finally vanished from sight.

———⚬⚬⚬———

My father and I stood in the doorway, unwilling or unable to go out or come in. "What on earth are you doing here?" I whispered through clenched teeth.

"I wanted to see you," he answered.

"Why?" I asked. I couldn't imagine my father even thinking of me, never mind wanting to see me. "Why would you come here? How did you find me?"

"It was easy," he told me casually. Easy? I had lived in the same place for years before coming to Sarah Lawrence, and that apparently had not been easy enough for him to find. I thought of that little girl who waited by the window, nose pressed against the glass. *Now* he shows up. And I recalled the bigger girl who showed up for him, hundreds of miles from home, who received little of his time and less patience and absolutely no love. Now he shows up, now he is interested in me. I struggled to fight back my tears of hurt and anger.

"I just wanted to see you, to see where you were going to school," he said. "I just wanted to tell you how proud I am of you."

That did it. My tears erupted.

"Go away," I whispered. I slammed the door and ran upstairs to my room. I cried the old tears right along with the new ones; I felt the old pain right along with the new, and the old shame right along with the new shame. For one brief moment I got the feeling that my father wanted forgiveness and was truly here because he needed me to forgive him. But I had both wants and needs of my own. All of my life I had just wanted him to love me and needed him to show me love. I had tried to cut him out of my life, so that he could never hurt me again. But this evening, I discovered I had not really been successful. I suppose it was impossible; he was part of me and to deny him was to deny myself, to hate him was to hate myself. When people asked me about my father I had created one . . . sometimes I created one who traveled a lot on business; other times I created one who was around but busy with his medical practice. I created stories about him, stories that were palatable to me and acceptable to those I told. But until I learned to accept him, I would be the one who suffered most.

I was still that very little and very lonely girl filled with longing. And no matter how hard I worked, I just couldn't work hard enough to be at peace with myself. And all that I had done was not good enough. All that my mother had accomplished was not right enough. All that my grandmother had overcome was not achievement enough. I cried myself to sleep. The tears were all too familiar.

About 3:00 in the morning an alarm went off in my head. I had not finished my paper. I eased out of bed and once again sat at the new Brother typewriter, my graduation gift. The paper would need to be finished by morning, and the paper would have to be perfect. I began to prepare for the time when the light of day would shine on me and I could present the ideal image. Perfection was not the same as flawlessness. On the contrary, it was a place to hide my flaws . . . my feelings of inadequacy and lack of self-esteem . . . my feelings of shame and lack of worthiness . . . my devastating pain and my longing . . . these feelings that hurt so deeply and that I could not control. And no one would know the pain I felt, or how incomplete I felt. Perfection would hide my wounds and conceal my flaws. Anyone looking at me from the outside would never guess that indeed I was perfect . . . a perfect mess.

And so I typed away and prepared for the day ahead.

Chapter Eighteen

One thing that we all have in common is the challenge of finding a way to survive our childhoods. In the process, we discover the tools we believe are the most crucial for our survival. Mine was the fine art of "perfection." Flawless, faultless, picture-perfect—I claimed these attributes as my own. My mother instilled it and I followed along; I needed to be the best good girl I could be. There was safety for me in the idea of perfection, but I guess that is why I never felt safe. Nobody is actually perfect.

But college posed no threat to my self-image. I did not have any trouble keeping up with the academics of college, taking it in stride, except for one all-nighter early on. I'd tried some NoDoz, which wound up making me lightheaded and faint. Unfortunately, my collapse was public, and I was sent to see my don, Mr. Clark, again. He was as warm and wonderful as he'd been the first time I'd seen him. Concern for me was all over his face, and when he brought up my academic load, I was relieved. Now *that* I could explain . . . after all, I was premed. Well, that was exactly his concern. Sarah Lawrence was (and is) a creative liberal arts school, and he wanted me to experience something more than just the sciences.

"Do you know what creativity permits, Robin? It permits us to bring something new into being—maybe even some new ideas about ourselves. Maybe you can learn something new about yourself. Maybe you can learn to be less stringent and open your mind a bit."

I could push myself to stay up all night, I could push myself to meet any challenge, but I wasn't sure I could fathom a course different from the one my mother had set for me in the second grade. But after all, we were just talking about a few classes to break up the all-premed-all-the-time schedule I had concocted. The thought of following up with my acting classes struck me, and as if he'd read my mind, Mr. Clark brought up the idea.

"Acting speaks to the human condition and can serve to remind us of our sensitivity and the need to safeguard that sensitivity." I must have looked doubtful, even though the same thought had occurred to me, because he continued. "How long have you planned to be a doctor?"

"Since the second grade," I answered, sure that my answer would impress him, just as it had my family.

"Well, I would encourage you to learn to experience things that you have not planned since the second grade," he told me gently. "Did you ever think of what you would do if you didn't become a doctor?"

I shook my head adamantly.

"Maybe you should," he said.

"Why?" I asked, trying not to panic.

"Because that is what we do here, Robin—*think!*"

I scooted out of there, determined never to be summoned there again. I changed my schedule and incorporated more drama. I loved my classes. And I determined that with this schedule I could still finish all my requirements by my junior year. I could accept that as almost perfect.

There was an ease to being at school, the kind of ease that comes when you are in the right place at the right time in your life—as if I had set sail on the right day under the right conditions for this journey to the other side of the world. And I was given the gift of ideal conditions for my crossing. The wind was at my back. And I encountered no major storms. I was perfectly on course.

I had good friends, and with the acting jobs that fit into my downtime, I was able to shop and dine out as frequently as my new roommates, who were all used to a more extravagant lifestyle. I was now in my sophomore year and had been lucky enough to land a room in the much sought-after Andrews Court. Ultramodern and sleek, Andrews Court was quite the opposite of my home freshman year, a cool place that almost every student wanted to call their home away from home. I was happy and so very excited to be among the fortunate ones.

I lived with Anna and Tinette, both from the Philippines, and Wendy, who was from Philadelphia. Anna and I would share the closest friendship. From shopping to romances, schoolwork to our lifelong dreams, there was nothing we weren't able to share. Whenever I felt a little bit lonely or unsure of myself, or experienced an increasingly deep and gnawing sensation of emptiness, Anna did everything a friend could possibly do to lift my spirits. She gave me the precious gifts of encouragement and acceptance. Anna was one of the few people who knew the truth about my father, what I'd wanted him to be and what he was, and the deep hurt of my few encounters with him.

One of her efforts to cheer me up led me to my first serious romance, with a young man named Eddie.

"Get dressed, Robin, we're going out. Put on something special," Anna told me one early evening. "I don't feel like going anyplace," I told her. "Well, too bad, you're going."

She had tickets to a comedy club. We arrived a bit late, so there was no waiting in line. We entered the club and spotted two empty chairs near the stage. As we tried to make our way past those already seated, the comedian suddenly stopped his routine and said, "Hey, you! Can't you see I'm working?" I gazed up. "That's right, I'm talking to you. You on C.P. time?"

A heckler answered for me: "Yeah, her friend's on C.P. time too—Chinese people time!"

Everyone laughed. But no one laughed more than Anna except the young comic, who jokingly chastised the heckler, saying, "Hey, I'm the one working here!"

The exchange was too funny for either of us to be embarrassed and laughter filled the room for a very long time.

"We'll wait for you to be seated, Your Highness," he said, looking directly at me. I hadn't been called "your highness" by anyone since my grandfather in Kentucky—and I loved the sound of it now just as much as I did then. I was flattered, and I thought for a second he might be flirting with me. Then I told myself not to be ridiculous.

Later, when I went to use the pay phone, I ran into him again. "You and your friend having fun?" he asked, smiling as if he'd expected to see me.

"Yes, we are," I said, hoping to appear much more poised than I felt. He was adorable, with sweet chocolate skin and a smile that lit up the dark room.

"I was just playing with you out there."

"I know," I said.

"You know?" He laughed a funny laugh, a strange and unusual laugh that seemed to tickle the back of his throat. And it made me laugh too. "I'm Eddie," he said, holding out his hand. "Eddie Murphy."

"Hi, Eddie. I'm Robin," I replied. "Robin Givens."

"Are you and your friend going out later?" he asked.

"No, we're going back to school," I told him.

"Oh, school," and he laughed that laugh again.

"What's so funny?" I asked, and my smile was as big as his laughter. He just said, "Can I call you sometime?"

I was so pleased and so stunned that words eluded me. When I didn't answer, he scribbled something on a piece of paper.

"Maybe you'll call me." He placed the paper in my hand and walked away.

When I got back to the table, I suppose I still had the stunned look on my face because Anna asked, a bit alarmed, "Robin! What happened?"

"He gave me his number," I told her, still a bit dazed. There was laughter in the air during our train ride home . . . and there was the promise of romance.

⎯⎯⎯ ⬯ ⎯⎯⎯

It was nice to be in love. I'd been longing for this for what seemed like my entire life, and now I had it . . . even if the love affair was a little one-sided. Whenever Eddie and I were together or talking on the phone, he was warm and wonderful, interested in me and my life and what I thought and felt.

"How was your day, Simone?" He always called me by my middle name—the only person who ever has. "It was great, Ed," I'd tell him—I was the only one who ever called him Ed. At the end of the date or the end of our phone call, he'd always say, "I'll call you tomorrow."

But tomorrow could turn into several frustrating days. Somehow this roller coaster of joy and misery only convinced me that this must be love. Otherwise, how could it hurt so much?

"I waited for you to call all weekend. What happened to you?" Sometimes I got the courage to ask, but my protests were very short-lived, because I was always so happy he'd called. He just ignored my disappointment, knowing it would fizzle and knowing I'd love to see him. It wasn't long before I would understand the meaning of every sad love song, because my life virtually became one. Despondent, dejected, then elated, ecstatic. A classic first-love scenario.

Many a morning, Anna would poke her head in my room. "You got in pretty late last night."

"Yeah," I would answer, with a big smile on my face.

"You having fun?"

And all I could do was say, "Yeah" again, because it was all my big smile would permit. And I curled up in bed, feeling warm all over, sure that this would last.

"Good to see you happy again," she'd say, as she closed the door.

Ed was so charming, so charismatic, so easy to love in spite of the disappointment . . . or perhaps because of it. Soon enough, my smile would fade as the uncertainty mounted, and the emotional roller coaster headed down.

Eddie called late one evening, after not having called for several days. "I have to be in L.A. for a test," he told me. And though I didn't quite understand what a "test" was, it was clear from his tone that it was indeed something fabulous, something we should both be excited about. "I'm being considered for a role in a new Nick Nolte film," he told me.

I forgot my annoyance, I was so happy for him. Then he asked, "How was your day, Simone?"

"Remember that national Pepsi commercial I auditioned for a couple of weeks ago?"

"Of course I do."

"Well . . . I got it," I told him.

"Wow! Simone, that's really great! I don't know how you go to college and do all that acting too." A few simple words of encouragement, and I was hooked, head over heels again. "Why don't you give me a ride to the airport," he asked in that charming way of his, knowing I would be flattered by his request.

Eddie's request.

I got up very early the next morning and had my hair done at Soul Scissors. I was determined to make an impression on Eddie that would surely last. I had always worn my hair in a ponytail, but I wanted to give him another look at me, one that he wouldn't forget. I left the salon with flowing curls that, as the hairdresser said, "Frame your face just *so!*"

When I arrived outside the *Saturday Night Live* studio at Rockefeller Center in my mother's new powder blue Monte Carlo, Ed was waiting. I popped the trunk from the inside and he loaded his bag in. After he climbed in the bucket seat next to me, Ed gave me a kiss and then stared at me for a moment. "I like your hair pulled back. It shows your cheekbones," he said, then fastened his seat belt. I just sat for a moment, crushed.

"Come on, let's go, Simone," he said. As always, he was cool, but it was obvious he was excited about this trip. And I was hopelessly insecure . . . wilting like a flower in the hot sun that someone had forgotten to water. I thought to myself, "I'll never go to that Soul Scissors again."

But on the drive to the airport, I convinced myself that there was indeed possibility for our relationship. In his silky-smooth, self-assured way, Ed talked about me coming to visit him in L.A. if he got the role, and I just nodded, for fear of saying something wrong . . . saying something that might ruin this glorious moment. He looked at me and just laughed that laugh, the one that was his alone.

"I'll call you later," he said as he boarded the plane.

I waited for several agonizing days and exhausting nights—sleepless nights, since it was difficult to sleep and will the phone to ring at the same time. He did call to let me know when he got the part—his first film, *48 Hours*—something I'd never doubted would happen. As always, he was interested and encouraging about my own acting ambitions and adventures. He had a way of making everything I did seem every bit as significant and promising as a starring role in a Hollywood film. For a few weeks, we talked frequently—or as frequently as we ever had—and it felt like our relationship was on track. And I suppose that's why it hurt so when the calls began to come too infrequently to really matter.

Now I knew for certain what a broken heart felt like.

My year only got worse. Anna had decided to transfer to Columbia to prepare for graduate school in architecture. For a long time I pretended she wasn't really leaving, but when junior year began without her, my heart broke a little more. I sat alone in the library, more focused than ever on school but now also feeling more out of place than ever. When a student asked to join me at what had become my table at the library, I felt a certain sense of relief and I was anxious for some company.

Lauren Holly was a lovely all-American blond, and though she had been modeling for some time, she seemed totally unaware of her beauty. More than anything, she was a free spirit, and I think much of her beauty came from within. We became friends and later roommates, and her friendship helped lift my spirits at a difficult time.

That St. Patrick's Day, Lauren and I ventured out to a local pub and—unwisely—accepted a drinking challenge. That night is a blur but I have a vague memory of walking back to the dorm in the wee hours, singing and dancing in the street. I definitely remember the next few days, which Lauren and I spent recovering from "the flu" at my mother's apartment on the Upper West Side. Lauren lay in my sister's twin bed, and we felt like sisters as we discussed life and men and hopes and dreams. I encouraged her to try acting and promised I'd introduce her to my manager. It was so wonderful to have a friend with the same interests and a similar taste for adventure.

Chapter Nineteen

My life was changing—almost by itself, as if all I could do was watch it happen. For so many years, my life had followed my mother's plan, the one she'd designed to be *perfect*, and now it was moving off in some unknown direction. And no matter how much I tried to control its independent thought and independent breath and independent pulse, it was screaming and kicking and fighting to be let loose. By the end of my junior year, it was difficult to keep it contained any longer. And I had become exhausted from trying. One afternoon after just completing an organic chemistry final, I went back to my room with my shoulders slumped. It wasn't because I'd done badly on the test or the material was too hard. It was simply because I knew by now that I did not want to become a doctor. And it was time to have the conversation with my mother.

I knew it wouldn't be a real conversation between equals, because I wasn't woman enough. I knew I would be begging for my life, for that part of me that I'd tried so hard to subdue to be given the chance to live.

I sat in my room at school and called my mother's office. She had a thriving computer consulting firm called Roper Consultants (although I was never certain why she'd kept using the name of a man who had been in our lives such a short time). Roper Consultants designed portfolio management systems for many of the major banks and brokerage houses in New York. Her firm had more than thirty employees and had been written up in *Black Enterprise*; she was, by all accounts, very successful and I knew she expected my success in life to surpass hers, especially since she had supplied me with so many more opportunities than she'd had. "If I'd had what you have . . ." Those few words, so often repeated, were meant to remind me of all that she had sacrificed, all that she had given me and all that she intended for me to accomplish. And as long as I stayed on track she forgave any of my lapses. Such as the time I ran up my American Express bill shopping and dining out with Anna and Tinette, and she paid off the eleven thousand dollars without too much of a fuss, insisting that I be more mindful. If I was on track, she could tolerate the occasional bump, maybe even a minor detour. But today I knew she wouldn't be very forgiving when I told her I wanted to stop the train and get off—this would be something she would not tolerate.

Everything about my mother's office was, like her, modestly elegant, from its location in a landmark building in midtown Manhattan to its tasteful, yet comfortable, décor. When I was in college, I got off the train from Sarah Lawrence at Grand Central and simply crossed the street to her office. It was so comfortable, so reassuring. I loved to curl up under her big desk and take naps on the floor.

An important, even essential, fixture in the office was my mother's assistant, a beautiful young Puerto Rican woman named Olga. She had been with my mother since the beginning of Roper Consultants and had become my mother's right hand. Both Stephanie and I felt some relief when our mother took Olga under her wing; the new focus took some pressure off the two of us. Soon Olga had become very much a part of our family. Indispensable to my mother, she could practically run the company on her own, but she also typed papers for me if I got behind, and on occasion she would even come over to our apartment and cook fantastic dinners for us. My mother always said Olga could make a great meal out of nothing but ice cubes.

Olga admired and appreciated my mother tremendously, but fortunately for me, she was a very different person. Olga became somebody I could talk to about my heartthrobs and my heartaches. She always sympathized with me because she was a hopeless romantic. As my mother put it, "Olga is simply in love with love."

For instance, Olga was my co-plotter when I got an idea to get Eddie's attention and win back his heart. I knew he had been house hunting, so Olga and I went to F.A.O. Schwarz and bought a grand dollhouse. We decorated it with elaborate furniture and sent it to Eddie with an adoring card that she helped me write.

Olga had *mucho gusto* for life and for love, with no strings attached and no agenda. This made her the perfect balance to my serious and intense mother, who firmly believed that every action had a goal, and every person a purpose in life. And if someone hadn't identified their purpose or wasn't progressing toward a goal, my mother was happy to help them get on track, whether they wanted her help or not.

That afternoon, as always, Olga answered when I called the office. "Hi, baby," she greeted me, in her sweet voice tinged with an accent, and I pictured her tossing her straight, jet-black hair as she smiled. "Your mom's on a conference call."

"Will she be long?" I asked.

"Are you okay, Robin? You sound a little funny."

"Yeah, I just need to talk to Mom," I said. Olga took it from there. No conference call was so important that my mother wouldn't come to the phone if I needed her.

"Robin, is everything okay?" Now Mom sounded a bit worried.

I started right in, not giving myself time to get nervous about what I was about to say.

"Mom, I'm tired. I mean, really tired, and I think I'd like to take a break after graduation . . . I mean, I don't want to go to medical school, at least not right away. I'll be nineteen at graduation; that's still young and I have time. And I'm just really tired, Mom." Not brilliant oratory, but at least I had gotten the words out.

"Of course you're tired, honey," she replied, with no real concern. "You work so hard . . . we'll go to the Bahamas for the summer and you'll be just fine." She couldn't imagine that she couldn't manage the flood of my emotions, keep that dam plugged, and preserve all her careful plans. I tried once more.

"Mom, I'm not talking about vacation. I think I just want a break before medical school. I was thinking maybe I could take some time to concentrate on acting for a while. Mom, I've worked hard at school and I am just so tired."

My mother's silence told me everything. When she finally spoke, her tone was not quite icy but it was definitely chilly, and she made it clear that she had no tolerance for my foolishness.

"Robin, *we* don't have time to be tired." This was another familiar refrain, and I knew that the "we" meant more than simply she and I. "We" bore the weight of all the black women who'd come before us, who'd had to struggle simply to survive, much less succeed. "Anybody who accomplishes anything is 'tired,' Robin. Don't you think I'm tired? Let me tell you something," she said, as if she had not already told me this hundreds of times. "We have to work—"

I interrupted and finished the sentence for her. ". . . twice as hard to be half as good."

"Don't get smart with me, young lady!" Now she was angry.

"I'm not, Mom," I said, starting to back down from her clear agitation, and I suppose her disappointment as well.

"And don't be disrespectful either!"

"I didn't mean to be disrespectful, Mom. I'm sorry." And now I was in full retreat. Once again, as always, I felt defeated.

"We'll go on vacation and you'll be fine. Now I've got to run." When I heard the click of the phone hanging up, I burst into tears of exhaustion and frustration. I was never able to stand up to my mother. And today would be no different. The only difference today was that my tears only fueled my determination to be free, to have a life of my own.

—— ⊗∞∞ ——

When I graduated from Sarah Lawrence, we had a magnificent celebration, a perfect day for us as a family to congratulate ourselves. It began with a small pregraduation party of family and close friends, with lots of caviar and champagne, and it ended with a celebration on Fire Island that included what seemed like everyone we'd ever known.

And in between was the proudest moment of my mother's life. The three of us pulled up in front of Sarah Lawrence in the limousine my mother had hired for the day. And when we climbed out, we collectively took a deep breath and let out a sigh of relief. We had done it. Jane Alexander, an actress that I had long admired, was our guest speaker and I looked to her speech for affirmation for my secret hopes and dreams. Accepting my diploma, I looked at my mother and noticed her crying—one of the few times I'd ever seen her cry. The day was everything she could have hoped for, perhaps a little more. As I looked at Mom, so proud and so pleased, I was proud of her too, and grateful. But I also knew that no matter how much I wanted to make her happy, by now my life had decided that it wanted a life of its own.

Chapter Twenty

I applied to Harvard Graduate School of Arts and Sciences. I hoped this would appease my mother and therefore ease the pressures on me—though I realized that both the ease and the appeasement would be temporary. I was maintaining the illusion of being on course, while quietly trying to change direction. As desperately as I wanted to be independent of my mother, I didn't entirely believe I was capable of it.

When my acceptance letter came, my mother was once again ecstatic, as the possibility for her dream was still alive. It wasn't medical school, but it was Harvard. Anna was in graduate school there, studying architecture, and I am sure my mother hoped Anna's discipline would rub off on me . . . and part of me hoped that too.

Sticking to the plan offered the comfort of safety. I was afraid to follow my emotions, afraid to follow a dream; most of all, I think I was afraid of discovering me. The future me, the future life my mother had planned and constructed was certainly appealing. I wanted what she wanted for me—but I wanted what I wanted too, even if I wasn't entirely sure what that was. And underneath it all was my enormous fear of messing it all up, all that she had done and all that she had given me. Her words echoed in my mind: "Each generation is supposed to do better than the one before it." I was not quite

sure whether it was the law of the land, the law of nature, or simply
the law that she was imposing on her children.

Anna and I talked about becoming roommates again, and even
looked for an apartment in Boston. It took everything in me to last
the short time that I did, and for the first time there was something
that I couldn't share with Anna. She was so reasonable, so practical,
so planned . . . so much like my mother. I didn't take an apartment
with Anna because deep down I knew I would not be there that long.
I felt terrible disappointing Anna and I felt terrible not being able to
share my feelings with her. But it was only because I didn't have the
courage to say them aloud.

⸎

It couldn't have been much longer than a month into school when
I got a call to audition for *The Cosby Show*. The number one show
on television, it represented a fresh new way of showing family life
on television. Although the Huxtables were a family of color and
proud of it, color wasn't the show's primary focus. All of America,
regardless of color, recognized their own families in the Huxtables,
and responded to the show's humor and humanity. "If I could get
this, maybe it would convince my mother to be supportive," I
thought.

After my first read with Peter Golden, the casting director, I was
asked to stay and join three other girls to read for Mr. Cosby. When
I met the man, he was as warm and caring in person as he was on the
show. I instantly had the sense that he cared about me and for me, as
a father would.

I read a scene with Malcolm Jamal Warner, who played Mr.
Cosby's son on the show. Malcolm helped make the scene so real that
I forgot there were other people in the room watching. Afterward, I
was asked to wait outside, and the four of us who had read for Mr.
Cosby sat in a waiting area making small talk. Finally the casting di-
rector returned and thanked us all for coming. As we gathered our

things, he asked me if I wouldn't mind staying a bit longer. I returned to the room where we'd had the reading.

"Congratulations, young lady!" Mr. Cosby said as he reached for my hand and shook it. "You're a good little actress and quite a lovely young lady. I'd be happy to have you on our show."

For a long moment, I just savored the feeling of my hand in his. I couldn't say a thing. Mr. Cosby was much younger than my grandfather, but he reminded me of Poppy. I got the same feeling when he talked to me, as if my thoughts and hopes mattered, as if I mattered.

"Well, we'll see you later," Mr. Cosby said, and I finally released his hand.

I nearly ran out of the room, so afraid that he would change his mind. I don't remember a thing about the subway ride home from Brooklyn to Manhattan. I was fixated on what I would say to my mother and on how proud I would be to tell her.

She wasn't as happy as I had convinced myself she would be. "Oh! That's nice," she said. "But just how long are you going to do this?" "This" being, of course, acting, which was merely a silly distraction, a deviation from the plan.

"Mom, Bill Cosby said I was a good actress," I told her, thinking, *Don't you understand what that means? Who he is?*

"Well, maybe once you've done this show, you'll have gotten all of this out of your system," she said. It was as if she were a doctor herself, who'd just diagnosed my disease and offered the cure all at the same time. My mother had a way of making me feel a way that was completely unique to her—tremendously capable and powerful, yet so small and weak at the same time. And that evening when she walked out of the room that I still shared with my sister, I felt like a lost little girl . . . capable of nothing and certainly not powerful.

I called Ed, who happened to be back in New York. Though we hadn't spoken for a while, he was as charming and as happy for me as always. We had dinner that night, and it was lovely to visit and catch up.

"I don't know what to do," I told him in the late hours when we'd gone back to his house in New Jersey. He played the piano with me sitting next to him on the bench, although he was playing around more than playing the instrument. It felt as if no time had passed at all.

"Sounds like you are doing just fine, Robin Simone Givens," he reassured me. And he laughed that laugh and kissed me on the forehead. I hadn't melted in a while and it felt wonderful.

Rehearsal for the *The Cosby Show* was as exciting as I'd dreamed it would be, and I loved every minute of it. I was scared to death, but in that way that's exhilarating, not paralyzing. I also got an early lesson in the ways "perfection" can work against the creative process. Phylicia Rashad, who played Clair Huxtable, Mr. Cosby's wife, changed a line during one of our scenes; I responded with a perfect reading of the line I'd memorized from the script, which now made no sense at all. I hadn't budged from the line I had studied and hadn't made any adjustment at all to meet her change. Actually, I had been so focused on my lines, I clearly hadn't listened to hers. Phylicia stopped and fixed her gaze on me.

"You're not listening, Ms. Givens," she said. She was a magnificently trained, very professional actress whose work had a grace and fluidity I admired tremendously. "In order to act—and act well—you must learn to listen. So, *listen.*"

It was definitely a rebuke, but it made me oddly proud to even be in a position to get such a rebuke, from such a talent. And I certainly took it to heart.

I talked to Mr. Cosby a lot during the downtime on the set. I'm not sure why or how I began confiding in him, explaining my mother's expectations and my dilemma. I suppose I felt that, as the father of five, he might understand my confusion and have some wisdom to impart. He supported my acting ambitions and even offered to talk to my mother on my behalf. He invited both of us to his house for dinner, and told me to leave everything up to him.

Well, he might be Bill Cosby, but he'd never talked to my mother. I promised I'd sit back and let him handle things, then crossed my fingers and hoped for the best.

On the appointed day, I met my mother at her office. We took a taxi to Park Avenue and Seventy-second Street and decided we'd enjoy walking the rest of the way to Mr. Cosby's home. "This is very nice of him, but I don't understand what this is about," my mother said, for perhaps the third time that day. "Does he do this for everyone who is a guest on the show?"

Soon we arrived at a beautiful brownstone, and a man in a crisp black suit answered the door almost before we'd even rung the bell. It was obvious we were more than expected. "Mr. Cosby is waiting for you in the library," he told us, showing us the way.

Mr. Cosby was hunched intently over an old record player, listening to Miles Davis. "Hello, Mrs. Givens," he said, not moving, as if he had to be an inch from the player to capture every note. "So nice to meet you." He moved his fingers and feet in time with the music. I knew he was a jazz aficionado, but I suspected this just might have been a tactic to disarm my mother. He offered her wine, choosing a bottle from a beautiful mahogany cabinet. "I think for a special occasion, this bottle will do just fine," he said, blowing dust off a venerable-looking bottle. "Oh, my mother has met her match," I thought.

We ate an exquisite dinner at a table elegantly set with lush linen, sparkling crystal, fine china, and heavy silver, served with perfect, unobtrusive attentiveness by the man who'd greeted us at the door. Mr. Cosby poured the wine and waited for my mother to taste it. "Oh, this is quite good," she remarked, smiling. He smiled in return . . . and then got right to the point.

"Your daughter is a good actress and I think she should have a chance to do just that," he told my mother. And for the first time, I felt what it would be like to have a father, a man who cares about what you really want, someone who sees your talent and appreciates your gift, someone who just wants you to be happy, someone who will stand up to your mother on your behalf. "That's why we're here," he said, seeming to read her mind. As he talked, he couldn't help but be funny, even though this was a deadly serious topic. And I wondered what my mother was thinking. She typically wore every emotion on her face but at this moment, her expression gave me no clues.

"What do you want her to do?" Mr. Cosby asked, genuinely interested.

Now my mother began to reveal her thoughts.

"I want her to go to medical school, like we'd always planned," she said, and now it was apparent that she was upset, and hurt; I could hear it in her voice.

"Don't you want her to be happy?" he asked.

She looked at him long and hard. "She'll be happy if she has a good, stable life."

He chuckled. "Actors can make a lot of money," he said.

"I want her to use the gift she's been given," my mother insisted. "She's a brilliant girl."

"She's a gifted actress," he responded.

My mother shook her head. "I want her to do something that really matters." As soon as the words were out of her mouth, she realized what she'd said, but Mr. Cosby didn't take it as an insult.

"Look, Ruth," he said, speaking to her as if they were old friends and he was offering her a rare bit of wisdom and insight. It was as if he knew that no one liked to learn more than my mother. "How about this? If Robin goes to L.A. and doesn't get a job in six months, not only will I agree with you that she should go to medical school, but I'll pay for her to go."

My mother was literally speechless . . . his confidence seemed to have found a crack in her iron will and absolute certainty. Just enough doubt seeped in to allow me that six-month trial period.

And suddenly, everything seemed to shift into fast-forward. Within weeks, my mother and I were settled in Mr. Cosby's house just outside L.A., a lovely home that wouldn't have been out of place in West-chester or Connecticut, with a big backyard and a white picket fence. The house was filled with photos and mementos of the Cosby children, and the family's diverse interests in art and music, and Mr. Cosby's il-lustrious career. There were memorabilia from his animated series, *Fat Albert*, as well as the earlier *I Spy*, which premiered in 1965 and made him the first black man ever to star in a dramatic TV series. It's said that some stations in the South initially refused to carry the show. Yet *The Cosby Show* had families across America, black and white, northern and southern, glued to their sets. What a dramatic change, in such a relatively short time. I felt awed by his accomplishments and so flat-tered that this man believed in me.

Both the house and its housekeeper were warm and welcoming but before we had a chance to settle in, we got a call from Mr. Cosby. He'd arranged a meeting for me with an agent at William Morris. The following morning, I met my new agent, and was informed that I'd be reading for a part in *Beverly Hills Madam*, a television movie star-ring Faye Dunaway. I'd always admired Ms. Dunaway and was thrilled at the mere thought of working with her. The evening after the reading, as my mother and I were sitting down to the wonderful dinner the housekeeper had prepared, the phone rang again.

It was my agent. I had gotten the job.

Chapter Twenty-One

If there were ever a time when the stars and moon and sun, all the objects in the entire celestial galaxy, were aligned—it was now. The Cosby home, Mr. Cosby's influence in my life and career, were nothing short of magical. I was certain nobody had ever had such an experience—not Cinderella, not Snow White, not Dorothy, not all of them combined.

One week after I arrived in L.A., I was driving down Sunset Boulevard, on my way to rehearsal with Faye Dunaway, with the acting job Mr. Cosby was so certain I would have. If I hadn't been living it, I wouldn't have believed it. As I drove toward the studio, I savored the moment, breathed it in, and tasted the aroma of independence . . . of working at what I loved to do. I had painstakingly prepared for this moment in time, and though it had not been consciously, somehow I had been conscientiously prepared. I had studied at the American Academy of Dramatic Arts. I had studied drama at Sarah Lawrence. I had studied voice with some of New York's top coaches and dance with some of its best.

Both in spite of and thanks to my mother's rigorous plan to raise an accomplished, well-rounded daughter who would attend a fine school and become a distinguished doctor . . . I was driving down

Sunset Boulevard, on my way to rehearsal with Faye Dunaway. A warm smile filled me as Nanny's words echoed in my mind, "Robin, God knows what He is doing, and He knows just how He's gonna get it done. And God is a patient God, so you just might as well be patient too."

I couldn't wait to call Nanny that night to let her know how right she was.

The director was awaiting our arrival, Melody Anderson and Donna Dixon were already there, and Terry Farrell and I arrived at the same time. Terry was very much like the girls I'd gone to school with and everything about her relaxed me. We were like two kids living our dream—actually, that's exactly what we were. As I talked with Donna, Terry, and Melody, I realized suddenly that I wasn't the student, the girl who acted on occasion and as a hobby, not even the precocious daughter. I was a working actress. I took another breath of independence, just as Faye Dunaway stepped into the room and made time standstill.

Faye Dunaway and Donna spoke as if they had known each other for years, though I don't think they knew each other at all. It was the kind of greeting confident women give one another, a kind of matter-of-fact acknowledgment of accomplishment and mutual respect. Not at all the greeting I could possibly extend. Terry, who certainly towered over me, was also a few inches taller than Ms. Dunaway but when the star shook her hand, she became an awed girl in the presence of a true diva. And now it was my turn to meet this legendary actress. She approached me slowly, deliberately, as if she was looking me over, sizing me up. I extended my hand, trying to radiate grace and calm. Ms. Dunaway smiled, warm and welcoming, and when she took my hand, she said, "You can close your mouth now, darling."

Throughout the shoot, at every spare moment, we all gathered around Faye Dunaway like students at the foot of a master and listened to the collection of stories she'd gathered over the years, gathering up these treasures she imparted. She became an ally, a teacher and supporter, and I soon felt comfortable going to her for advice and encouragement.

One day we shot a scene with just the two of us. Ms. Dunaway, of course, played the magnificent madam who, like a headmistress in a finishing school for call girls, was meticulously molding each of us. And the four of us, her students, were quite studious, diligent, and terribly serious about our chosen profession. For this scene, I sat at a vanity table, while Ms. Dunaway stood over me, brushing my hair and grooming me for my next client. She was wonderful and I was awed by her acting . . . but I could tell something wasn't quite right. This accomplished actress was not pleased, and I wanted nothing more than to please her. At last, she whispered in my ear, "You keep getting in my light, darling."

"Oh, my goodness! I'm so sorry."

After that, she gently moved me to and fro, back and forth and side to side, insuring that she was beautifully lit. I didn't care where the light hit me or if it hit me at all. I just wanted her to be happy.

Faye Dunaway was one of so many extraordinary women I've been fortunate enough to encounter, and all have been happy to share the many lessons they've learned.

Mr. Cosby had promised my mother, if she doesn't have a job in six months, I'll make sure she goes to back to school. Well, it looked like that wouldn't be happening. My mother's dream was fading while mine was being given breath and life and hope.

My agent had set up some readings for a new ABC series called

Head of the Class, as well as a new show being developed by Ed. Weinberger, who'd produced classics such as *The Mary Tyler Moore Show*.

I hadn't thought anything of either of these auditions. They were just part of what a new actress did to get her career started.

A few days later, I'd just gotten home from filming for *Beverly Hills Madam* when the phone rang. It was my agent. "Well, Robin," he said, "both shows want to take you to network. You have until tomorrow to decide which one you want in first position. I think you should go with the ABC show. You're not shooting tomorrow afternoon, so you'll test at four." He was talking so fast, and I didn't understand most of what he was saying. "Taking you to network"? "First position"? Then he said again, "I think you should go with the ABC show."

As I stood there holding the phone, I wasn't sure what I was feeling. I can't say I was excited. I didn't know enough at the time to realize I should have been. So I just didn't say anything, until my agent said, for the third time, "You'll test for ABC, okay?"

"Okay," I said. I was uncertain about what I was feeling and I'm sure he could hear it.

"Robin, this is all very good," he assured me. "Be happy."

"Okay!" I said, a little more confidently.

I gave my mother the good news. She was still in L.A., conducting most of her business over the phone. Stephanie was attending boarding school, so Mom felt the comfort and freedom to stay with me as long as she thought necessary.

"This is all happening very fast, isn't it, Robin?" For once, my mother sounded as unsure as I felt.

"Yes, but I think we should be happy," I said, feigning confidence and repeating what my agent had told me. And we finished our dinner without speaking another word.

"Beginner's luck" has nothing to do with luck and everything to do with an innocent courage . . . before you know all that is involved, before you realize the procedures and the politics and the pressures, the opportunities seem to come your way almost unbidden. It's a time when we are trusting and receptive to the good that life holds for us.

I had been in Hollywood for less than a month. I had a role in a TV miniseries starring a Hollywood legend. I had gone to network and gotten my first series, *Head of the Class*, which would debut in 1986. "Robin Givens as Darlene Merriman," the credit would read.

But, no, it wasn't beginner's luck at all. It was my fearless belief in the magic of life—in the *goodness* of life.

⸎

Leaving Mr. Cosby's home felt sad but exciting, a lot like what I imagined a child feels leaving home for the first time, leaving the comforts of the nest. But I could only imagine that, since in many ways, I had not really left home at all, despite my half-hearted attempts to stand on my own.

My mother found a beautiful little house for me to rent in the hills of Bel-Air. It was a bit rustic, yet elegant, with big wooden doors opening to a courtyard, with a pool and Jacuzzi. Bedrooms and living areas faced the courtyard, and atop the first floor was a wonderful dance studio with mirrors and a dancer's barre. It was a fairy-tale house, part of the fairy tale that my life had become.

No one loved this house more than Nan. When she came to visit me, I was amazed by how comfortable she was sunbathing in the courtyard and wading in the pool. I had never seen her do anything like that before. I had seen her watch *The Tonight Show* every single night, so I arranged for her to see a live taping of the show during her visit. Nanny told everyone it was the high point of her life.

Mom filled the house with all the necessary furniture and fixtures, down to the most minute detail. She stocked the fridge and cabinets with enough groceries to last a lifetime. And when all of her work was done and she had no excuses left, she reluctantly boarded a plane home.

And ready or not, I was on my own.

Chapter Twenty-Two

Olga sat right outside my mother's office—it was her responsibility as assistant to keep my mother from trivial interruptions and therefore free for more critical tasks. Stephanie and I both thought our needs, however trivial, were among the critical tasks, but certainly we were two of the biggest interruptions and distractions. For both Stephanie and me, Olga became not just a trusted friend, but at times a kind of surrogate mother and honorary sister. Her loving care and attention were among the many things I missed when I was in Los Angeles working on *Head of the Class*, and I was happy to get home as often as possible.

In the fall of 1986, one of the trivial distractions Olga shielded my mother from was a series of persistent phone calls from a certain young man who wanted to meet me. Because he was so persistent, Olga got to know him a bit. He was about my age; he'd had a rough childhood in Brooklyn and grown up in upstate New York; he was very successful and very smitten with me. He was a professional boxer, and his name was Mike Tyson.

Olga tried to run interference for him, with no luck. "That young man is on the phone again," she said.

"What young man?" my mother asked, wondering why she was being interrupted.

"The one I've told you about, the one who keeps asking if he can meet Robin—that boxer."

My mother waved her hand dismissively. "Oh, Olga, please. I'm busy."

"Ruth, she might want to meet him," Olga said. My mother often said Olga was in love with love, enchanted with the idea of romance. As far as she was concerned, this was just Olga being Olga.

My mother didn't even bother looking up. "Over my dead body."

Olga turned to leave, but not before she spoke her mind. "You won't be able to control her life forever. Sooner or later she will insist on making her own decisions."

Olga had seen up close—and, to some extent, experienced—what it was like to be my mother's daughter. It meant that she was permitted to criticize every move you made, often before you even made it. You were subject to the harshest criticism and the most vigilant scrutiny in her effort to bring you to perfection. She would shield you from the pain of your mistakes simply by not permitting you to live outside the boundaries of what she felt confident would bring positive results. To be my mother's daughter meant she controlled your life.

———— ✸ ————

I was home on hiatus from *Head of the Class* and was meeting my mother at Domenico's that evening. She, Olga, and Tom Sapienza, sales director for my mother's consulting company, gathered there to have a drink before I arrived. They routinely met at Domenico's after a hard day at work. Tom was a handsome, wavy-haired Sicilian who was the nicest guy you could ever hope to meet.

Obviously, Olga's interruption had made more of an impression on my mother than she'd let on.

"Do you know Mike Tyson?" my mother asked Tom.

"Sure!" Tom said. "I mean, I know of him. He's a young heavyweight boxer."

"He keeps calling the office asking if he can meet Robin," Mom told him.

"And Ruth won't even tell her," Olga spoke up.

Tom shook his head. "By the time I was Robin's age I already had Chris," he said, referring to his daughter. "Ruth, when you were her age you already had two children. You can at least tell her he wants to meet her—hell, I'd like to meet him myself."

Just then, I walked in the door and was greeted with hugs and kisses from Olga and Tom, as well as Mom. We all settled in at a table and after we ordered, Tom turned to me. "How's it going out there?" he asked.

"I'm having a ball," I said. "But I get a little homesick."

"Yeah, I noticed," Tom laughed. "Any other girl would be glad to be rid of your mother."

My mother hit his arm playfully and he pretended to wince. "Ow! Your mom packs quite a punch. And speaking of punches—" She hit him again, less playfully, and he didn't finish the sentence. I hadn't been let in on the joke, so I just shrugged it off.

The food was delicious, as always, and I practically inhaled my osso bucco as the conversation carried on. Finally, over coffee, Tom returned to his earlier point.

"Ruth, don't you have a message to give Robin?"

Tom was one of the few people who was not afraid to say whatever he pleased to my mother. I think that was why she liked him. I would have thought nothing of his question, I would probably have not even heard him, had it not been for my mother's anger, which I felt spill over him.

Along with her anger, it was his glass of bourbon that flooded the table when her agitated reaction tipped it over. While the waiter was mopping up, I asked my mother, "What message?" She was picking up scattered ice, and her face was as frozen as the glittering cubes. It was a look that I did not quite recognize, one I had not seen before. She looked up and fixed her gaze on Tom, daring him to answer me.

"Some jokes aren't innocent," she said through her teeth. "And that's something Tom doesn't get." I figured this must be something between the two of them—something very touchy—and I decided to leave it alone.

The smell of the bourbon lingered at the table, and so did my mother's anger. The tension made it harder to enjoy our delicious dinner.

My mother always had a way of smelling trouble . . . a fine art that I think was an inherited skill honed by experience. She loved the aroma of bourbon on a man's breath. When she brushed her cheek against Tom's to greet him, she said it was better than any cologne that a man could buy. Tom had helped my mother build a business and that, mixed with the bourbon, was the sweet smell of a man who would help a woman do anything.

But some men just smell like trouble, she once told me. The distinctive odor of trouble was one she could sniff out from miles away. I guess she sensed trouble in Michael long before she'd even spoken to him.

———— ✤ ————

I left early the next morning for a trip to Washington, D.C. One of the commercials I'd done had been an antismoking spot for the American Cancer Society and they had recently asked me to be a spokesperson and give a speech at their annual gala.

When I walked up to the podium, I was in full Hollywood glamour mode. I wanted to look my absolute best because this speech, and this organization, meant a great deal to me. As I said that night: "More than ten years ago, when I was far too young, lung cancer robbed me of the man who had loved me most of all and best of all— his name was Poppy. 'Never' is always the best time to lose someone whom you love and 'too soon' is absolutely the worst time to lose someone who loves you. I have experienced personally the devastating effects of cancer. Yours is a noble cause, a much needed and necessary cause, and I thank you for permitting me the honor of speaking on your behalf . . ."

The words were heartfelt, and the crowd seemed genuinely to appreciate them. Afterward, many people approached me to thank me for the speech and to share their own stories of loss. I was proud to have made even a small contribution to this worthy cause.

By the time I reached the hotel, I was tired but exhilarated. It had been a lovely evening. The phone rang just as I entered the room, and I sat down at the gilded desk to answer it. It was my mother, and I tucked the phone under my chin while I tried to get myself out of the gown. It was very beautiful but not nearly as comfortable, and I felt like a pageant contestant.

Our conversation started out as usual, as I filled her in on the event, but at some point I realized that my mother was trying to tell me something, something she was having trouble putting into words.

"Maybe I should have told you before," she said. "Maybe I shouldn't tell you now. I don't know."

"Tell me what?"

Finally, I peeled off the dress, and tossing it across the sofa, I took in a long deep breath and let it go with a sigh of relief.

"I just don't know what the right thing to do is."

"Mom! Just tell me!"

I heard her take a deep breath, and when she spoke it was all in a rush, as if she had to say everything immediately before she could have second thoughts.

"Do you know who Mike Tyson is? The boxer. He wants to meet you. He keeps calling the office, asking for your number."

"How long has he been calling?" I asked. Now my cheeks were warm, and I wasn't sure if I was blushing because I was flattered or flushed with anger at my mother's controlling behavior. I think it was both.

"A while," she said.

"How long is 'a while,' Mom?"

"I'm not sure, Robin. What difference does it make?"

"Well, don't you think I ought to be able to at least meet the man and decide whether or not I'm interested?"

My mother had a certain kind of man in mind for me, one that fit the image of what she thought my life should be. She'd set me up on a date with a "perfect guy" once before. He was tall, smart, and handsome enough, all of which met with my mother's approval. But the real clincher was the fact that he was studying at Harvard Business School. As I recall, he was perfectly nice and we had a pleasant dinner together. If my mother hadn't pushed him so hard, I might have been open to seeing him again, getting to know him better. But though I didn't articulate this, even to myself, I'd already decided that the man I chose would be absolutely nothing like my mother's Mr. Right. And so what my mother said next guaranteed that I'd be interested in this mysterious admirer.

"Robin, this boxer is not your type." She said "boxer" as if it were something distasteful, as if she were describing a person with the plague.

"That's not for you to decide," I said. To myself, I added, "How do you know what my type is, anyway?"

"Everything is so nice in your life right now," she said. "Why risk messing it up? This young man smells like trouble to me."

"Mom, it's just a message, not the end of the world. And it's really wrong for you not to pass along my messages."

"Robin, I've worked too hard—" She corrected me sternly.

Now I was furious. "Why is everything about you? This isn't about you; it's about me and what I want. Nothing I've ever done has been about me or for me, for that matter."

There was a shocked silence, then she said, "Everything I've ever done has been for you and Stephanie . . . to make sure the two of you have good lives." Now she was really angry. "I've never had the luxury of thinking about myself."

I softened my tone but refused to back down. "Mom, you can't control my life, no matter how right you think you are. Or how wrong you think someone or something is for me." She said nothing. And I think she said nothing because she knew I was right, but she knew that she was right too.

"Please give him my number the next time he calls," I said. "I would love to meet him."

My mother—or, more likely, Olga—did give my number to Michael. We couldn't find a good time to meet, since *Head of the Class* was back in production and he was training for his next fight. It would be a while before we could work it out.

On November 22, 1986, Michael scored a second-round knock-out against Trevor Berbick, the reigning World Boxing Council heavyweight, to become the youngest heavyweight champion ever.

Between the frenzy that surrounded the new champ and the usual holiday craziness, it wasn't until January 1987 that Michael flew out to Los Angeles.

I suggested we meet at Le Dome, a restaurant on Sunset Boulevard. It was the restaurant my agent took me to when I first arrived in L.A., and since I'm a creature of habit, I went there often. Le Dome was comfortable and familiar, and I felt quite at ease meeting a blind date there. This wouldn't be just any blind date, though. Not only was I meeting the heavyweight champion of the world, I was bringing my family with me.

Some time before, my sister, Stephanie, had decided to pursue a tennis career and was working with coach Nick Bollettieri, alongside Andre Agassi, Jim Courier, and Monica Seles. Stephanie's first professional satellite tournament was held in Japan, and she and my mother were in Los Angeles on a scheduled stopover so that we could all visit.

Which still doesn't explain why they went with me to meet Michael. Stephanie's presence is perhaps understandable. She's always been able to relax me, to make me feel at ease, and she's such a sweetheart that she can smooth out the most awkward moments. If she was there, then no matter what, we'd have fun.

I can't, even to this day, say how my mother came along. I don't think she ever asked and I know I never invited her. I don't think an invitation was ever extended, but simply assumed, and I didn't have the courage to tell her not to come. If I had had the courage, I'm not sure she would have listened anyway. Would it have made a difference in everything that came afterwards? I have no idea.

So we were all together in this meeting of Michael, just as we were together in everything that came after.

The three of us arrived at Le Dome a few minutes early. My mother hated being late for any engagement, even one she wasn't particularly happy about attending. Mom had on a burgundy pants suit, with lush black velvet collar and cuffs, which was formfitting at the waist and she still had the tiniest waist. She looked stunning. Stephanie wore jeans and a blue Ralph Lauren blazer atop a crisp blue and white shirt, with her usual pearls—a gift from our grandmother—along with a paisley silk scarf, another of our grandmother's treasures, a gift from Poppy.

I wanted to look as if I'd casually thrown on something that just happened to look wonderful. So I tried on everything in my closet and every combination of accessories before choosing a black velvet Betsey Johnson dress. It clung where it was supposed to cling and it flowed just right in other places—such as the hem, where it touched the floor and revealed the flip-flops I had decided to wear just to emphasize the statement that I was attempting to make: I was comfort-

able, I was casual, and this meeting really wasn't all that important to
me . . . though that was not quite true. The truth was that it was incredibly important to me, but I was unprepared and, to some degree,
unable to put the thought into it that I should.

I wanted this date to go well. This was the first time I'd defied my
mother so openly, and I didn't want it to be a wasted effort. My mother,
to her credit, was trying. That morning, when I told her about the date,
she'd smiled and said brightly, "Well, what's the worst that can happen?"
If I'd had any idea of how bad that worst would get, we'd have ordered
takeout that night.

Instead, there we were at a quiet table at Le Dome. We hadn't
been there long when the host approached our table with a message:
Mr. Tyson is running a bit late.

"How late?" I asked sharply. Was I about to be stood up?

"Oh, not very late, madam," he assured me, as if he really had a
clue. "He asked me to make sure that you're treated well, that you
have everything that you need and anything that you want."

And in that instant I melted. Truth be told, even having a date
call to say he was going to be late was a new experience for me, and
ever so appealing. I ordered a glass of champagne, my mother had her
usual martini, and Stephanie, a beer connoisseur, asked for her favorite import.

Perhaps twenty minutes or so went by when the host returned with
yet another message. "Mr. Tyson called again. He is terribly sorry. He'll
be here shortly. May I get you more drinks?"

"No," my mother answered for us all. "But thank you very much."
By now she was visibly annoyed. Stephanie overruled her and ordered
another beer. I envied my sister's willingness to incite our mother's con-
demnation. She always had a gift for enjoying the moment . . . and I
began to enjoy it too. We talked and laughed, and it wasn't long before
we had all forgotten why we were there.

We decided to order something to eat, and Stephanie got her
favorite—steak tartare. I ordered the mussels and another glass of

champagne. By now, Mr. Tyson was more than an hour late. Finally, I said, "I don't think he's coming." Those words relaxed my mother far more effectively than one martini, or even two, could have.

"That's okay, darling," she said. "It's probably for the best." I knew she was right, but I hated feeling that she'd won, that my first moment of independence had been such a disappointment. I'd really been looking forward to meeting this man who seemed so eager to meet me.

And suddenly, there he was. I think I saw his shadow before I actually saw him. Or maybe it was the sense of him, some aura of power and danger and magnetism that I sensed before any of us actually noticed him. Maybe it was that smell of trouble my mother warned me about, the same smell Aunt Ruth had picked up from my father. I'd had nearly two hours to come to my senses, to admit to myself that perhaps my mother was right, and I was childishly disagreeing with her for the sake of disagreeing, just to prove that I was my own woman. But that moment had passed, and now it was too late.

The young man walking toward us had his head down, his huge muscular frame closer to the floor than I'd imagined. He was impeccably dressed in a navy blue Armani suit, a crisp pale blue shirt and a black and blue silk tie. He looked more like a very fit banker than a brawler, down to his sober and conservative shoes, which were in stark contrast to my own.

And so we met at this point in our lives. I was the well-bred, well-educated, overachieving young woman in flip-flops, wanting to appear cool and relaxed, as if everything came easily to me, including a man. The truth is that my upbringing and my education were not casual at all. They were well planned and executed with precision. And they had not come easily at all. They had literally come at the expense of my mother's blood, sweat, and tears. But Mom had a way of making some of the most difficult things appear easy—and I don't think either Stephanie or I had a real appreciation of what it took.

He would have been thought by most to be the kid from the

wrong side of the tracks, wearing the uniform of mainstream dignity and authority to convince everyone tonight—including himself—that he had crossed over to the other side. And though, in an odd way, we had some things in common, there's no doubt he'd had a much more challenging journey to reach this point.

Michael grew up in Brownsville, Brooklyn. It was a rough place, one of the roughest in the city. He was the youngest of three, with a brother and a sister. I don't think Michael ever knew his father, and I am going to dare to say that is where our connectedness lay. As a mere boy it would be a correctional facility that he would call home. But Michael was blessed to have caught the eye of a man of vision.

Cus D'Amato had a way of seeing what could be. He had a vision and he had a way of making hearts hardened by a lack of love believe too. Michael latched onto the dream Cus dreamed for him.

D'Amato was a legend in the boxing world who'd trained Floyd Patterson, another boy from a rough neighborhood. From that first day, Cus was Michael's trainer, mentor, and father figure and at age twenty, Michael realized a dream. He became the youngest heavyweight champion of the world.

Most unfortunately, Cus D'Amato missed seeing Michael's triumph. Cus had died of pneumonia on November 4, 1986, and his departure left a huge vacuum in Michael's professional and personal life. It would take a long time for the effects of this loss to play themselves out, and for all the destructive survival techniques Michael had learned as a boy to overtake whatever progress he'd made with Cus. And I'd have not just a front-row seat but a starring role in that drama.

"I'm so sorry I'm late," Michael said, in that soft voice that belied the massive presence. "Please forgive me." His hand swallowed mine, but his grasp was warm and gentle.

Now I was a little embarrassed that I'd brought chaperones. "This is my mother, Ruth, and my sister, Stephanie," I said. As if he could read my mind, he told me, "I was nervous about coming alone too." His smile was incredibly sweet, and I hardly noticed as he introduced us to Rory, who was his oldest and closest, and I would daresay dearest, friend.

Then Michael turned to my mother. "Ma'am, I'm so sorry for being late. I was so nervous about meeting your daughter, I couldn't decide what to wear. I have suits lying all over the room." He laughed softly. "To tell you the truth, I've been pacing around in my drawers for the last two hours." His laughter was infectious, and we all laughed with him, even my mother.

He and his friend joined us at the table. Michael turned out to be effortless to talk to and even easier to listen to. I stopped bobbing my leg up and down, a nervous habit I'd had for as long as I could remember, and relaxed. We talked about New York and about our careers. Our focus, our drive, and our commitment, even as children, seemed to give us an immediate sense of connection. Each of us could appreciate what the other had accomplished and the effort that had gone into it. Stephanie had seen him box when she and her basketball team were competing at the Empire State Games, and he shared some stories about how nervous he was before that fight. It was simple and easy, and though my mother refused to really participate, I think she was surprised by his warmth, by how comfortable we all felt in his presence.

Finally, he leaned close and said, "I was so nervous about meeting you, but you're just like a girl from my neighborhood." It felt like the ultimate compliment, even more flattering than if he'd compared me to Princess Diana. As if prompted by my enjoyment, my mother spoke up. "Well, it's getting late," she said. "I think we should be leaving."

Michael glanced at his watch. By now I felt comfortable enough to tease him: "Oh, so *now* you want to check the time?"

Laughing, he asked, "Would you like to go somewhere else for a little while?" Then he turned to my mother. "Is that okay with you, ma'am? I'll take good care of her, I promise."

Before my mother could answer, my sister jumped in. "Robin is a big girl. She can decide if she wants to go or not!"

So he turned to me. "Do you like comedy? We could go to the Improv for a while and I promise to get you home early."

Stephanie said, "That sounds reasonable, doesn't it, Mom?" Michael rose from the table and made the gesture to pull out my seat, but I did not budge, still wanting the approval of my mother. Still in deep thought, she didn't quite approve, but she did acquiesce.

"Give me the key to the house, darling, and we'll see you very shortly." With her words, I rose from the table.

Michael turned to me as we approached his car, with the driver holding open the back door. "Are you okay?" he asked, offering his hand to help me in.

An ease that I had not planned, that I could not have imagined, washed over me. "Yes," I answered him as I placed my hand in his. When he had climbed in beside me, the driver closed the door.

And we were off—alone.

⚬⚬⚬

The drive was quiet; no one forced conversation. For the first time ever, I didn't feel insecure at all with a date, and I wasn't the least bit nervous. I didn't wish I was taller or thinner. I didn't question what I had worn or anxiously review what I had said. I didn't worry about me at all, because I really felt like it was something he was going to do. And without that burden, I was free to float on air. He simply made me feel as if whatever I was, was good enough. *More* than good enough.

As the driver pulled up to the club, Michael said, "We won't stay very long." He helped me out of the car and held the door of the club so that I could enter. There was a murmur among the crowd as we entered but there were always celebrities at the Improv and no one ever made a big deal about it.

Michael and I talked about everything and nothing at all, and we laughed at the acts and each other. Then he looked at his watch. Without saying a word, he rose and stood at the back of my chair. "I said I'd get you home early," he told me. Once more he took my hand and led me back to the door. Could this really be that rarest of creatures—a man who keeps his word?

———— ❧ ————

We climbed back in the car, and once again the ride home was quiet and still. Not a stillness that's unnerving or a quiet that echoes. Not for a moment did I wonder what I should be saying, nor did I have the least bit of fear that perhaps I might say the wrong thing.

"Can I see you again?" he asked as the driver pulled up to my house. I answered without a moment's hesitation. "What would you like to do?"

"I'll do anything you want to do," he said simply. "I'm only in town to see you." No playing games here! I gave him my number and he repeated it to himself as he walked me to the door.

"I'll call you in the morning," he said as I stepped inside.

"I'll be waiting," I replied.

As I closed the door I spoke aloud to myself, in a whisper that was almost a prayer: "If I'm dreaming . . . let me dream on."

———— ❧ ————

The phone woke me from a deep sleep the next morning. Hoarse and groggy, I said, "Hello."

"So am I gonna get to see you today?" There he was again, picking up right where he had left off, doing just what he said he would.

Wide awake, I quickly sat up, wanting to take in this new feeling. Reflecting the joy in my heart, I simply couldn't stop smiling. I had always wanted a man who was dependable and reliable. A man who called when he said he would call and arrived at the appointed hour.

"Are you hungry?" he asked. "Do you want to have breakfast?"

I don't know what possessed me to respond the way I did. "Sure, why don't I make breakfast? You can come here."

When I hung up, I remembered that I can't cook. So I did what I did every morning when confronted with a dilemma. I screamed, "Lucy!" and she came running, as she always did, muttering, "*Dios mio!*" as she always did.

"We need breakfast," I told her.

She frowned. "You know I make breakfast every day, Ms. Robin. I'm making eggs Benedict with salmon, just the way you like it."

"We need breakfast for a *man!*" I told her, reveling in the thought. "Do we have any bacon and eggs? Maybe we can make home fries." I included myself in the "we" as if I could help. And then a thought occurred to me. "I know how to make chocolate chip pancakes, Lucy! Do we have any chocolate chips?"

With pride in her ability to run a house smoothly, she said simply, "*Todo, yo tiene todo.*"

"I'll take that as a yes. I'll get in the shower. You start, and I'll be right there"—as if she needed my help.

"Very funny!" she told me, in English to make sure I understood.

I took a shower as fast as I could, threw on my sweats, and pulled my hair back in a ponytail before I galloped off to the kitchen. The air was filled with the smell of a hearty breakfast, bacon and eggs, and, yes, home fries. I set the table with confidence, and then I started the pancakes. Actually, I made a mess because that's my chief skill in the kitchen.

"Where are my mother and Stephanie?" I asked Lucy, spilling pancake mix all over the floor. Poor Lucy was trying to both cook and clean up the mess I was making.

"Your mommy said to tell you they would be back soon. They went to practice." Then I remembered that Mom had arranged for Stephanie to practice with Robert Lansdorf, an L.A.-based coach who, like Nick Bolletieri, had a reputation for grooming some fine professional players.

I poured the pancake batter onto the griddle, getting as much batter on the floor and the counter as on the griddle itself. When the doorbell rang, I was just buttering the first stack. Lucy started for the door.

"No!" I cried out in a bit of panic.

"Don't you want to let him in?" she asked, confused.

"No . . . I mean, yes, of course. But I'll do it. I'll let him in."

I was so caught up in wanting breakfast to be just right, I didn't notice that I was covered in a combination of pancake mix and pancake batter. I opened the door quickly before I lost all of my nerve. He looked at me and he smiled. Instantly, I relaxed. I smiled too, and his smile grew bigger and brighter.

"I have a feeling that you don't cook breakfast very often."

"What was your first clue?"

When we reached the kitchen, we found Lucy cleaning feverishly, but not fast enough to get rid of the mess I had made. Somehow I wasn't embarrassed at all. I introduced Michael and Lucy, and showed him to the one place in the kitchen that wasn't a mess, the table I had set perfectly. Then I noticed the flowers he had hidden behind his broad back.

"Maybe you can put these on the table," he said.

"They're beautiful!" I said, almost embarrassed by his gesture.

"Now, dig in." I found a vase and began arranging the flowers as he piled his plate high. It barely put a dent in all that had been prepared.

"Where's Stephanie and your mom?" he asked. "This is way too much food for just you and me! Hey, Lucy, have you eaten? Grab a plate."

"No, no thank you," she told him.

But he began to pile food on another plate. "Lucy, you have to eat. This is way too much food." Michael walked over to the sink and took Lucy by the hand, brought her to the table and pulled out a chair for her. "Now, please sit down and eat. It's good!" As she took her seat, he said, "Lucy, let me ask you one question. Did Robin help at all?

"Did you see this kitchen?" Lucy said, laughing, "Oh, yeah, she helped."

And now we were all laughing, and the laughter filled the kitchen already overflowing with the fragrance of flowers and good food.

Then silence fell, and I noticed my mother in the doorway. I wondered how long has she had been there, watching.

Stephanie walked past Mom into the kitchen. "Wow, that smells good," she said. "Hi, Michael. How are you this morning?" She spoke as if he were there every morning.

"Good—and full. Robin invited me to breakfast," he told her. "She was telling me you were practicing with a coach here in L.A."

"Yeah! I liked him a lot."

We all went on eating and talking and laughing, as if we had done this every day of our lives. Except for my mother. The next time I looked up, she was nowhere in sight.

─────── ∞∞ ───────

Our next few days together were very much the same, except we were together—alone. My mother and sister had left for Japan. Each of them had parting advice for me. My sister was almost giddy when she said, "Don't do anything I wouldn't do."

And my mother . . . well, my mother had obviously given serious thought to what she would say, and there was nothing giddy about it. "I don't know what you are trying to do, or what that boy is all about. I don't know who you are trying to hurt. Sometimes I believe it's me, because you think I demand too much. And other times, I feel it's yourself, because you're worried you can't live up to what I demand. But I do know one thing. When you play with fire, you're bound to get burned . . . and you mark my words, some things are just too dangerous to play with."

"Mom, what in the world are you talking about?" I asked. And she answered with the phrase I'd heard my whole life. "I've worked too hard to have you throw it away on some—"

I stopped her before she said something that she might regret and before I heard something that I didn't want to hear. "Mom, we're just having fun. Don't you think I deserve to have some fun?"

Chapter Twenty-Three

Michael's morning calls came like clockwork, and we were like two kids playing hooky from school, taking a break from the pressures and responsibilities of our lives. We did a little bit of everything and a whole lot of nothing. Sometimes we'd stroll through the mall and sit at the pet shop playing with puppies for what seemed like hours.

At night we'd watch television or take in a movie. I introduced him to sushi, and from toro to octopus, he tackled it like the champ he was. When he bit into the salmon roe and liquid oozed out of his mouth, he wrinkled his face, grabbed his stomach, and feigned sickness. "You can't be serious. You eat this stuff?" Never had sushi been so much fun, and never had a relationship been so easy. It was as if each of us had found something in the other we desperately sought.

One evening after dinner, we walked hand-in-hand down Sunset Boulevard, and I felt like we were a couple. Then my insecurity kicked in, and as if he felt it, Michael asked, "What's wrong?"

"I got a call to leave town the day after tomorrow. I'm hosting an MTV show in Vail."

"Do you ski?" he asked.

"A little. Do you?"

"Hell, no," he said, laughing. And the thought of him on skis made me laugh too. "I still don't get what's wrong," he said, not about to let me off the hook.

"I guess I'm gonna miss you."

"Well, you're not gonna be there forever, are you? Tomorrow we'll have a special going-away dinner." He pulled me closer and held my hand tight. Even this small gesture, from this strong man, relieved my unexpected anxiety. I'd never experienced such devotion, and I had to admit, it was intoxicating. And addictive.

The next afternoon, we went to a movie and made a stop at the pet store to play with the puppies. There was a little black chow I thought especially cute. He gnawed at the other dogs' legs and tails and I told Michael somebody needed to give these puppies a break and take that little terror home. When we returned to his car, he said, "Hey, let's get dressed for dinner tonight!"

"Are you trying to say you don't like my sweats?'

"I love your sweats, but just for variety, why don't you try this?" He reached in the car and pulled out a box. "I hope you like it."

I just looked at him, unable to say a word, and I hadn't a clue what the right words would be. I was not at all used to men giving me presents. "Don't open it now. Open it later. I hope you like it," he said again.

"I'm sure I will," I said.

As soon as I got home, I opened the box to discover the most beautiful dress I'd ever seen. It twirled out of the wrapping and waltzed out of the box. It was black satin, smooth and lustrous. It didn't hug too much and it wasn't too revealing. It was perfect, and it had been hand-picked by a man just for me. I loved it. As I stood at the mirror admiring it, I felt prettier and happier than I think I ever felt in my life.

When Michael arrived early for our date that evening, I wasn't at all surprised. He and Lucy talked while I finished getting ready, taking extra care with my hair and makeup. When I walked in wearing the dress he'd given me, he simply said, "Damn!" Lucy said, "Oh, yes, Miss Robin. I agree."

We had dinner at Nicky Blair's, a place I'd never been. As we walked in, I felt all eyes on us for the first time. At first I felt a bit uneasy, but he was comfortable enough for both of us. A few minutes after we arrived, Sylvester Stallone walked through the door and the room went abuzz. In the mid-eighties, there were few stars bigger than Stallone. Michael whispered in my ear, "Watch this, Robin. I'm star to the stars." So I knew that Michael wasn't the least bit surprised when Stallone approached our table and greeted Michael warmly. Michael was cordial enough, but didn't really encourage conversation. "I don't want anyone interrupting our time together!" he told me after Stallone left. Now I was far beyond flattered.

⸺⸺⸺

We drank loads of champagne and laughed and danced and had a glamourous, glorious time. On the ride home he laid his head on my lap and fell fast asleep. I placed a hand on his cheek and touched him gently. If sweet could walk the earth, at this moment he was it. When the car came to a stop he woke.

"Damn!" he said. "I was drooling on your leg." Everything about him made my entire body smile.

He walked me to the door and said. "It's too late for me to come in." Then he cupped my face in one enormous hand, wrapped the other around my neck, and pushed me passionately against the door. Our first kiss. All I could think was, *What took you so long?* He held my face tightly in his hand, looked deep into my eyes, and made sure he had my attention.

"Listen to me," he said. "You're gonna be my woman and I'm gonna be your man and that's the way it's gonna be, okay?"

All I could say, all I wanted to say was, "Okay."

And now he kissed me again and headed back to the car, as if he had accomplished his mission for the night. The driver held the door, but before Michael climbed in, he turned back to me.

"I don't think your mother likes me very much," he said, "but don't worry, she will."

Chapter Twenty-Four

It was difficult to believe that this could last, simply because I felt undeserving of this kind of love and attention. I was certain Michael would wake up one day and change his mind about me. He'd slowly disappear, or one day simply not show up.

I'd never been one to savor each moment. Instead, I worried about where the relationship was going, or what he meant by something he said or did. But with Michael, each moment seemed to lead into the next, and he never gave me enough time to worry.

The next morning, Lucy knocked on my door, poked her head in, and tried to wake me up. "Ms. Robin, there's something for you at the front door."

We'd been out late, and I desperately wanted to stay in bed just a little while longer before I had to fly to Vail. "Good, Lucy. Please get it."

"No, Ms. Robin, you must get it." Now there was a hint of a giggle in her voice.

"Lucy, just let me sleep," I said, and pulled the covers over my head.

I quickly sank back into deep sleep, and I had the strangest dream . . . a little black puppy, the chow we'd played with at the pet store the afternoon before, was licking my face as I lay in bed. Only now, he had a big red ribbon tied around his neck. Then I heard Lucy scream, "*Dios mio*, I think he's going to pee-pee!"

I opened my eyes to see Lucy scooping up the puppy and rushing for the backyard. I chased after them, and in the kitchen, the puppy wiggled out of Lucy's grasp as she tried to open the door. Watching the puppy scramble around the kitchen (he did pee-pee), I was overwhelmed by a happiness I'd never felt before.

The doorbell rang not long after I'd gotten dressed. It was Michael, of course. I ran into his arms and kissed him all over his face. "I guess you like him," Michael said.

"I like *you*!" I said, between kisses. He put me down and asked, "Are you packed? You'll be late for the flight."

"I'm fine. The show is sending a car for me." How sweet of him to be concerned!

"No, I'm taking you," he said. And that ended any discussion of how I'd be traveling to the airport. My bag was mostly packed, so I just threw in a few last-minute things.

"Bye, Lucy! Take good care of him!" I kissed the puppy in Lucy's arms and smiled up at Michael. "I think I'll call him Mikki. After you, of course." And I kissed Michael too.

He was quiet on the way to the airport, almost brooding. I immediately started to wonder if he was starting to reconsider, wondering how to get out. But then he asked me, "Will you be all right?" I put my arm around his neck and lay my head on his shoulder. "Except for missing you, I'll be fine." I took his hand and held it tight the rest of the ride.

———— ⊶⊷ ————

As I settled into my seat on the plane, I was in a state of delighted disbelief. I closed my eyes, remembering the good-bye kiss he'd given me. And I thought, *Even if I never see him again, as sad as I'd be, I will be forever grateful, because he's unleashed in me a happiness I've never known before.*

Soon my thoughts turned to my father. Not for the first time, I wished he could be closer to me. I wondered what it would be like to have a father to talk to about this new man in my life. "Mom's not crazy about him," I'd say, "but he treats me so sweet! You're a man—what do you think?" I smiled to myself as I imagined his response, felt it echo in my heart: "You deserve to be treated sweetly. You're a sweet daughter, a sweet woman." As the plane began the descent into Vail, the words faded, and I realized that whatever I'd heard was my own wishful thinking.

—∞∞∞—

At the hotel, we had a quick meeting about the show, and then I rushed up to my room to take a nap and get ready for dinner. I was disappointed to see that Michael hadn't called, but then I checked the time and realized that he was still on his flight back to New York.

Dinner with the MTV people was fun, but I felt very tired; my nap hadn't refreshed me at all. By the end of the meal, I was so exhausted I could barely walk. By the time I reached my room, the walls were spinning. I lay in bed with my eyes shut, feeling my stomach churn. What was wrong with me? Soon I began getting chills and cold sweats. Now I was really panicked. The phone rang and I grabbed it. I was so very happy to hear Michael's voice on the other end.

"Michael, something's wrong," I said. "I feel so sick."

"What happened?"

"I went down to dinner—"

He broke in, asking, "Who'd you go to dinner with?"

"Just some people from the show—oh, I'm going to be sick!" I slammed down the phone and ran to the bathroom.

Michael called back immediately, seriously worried. "Robin, what's wrong with you?"

"I don't know," I said.

"Hang up," he said. "I'll call you right back."

So I lay back on the bed, weak and sick.

The phone rang again, but this was a voice I didn't recognize. "Ms. Givens, I'm the hotel concierge. Mr. Tyson just called and he's extremely worried about you." The concierge said that Michael had demanded that the hotel send up a doctor, and that he'd be happy to do so, if I liked. "But, Ms. Givens, I'm reasonably certain that you're suffering from altitude sickness, and the symptoms will subside within a few hours as your body acclimates." I thanked the man and said I wouldn't need a doctor.

As soon as I hung up, the phone rang again. Michael, of course.

"I talked to someone at the hotel," he said.

"I know," I said. "Thank you."

"He said you're gonna be okay, and you just need to get some sleep."

All I could do was repeat, "I know."

"You try to sleep now, Robin, okay?"

"Okay," I mumbled, barely able to keep my eyes open.

"I love you."

The words jolted me awake. All of his attention, his care, his concern—and now this, another amazing first. If the altitude had sent my head spinning, Michael now had my heart spinning in tandem.

I lay back and closed my eyes, but I didn't want to sleep. I just wanted to hear his words over and over again. "I love you . . . I love you . . . I love you . . ." But I must have drifted off to sleep because I was awakened by a knock on the door. "Who is it?" I asked, still feeling a bit woozy.

"It's me," answered the voice on the other side of the door. I threw it open and jumped into Michael's arms. "Sorry it took me so long," he said.

Sorry it took him so long? I couldn't believe he was there at all. But he was, and as he held me close, I was flooded with emotions I'd never felt before. I rested my head on his shoulder and simply said, "I love you too."

Chapter Twenty-Five

The next day it was official: I had a man who loved me. I was filled with excitement, from the top of my head to the soles of my feet. It was as if a part of me that had been missing had been found. We'd spent the night holding each other and talking. He'd told me he belonged to me and I belonged to him, and it all felt so comfortable and comforting and normal and natural . . . it all seemed so right. He knew what I was thinking, what I wanted, what I needed, and what I hoped for. He knew me, in a way I had never been known before. He satisfied a need so very deep inside me, a need I barely knew I had. He breathed life into a part of me that may have been best left unknown. But he knew me . . . he knew me so well. Perhaps he knew me better than I knew myself, and that is an awesome knowledge. This perception and understanding of one's partner must be aligned with a good intent, or it becomes dangerous.

But for the moment my need was indeed both awakened and satisfied. I was too young, far too inexperienced, and far too unaware of my own self to realize that some needs are better left unmet . . . that emotions rarely lead us in the right direction. And at that moment a young woman who had never been in love, had a man who loved her more than anyone else; who had never known a man who kept his promises, had found a man she trusted.

We left Vail together, and on the flight to New York, he promised to love and protect me always. He hugged me close and said, "I'm never going to let you out of my sight again." That sounded just fine to me.

After we left Vail, we went to the Catskills. Michael wanted to introduce me to his friends and family upstate, and so a car met us at JFK to take us on this two-hour journey to Michael's world. Michael wanted me to meet Camille, the woman he called his mother. When Cus rescued Michael from the boys' home and opened his home to Michael, Camille became the woman who kept the house, cooked the meals, and took care of Michael in a way no one else had in recent years. And he sincerely appreciated this tall, striking, European woman, and he liked referring to this elegant, cultured lady as his mother.

Michael already knew my world, and I was delighted and awed by just how comfortable he was in it. It was the eighties and black culture—always enticing but on the fringe—was beginning to have profound effect on popular culture . . . it was permeating it. A new-found sense of freedom was being expressed in rap music and even in fashion, and this new cultural influence was becoming a lucrative industry. The hip-hop culture was emerging.

We behave as if blacks have always had the freedoms we enjoy now, all too often with a lack of appreciation for how far our people have come, how much we have grown as an American society that permits a lack of appreciation for our history and ourselves. Together we overcame and together we will just keep getting better. My mother—not an old woman, by any stretch of the imagination—can describe walking through the alley to climb up into the balcony to see a movie at the theater on Main Street in Lexington, Kentucky, and that was permitted only one day a week.

Just as the black migration from south to north, the civil rights movement, and the women's movement could not have happened at a different time than they did, Michael became very much part of a particular time and place. He was part of the advent of hip-hop culture. Though it's now such a part of our world that it seems it must always have been here, there was a time when a brilliant innovative Russell Simmons simply had an inkling and an idea. And no one else dared dream of Phat Farm. Michael was very much a part of this new black-and-white culture. He helped usher it in and he was ushered in by it—who knows what comes first. We became part of a time and helped define it, all at once. It was a culture that considered him king.

Yet simply inherent in this young man was an element of high culture too. Culture, according to T. S. Eliot, is the one thing at which we cannot aim. My mother had long since been aiming at it and was doing quite a fine job; I suppose that is what made him so comfortable with us, and me so comfortable with him. What my mother hadn't realized was that culture is not merely erudite, and nor is it found only in the confines of an institution such as New Rochelle Academy, or the Master's School where my sister had boarded, or Sarah Lawrence College.

I don't know if my don at Sarah Lawrence was quoting someone, or if this was his own insight, but he once told me, "Culture may even be described simply as that which makes life worth living." By that definition, Michael was the most cultured man I had ever met. And no matter how one might define themselves or their culture, in some ways, everyone loved Michael or at least they were fascinated by him.

Michael was taking me to the place he considered home. While this beautiful old structure would not have looked out of place among the historic houses of Bronxville, it had been home to, as well, some of boxing's elite and society's rebuffed, including Floyd Patterson. But, as I said, it was the eighties; radio and television were closing the gap between the two.

Camille was gracious to me but a little aloof. She was an imposing woman, in her eighties but looking far younger, thanks to her strong stature, boundless energy, and smooth skin.

That night, Michael and I lay awake sharing stories of our childhoods, his in Brooklyn and mine in Westchester. I told him about all of the happiness that I had experienced, and my few yet deeply hurtful disappointments, all centered on my father. Michael's father had been absent so long that he believed he didn't miss him at all. In fact, he could hardly recall him. I told him about the Christmas I waited all day for my father, who never showed up. And it was as if Michael could feel my pain and wanted to take it all away. He kissed my cheek like a brother might and said, so sincerely, "I would never disappoint you."

He seemed to feel so comfortable, telling me the darkest stories. Though I liked his sharing his stories with me, they made me just a bit uncomfortable. As he talked, his Shar-Pei puppies licked our toes, their innocence and sweetness such a contrast to the bleak stories. The streets of his childhood were pretty mean, and some of the meanest characters became his mentors. But with Cus he had learned to control and discipline all he had learned and all he had become. And because of Cus, this young man initially groomed by thugs had become The Baddest Man on the Planet. Beyond Brooklyn, beyond New York, he was the international bad boy. Everyone loved him, and I loved him too.

"Back in the day," Michael said, "I'd ride the subway looking for somebody to rob. And women would know what I was there for. They'd clutch their purses close, knowing what I'd do. I'd watch the fear in their eyes as they boarded the train. I'd take a seat and close my eyes, and still the fear was so obvious. I could smell it." He paused for so long I thought that might be the end. But then he spoke again. "Think about it, Robin. Women knew I'd come there to steal from them. They knew to beware, and I took what I wanted anyway. Didn't matter what they did. They still lost whatever it was they were protecting."

He picked up one of the puppies and cuddled it, scratching its belly. "Do you understand, Robin?"

I felt deeply uncertain, entering territory completely new to me. "I'm not sure, Michael."

He picked up both dogs and carried them out of the room. Then he came back to bed and leaned close, held my face in both of his enormous hands.

"Are you afraid?"

"No!" I said quickly, not giving myself time to think. "I want to know everything about you. I want you to share everything with me."

Michael had never talked about his own fear. Instead, he was the architect of fear and intimidation in others. For many of us, certainly many men, it's easier to deal with someone else's fear and pain rather than their own. Certainly that was true of Michael.

I stayed in Catskill for several days, and in some ways this was one of our happiest times together. Being in this home allowed him to return to the safety of the better (if not perfect) years of his childhood. This was familiar ground, and its people were familiar to him, and with him. They knew the good in him, as well as the bad . . . they knew all he was capable of producing, building, and creating, as well as they knew what ruin and destruction he could wreak.

One afternoon we were sitting in the barren old gym where he'd trained with Cus. We were both cross-legged on the floor, and I was enfolded in his arms. In this safe harbor, I began to tell him about my frustrations, my lifelong sense that I would never be good enough to please my mother, that every success landed me at the bottom of yet another steep hill to climb. He wrapped his arms around me tighter and whispered in my ear, "You're perfect." And for that brief moment, I believed him.

Then he cupped my face in his big boxer's hands and said, "I've done so many things wrong and it just hurts so bad . . ."

"It's okay," I said. "I love you, and I'm going to love you until all the pain goes away."

He looked up and stared into my eyes. "Do you promise?"

"I promise." My gaze held his.

"No matter what?"

"No matter what."

And he again rested his head on my shoulder.

I told myself that my love was powerful enough to save us both. How wrong I was.

The fact is that darkness is powerful. As he told me more and more about his past, I began to think of these revelations as a kind of initiation, a test to see if I was worthy of this deep dark intimacy. And so the darkness swallowed us both, two kids lost in a big world.

That's the answer to a question I'm so often asked—"Why didn't you leave?" I didn't leave because I didn't think I had any reason to. When Michael looked deep into my eyes, I felt no fear, no anxiety, only love. I realize now that I saw what I wanted to see—yet there was real love there too.

Just not enough to save us.

Chapter Twenty-Six

No, culture is not erudite . . . it is not studied. I would liken it to one's relationship with God, and I believe it has a close kinship with one's spirituality. It cannot be taught . . . it can only be experienced.

I would learn many, many things over the next couple of years. In many ways, I was forced to learn them in order to survive. I had to learn who Robin Givens was in order to recognize who she *wasn't*, even though the media often insisted on writing about her. There was a time when much of what I had learned . . . I wish I never knew. I learned about Michael and I learned much about the workings of the world . . . but what I learned the most about was myself. There was a time when I was confused about who I was; when one is not firmly rooted in one's identity, that confusion is easily created. And when one is not firmly rooted in God, that confusion reigns supreme.

But I'm getting ahead of myself. I wouldn't learn any of this until much later.

Between Michael's commitments and mine, plus the passion of new love, we lived life at record speed . . . the next few weeks became a bit of a blur . . .life became a bit of a blur . . . Planes back and forth across the country so we could be together every possible minute; parties and champagne and late, late nights when we were together. When I was in New York, I stayed in my old room on West End Avenue, and my mother and I had many arguments about Michael and my new lifestyle.

One night I sat in the bedroom I shared with Stephanie, waiting for Michael's next call. Whenever we had to be separated, he called me as often he could, sometimes every fifteen minutes, like clockwork, just to say he loved me. I sat curled up on my bed, the phone extension in front of me. When the phone rang, I picked it up as fast as I could—but my mother beat me to it.

"Hello, Michael," she said, her voice soft yet cold. "You've been calling all night. Don't you think that's enough for now? You can talk to Robin tomorrow."

"Mom, please!" I was embarrassed, and afraid she'd ruin this wonderful thing of ours.

"Robin, don't be long. I need the phone." And I heard the click of her hanging up.

"What's wrong with her?" Michael asked, without much interest.

"I don't know. What's going on?"

"Nothing. I just called to say I love you."

"And I love you." We went on like that for quite some time, and then there was my mother once again.

"Robin, I need the phone."

"Mom! You can't just pick up the phone while I'm on it." *Click*, and she was gone again. I was a little embarrassed, but Michael immediately put me at ease, made me feel that everything about me, even my controlling mother, was lovable. So we talked for a while, until once again my mother picked up the phone, determined to speak her mind.

"Robin, you have to stop this. I really can't take it anymore. You're out all hours, talking back to me. I really don't recognize this behavior. And the way you speak to me is something I am completely unfamiliar with."

Michael tried to break in. "I would never let anything—"

But she cut him off. "Let me tell you something. I know men like you—men who offer poison and call it love." Her tone having turned bitter, she caught herself and resumed speaking in a way that was so matter-of-fact, yet so cold. "I am sure you feel you do love her, but for some people there seems no greater pleasure than destroying the ones they claim to love."

I was shocked. "What are you talking about, Mom? He loves me!"

"I've protected you, Robin. Maybe too much . . . maybe so much that you're just plain stupid about some things. He knows that, and that's what he loves about you."

"Mom, that's not Michael. You don't know him."

"Well, I may not know him but I darn sure have known men like him. And I sure as heck know you. I know you better than you know yourself."

My relationship with my mother has always been a beautiful thing, and in spite of my need to be my own woman, it still was a beautiful thing. In spite of my childish, unaware, insensitive ways . . . still, it was beautiful. I would come to learn that those who are hell-bent on destruction always look for the most beautiful things to destroy.

Finally, my mother hung up, defeated in this battle, if not the war.

"No one's ever defended me like that," Michael said. "And I know that wasn't easy for you. But now I know you really do love me."

—⚭—

This confrontation had been a long time coming. Truth be told, the confrontation was far less in defense of Michael than in defense of myself.

Undoubtedly this is something that everyone goes through, a rite of passage for every young lady and every young man. Timing is everything in life . . . a situation arises at a time that permits it, or it occurs at a time that does not allow it to proceed. The civil rights movement could not have happened at any other time . . . the women's movement could not have happened at any other time. And the explosive situation that was Michael's and mine could not have occurred at any other time. But time is also something that God uses to reveal Himself. In time, He reveals the awesomeness of His purpose, His plan, and His power.

———∞∞∞———

Over and over, my mother warned me that she wouldn't tolerate my behavior forever. She especially hated my late nights, when I came home at four or five o'clock in the morning, after drinking too much champagne. But the behavior continued.

Late one night—rather, early one morning—Michael's car pulled up in front of our building. Michael followed me into the lobby after I'd hurriedly told him goodnight, and he slipped into the elevator with me just before the door closed. Suddenly, I began to feel claustrophobic. I was worried about what my mother would say, and Michael was standing so close to me I could barely breathe.

"Come home with me," he said, over and over. I pushed him away, saying, "I can't, Michael. You know that." I lifted his arm to check the time on a massive Rolex that had diamonds instead of numerals. It was after three.

"My mother is going to have a fit," I said.

"Forget her," Michael answered. "You can do what you want; you're a grown woman." But I wasn't grown, not really.

"Come home with me," Michael said again. "No, Michael," I said again, as we got off the elevator. Michael could be so very playful, and he walked backward in front of me, clowning as he continued his pleas, but I wasn't at all amused. I didn't have my keys; I'd have to ring the bell, and oh, how I dreaded it. "Shhh, Michael," I whispered, but he just kept up his teasing.

I was so focused on keeping him quiet and figuring out what to say to my mother that I tripped over the luggage before I saw it. A matched set of Hartmann bags, three brown-tweed suitcases monogrammed with the initials "R.S.G.," neatly stacked in front of the door. They looked very much as they had a few months ago, when my mother had given them to me. But now they were filled with my clothes.

I was so shocked I couldn't move, much less speak. Michael wrapped his arms around me and once again I felt claustrophobia setting in.

"Great! Now you've gotta come with me," he said. I shook my head and wriggled out of his grasp enough to ring the bell. "What are you doing?" he demanded.

I rang the bell again. Still no answer. I knew my mother was there, listening. I rang again, and again, more and more insistently as panic mounted. Finally, I heard the bolt slide back and the door opened—but only a few inches, enough for my mother to peer out at me. She stared at me as if she didn't recognize me at all, as if I were an unwelcome stranger at her door.

"If you're going to live like this," she said, "I won't be a part of it."

"Oh, come on, Mom! It's late but not that late. Let me in."

She shook her head, refusing to listen to my pleas. Finally, as if she could no longer bear to see me, she slowly closed the door, and I heard the thump of the dead bolt.

Michael grabbed me in one arm and the suitcases in the other, and headed back down the hallway to the elevator. At first I let him carry me along, too stunned to react. As much as I'd been struggling to break free of my mother, I couldn't quite believe she'd actually kicked me out. Despite all my rebellious behavior of the past few weeks, I never imagined things would reach this point. I needed to make things right with my mother.

By now we were in the lobby. "Michael, I can't go with you," I said. "I need to think."

"You don't need to think. You just need to come home with me, where you belong."

A week, a day, an hour ago, his words would have thrilled me, would have seemed deeply romantic. Now they filled me with panic. All I could do was repeat, "I need to think."

Now we were out on the sidewalk, at his car. Michael gave my bags to his driver, who began loading them into the trunk. "No!" I yelled. Then, calmly and slowly, to show that I wasn't the crazy woman I must have appeared to be, I told the driver, "I'm not going. Please take my bags out of the car." The driver ignored me, completely ignored me, as if I hadn't spoken at all. He slammed the trunk lid shut and retreated behind the tinted glass of the car.

By this time, I was furious, screaming with rage. "Michael, get this through your head—I am not going with you!"

If I was angry, so was Michael. "Get in the car, Robin," he said, no trace of tenderness left.

Suddenly the chaos in my head cleared, and I spoke with utter composure and clarity. "You know what?" I said. "Keep the bags. I'm leaving."

I turned to walk away, but before I'd taken a step I was yanked off my feet and swept into the car, with the door slammed behind me. It all happened so fast that I couldn't make a sound. Now all I could do was scream, so I did. Both Michael and the driver ignored me. This wasn't the first time Michael had overpowered me physically, but it was the first time that there was nothing playful or sexy about it. This felt dangerous. "Let me out!" I screamed, again and again. "What the hell are you doing?"

Finally, Michael answered. "You're coming home with me, and that's it," he said. "Now shut the hell up."

"I am not going home with you! What part of 'no' don't you understand?" I was all up in his face, all 105 pounds of me, as if I could pose any kind of threat to him. But in my powerlessness and fury and fear, this was all I could think of to do—like a frightened animal bristling its fur to look bigger than it is. He sat there while I screamed, facing straight ahead, not moving a muscle. Then finally, he spoke, in a tone that chilled me to the bone. "Get out of my face," he said.

And I dropped back against the seat, scared into silence at last.

<hr>

We arrived at Michael's apartment building, and the car had hardly stopped before the dutiful driver was ushering Michael out. He came around and opened my door, but I refused to move.

"I'm not going in," I said. I just couldn't believe that I really had no say in this.

"Robin, get the hell out of the car," Michael said.

"*No.*"

Michael moved closer and I grabbed for the door handle, the seat belt, anything. He bent down and wrapped his hands around my ankles and, while his driver politely held the door, Michael yanked me out of the car and onto the pavement. I sat there on my backside a moment, hurt and humiliated, then leaped up, even more furious. Ignoring me, the driver slammed the door behind me, and the doorman began taking my bags out of the trunk. As if we were returning from our honeymoon, Michael scooped me up in his arms and carried me over the building's threshold. But this was no honeymoon.

"Let me go, you jerk!" I yelled. "I'm not staying here with you."

The doorman held the elevator door for us. We rode up in silence, until we reached Michael's floor. I decided I wouldn't help him humiliate me any longer, so as he stepped off the elevator, I said, "Please put me down now."

We were nineteen floors up, so I guess Michael figured there was no place for me to go. He set me on my feet, and I tried to straighten my rumpled clothes and tangled hair. At this point, arrogance was my only defense, and I walked down the hallway with my head held high.

Michael handed the doorman the apartment keys, and he set the bags down in the foyer, nodded at Michael, and left. He hadn't looked at me once. As the door closed behind him, I began to realize how truly alone I was. I didn't move, didn't make a sound, but inside I was screaming and struggling against the darkness that surrounded me.

Michael walked past me into the living room without a word. He stood with his back to me, still not speaking, while the screams echoed in my head. I forced myself to speak quietly and calmly.

"Michael, listen to me. Please listen to me. I have to go."

Silence. I began to walk toward him.

"Michael, are you listening to me? I have to—"

I never finished my sentence. Even with all that had come before, it was a complete surprise when it finally happened. Michael turned and his face was completely blank—no anger, no sorrow, nothing. But the fist flying toward me was full of rage. Time slowed and I thought, *No, he's not going to do this. He's going to realize what he's doing. He'll stop himself. He loves me.* But I watched from somewhere outside myself as that massive fist, the fist that had knocked out so many men, landed on my left temple. I felt no pain—that came later—just raw disbelief as I flew into one wall and bounced across into the adjoining one.

As I crumpled to the floor, I looked up at Michael's face. It was blank, even peaceful, and I wondered how I had come to this place.

———∞∞∞———

When I came to, Michael was standing over me dispassionately . . . disconnectedly . . . as if he didn't know me at all . . . much less love me. Neither of us spoke as I got to my feet and staggered out of the apartment.

I went straight to the apartment of one of my closest friends. She was rarely in New York, but now she was here to play the U.S. Open. I was so deeply ashamed of what had just happened, and so confused . . . and I needed to share it with someone without feeling I was being judged. Lori had always been so candid about the frailties of her family and the flaws in her life. I was confident that she would not judge me and hoped that maybe she would help me to understand.

When Lori answered the door, I couldn't even speak. I just stood there, silent, with tears running down my face. "What's wrong?" she asked, pulling me inside. I finally found my voice enough to speak . . . but I could never find the words to share what was wrong. There was so much I didn't know, and what I did know made me feel so ashamed.

"Can I just stay here? I have nowhere to go. I can't go home."

"Of course you can stay. Where's Michael?" she asked, and the sound of his name was like a knife to the heart. I collapsed on the sofa and cried until I was drained of tears and every ounce of my emotional strength.

Lori made me tea and we sat together quietly on her couch. Finally, when I had composed myself a bit, when the tears stopped running like an open faucet, she asked, "What happened, Robin?" As I'd known it would be, her voice was gentle, without a trace of judgment.

Yet even so, I could not bring myself to tell the truth, not all of it. "He pushed me and I fell against the wall," I said. It was all I could manage. She clearly knew I was leaving out a big portion of the story, though she didn't press me for more. "Are you hurt?" was all she asked.

"I'm not sure," I said, touching the lump just above my left temple.

"Do you need a doctor?"

"No! No doctor," I said, panicking. I couldn't possibly tell a stranger about this.

"Relax, Robin," Lori said. "It'll be okay. I'll get you some ice."

And that was the first time I sat with a bag of ice pressed against some part of my body that ached, wondering what I had said or what I had done to make Michael hit me.

My mother agreed to let me come back home, on the condition that I go back to being the old me. I was scared . . . I felt so alone, and truly sorry I'd upset her so much, so I readily agreed. Plus, there was comfort in going back to the familiar rules that had been imposed my whole life, in letting my mother be the grown-up for us both.

But underneath I was struggling. More than ever, I was confused about who I really was, and the murky, mixed-up chaos that swirled around in my head was more overwhelming than I could ever have imagined. Worse, I felt I couldn't talk about any of this. What little confidence I'd built up, trying to break free, had been shaken to the core. The questions rattled in my head constantly: *What had I said? What had I done? What could I have said or done differently?* But the questions, and my fear that I really wasn't capable of controlling my own life, remained my secret.

I didn't talk to my friends because of some degree of misplaced pride (*I can handle this . . . I can fix this . . . I am not a victim!*). I didn't want to admit how vulnerable I was, and I feared that talking about my fears would make them even more real.

And I felt that my tower of strength—my sound, sober, sensible mother—was the last person I could be honest with. Certainly, hearing her say "I told you so" would be more than I could handle. She'd welcomed me back, yes, but she was wary, still a bit chilly.

I could not even share what had happened with my dear, sweet sister, Stephanie, who had always been my confidant. Where would I begin? What reason would I give? What could I offer as an excuse? I was so disappointed in myself. I had somehow lost my man, my new best friend, my lover—and myself. I checked myself repeatedly in the mirror, looking for some indication of change, some mark that showed the difference I felt . . . I felt so unlike myself. There were none . . . no cuts or bruises, and no visible sign of how much I'd changed. I looked much the same though I was becoming a person I didn't quite recognize. Isn't that what my mother had told me might happen, a warning from this young and yet wise woman. A woman who had encountered so much, overcome so much . . . who had experienced what I was trying to hide from her. Certainly, she expected more from me than this.

———— ✐✐✐ ————

I didn't speak to Michael for the next three days. Our time together as well as our phone calls had been a lifeline, my lifeline, my connection to the independent life I so desperately yearned for, to the love I so desperately hungered for . . . and it had been mine . . . he had been mine. I made the choice to suffer the agony of being without, though his calls were incessant. Once the phone had never been more than inches away from me. Now I never answered it, and I refused to come to the phone when Stephanie or my mother told me Michael was calling. And he called incessantly.

Stephanie asked again and again what was going on, pushing ever harder for me to tell her. "Why won't you come to the phone? What happened, Robin?"

I would have been telling the truth had I said, "I don't know," but instead I chose to tell a lie. "Nothing happened," I told my sister. I began to convince myself of that lie. I just wanted to forget about what had happened. I was too embarrassed to admit to myself or anyone else what had truly happened. It would have been impossible for my mouth to form the words. Even my mind had put it away in a safe place so as not to have to relive it over and over again as I had the evening that it occurred. At the very least, I had persuaded myself that this was an aberration and never could happen again.

At first, my mother was delighted that I wasn't taking Michael's calls, and she followed Nan's advice about not troubling trouble by not asking anything about my sudden change of heart. But she knew I was keeping something from her, and she grew more and more curious about just what that was. When she finally asked me what had happened, I told her the same "nothing" lie. She didn't believe it any more than Stephanie did, but she was considerably more assertive than my sister. "Well, if you're not going to tell me, the next time Michael calls, I'll just have to ask him."

The next time the phone rang and my sister yelled, "Robin! It's Michael again!" I ran to the phone. I couldn't bear the idea of my mother talking to him before I had. My voice cracked with uncertainty as I said, "Hello." I was confused by what I was feeling and uncertain of what to say. I wanted an explanation. I wanted him to tell me exactly what I'd done to deserve his rage. I wanted him to make the confusion and pain I was feeling go away. I wanted him to make it make sense. I wanted to love him, and I wanted him to love me. All these thoughts raced through my head in the tiny space between my speaking and his response.

"I'm sorry, Robin. How long are you going to be mad at me?"

He seemed so relaxed that the thought rose up inside me, "Maybe I did make far too much of this." I was confused by his tone and more confused by my own thoughts. I reminded myself of the truth: *You're not making too much of it.*

"Michael, how could you do that to me?"

"You know how much I love you," he answered. "I love you so much I can't think straight. It's driving me crazy."

"That's not an answer, Michael." Tears began to well in my eyes and trickle down my cheeks, and before long the tears began to pour and my voice was choking with tears. "Why?" I asked again. "Why did you do that?"

"Don't bring it up again. I feel terrible. I can't take how bad I feel. You say you love me, but if you loved me, you'd want to be with me. No one would stop you, not your mother, nobody. How do you think it makes me feel that you want to make somebody that hates my guts happy?"

"She doesn't hate you, Michael. She—"

He cut me off before I could finish. "And how do you think it

makes me feel that the only way I can get you to be with me is to—"
His sobs choked him, and now we were both crying.

"I do love you," I told him. The tears ran down my face and
seeped into my mouth, and the taste was oh, so familiar. They had
the taste of the tears I had cried for my father. And I wondered for a
moment which were for my father and which were for this man I now
found myself in love with.

"I love you. I do, Michael, I do love you," I told him over and
over again, trying to comfort him. And for just a split second it was
as if I were watching someone else, but then I realized I was watching myself, and for that instant I wondered what I was doing. Now,
together we were crying, and not for one moment did I think: I am
the one who was bounced off of the wall, I am the one who was
bruised, I am the one who was battered. And not once did I think I
was the one who should be comforted. All I could think was, *What
do I have to do to convince him that I love him? I'll do it, whatever it is,
and I will never do what I did again* . . . though I wasn't quite sure even
then of what that was.

That evening, Michael and I were sitting in the back of a limousine in front of my mother's apartment, the place I still called home.
His head rested in my lap as he clutched his arms around my waist
and cried and cried and promised me it would never happen again.

"What did I do?" I asked him.

"Nothing. Nothing. I just love you so much it makes me crazy. I
want you to love me like I love you. But you have so many people to
love—so many people that love you. I don't know if I could ever come
first in your life."

For as long as I could remember, I had longed for a man's love.
Certainly I had dreamed of having my father's love bestowed upon
me. Poppy loved me with all his heart, a heart like Mt. Everest but
made of gold . . . yet still, there seemed to be something missing from
this love that he gave so generously. Somehow his loving kindness, his

gentle goodness still could not satisfy my longing . . . the longing I later realized was the legacy left me by my father. Somehow that evening, when I lifted Michael's face from my lap and wiped his tears away, to me this felt like love and certainly it satisfied my longing. . . . this felt like everything I had ever wanted . . . and so I told myself this must be love . . . this must be what it feels like to be loved by a man . . . to love and be loved. The hurt was so powerful, so strong, so deep, I knew that this just *had* to be it—a man's love.

I looked deep into his eyes, convinced now that his deep love for me had caused him to do such a terrible thing. *But if I can just show him how much I love him too, it will never happen again, just as he had promised*, I thought to myself.

I accepted the responsibility of doing just that, and in accepting that responsibility, I think that, in some small way, I accepted some responsibility for the awful thing that had occurred. And all I said was, "I love you too. I'll never mention it again."

Michael showed up with the first of many peace offerings, expressions of "his true love," symbols of his guilt and regret. Up to that point, Michael's gifts had been part of our celebrations, one of the elements of our whirlwind of excitement and intoxication, the intoxication of new love that can cloud the senses as much as any drug.

This first gift was a diamond necklace fit for royalty, along with a red leather suit. He intended for me to wear the outfit to a press conference about an upcoming fight.

The suit was made of soft, buttery, bright-red leather, the jacket tight and low-cut and beautifully tailored. The skirt, what there was of it, was also beautifully tailored and oh, so tight. I liked clingy clothes but this simply was not my taste. But I put it on, to please Michael. As I looked at myself in the full-length mirror, I felt that I should be walking the red-light district on Eleventh Avenue in Manhattan . . . before they cleaned it up, that is. The jacket barely covered my bust and the skirt hardly reached below the fold of my buttocks.

Michael came up behind me and clasped the diamond necklace around my neck. It—like my cleavage—was perfectly framed by the jacket. "You look beautiful," Michael said. He looked wonderful in a charcoal gray Armani suit. Michael always had excellent taste in clothes—his, at least. "You look beautiful," he said again, whispering in my ear. I loved his words, longed for them . . . but I hated how this getup made me feel. I stared into the mirror, wondering who this woman was staring back at me.

———

We left the building arm in arm, and the doorman greeted us like royalty. And we were, in a way. He was the king of the ring and I was his queen. Why wasn't I happy? Instead, I felt a strange numbness, yet the part of me that could still feel, felt dread. My legs felt almost too heavy to move. He sensed my unease. "Come on, baby, you really do look beautiful," he said, guiding me into the waiting limo. "I can't wait for everyone to see you."

"Thank you," I said quietly, glad he was happy but still intensely uncomfortable. I took a deep breath—there was so little air in the limo. "Roll down the window, please," I asked.

"No, I'll turn on the air," Michael said.

"Please just roll down the window," I said, my voice tightening with panic. "I'll be okay if I can just get some air."

The window rolled down, and for a moment the breeze against my face gave me some relief. I put my hand to my throat and tried to loosen the necklace a bit. Never before had the word "choker" seemed so apt. I fidgeted with the skirt and jacket, trying to reveal just a little less and so I could feel just a little more comfortable. Finally, I just sat back in the seat.

I'd never felt so disconnected from myself. This outfit was uncomfortable in every way. I was physically uncomfortable, but I was most uncomfortable with the way it made me feel. I heard his words in my mind again: *I can't wait for everybody to see you.* If we're comfortable with ourselves, clothes are very much an expression of who we are . . . though sometimes they are merely an expression of what we want the world to see. I felt vulgar in this suit. The woman in this outfit was not someone I wanted to reveal to the world, and without a doubt she was not an expression of who I was.

We were headed south on West End Avenue, and the traffic was growing worse. The limo slowed to a crawl, and I was suddenly overwhelmed by a wave of anxiety. My heart was pounding frantically, I could breathe only in short gulps, and suddenly I was sweating profusely. The limo stopped at a red light, and without thinking, I threw open the door and ran back up the avenue. I heard Michael call my name, but I didn't look back. I kicked off my pumps, grabbed them in one hand, and kept running in bare feet. I paid no attention to traffic lights, dodged in and out of cars, and just kept running. By the time I reached my apartment building, I was sobbing uncontrollably.

In my old bedroom, I peeled off the jacket and skirt, dropping them on the floor. I crawled into bed and pulled the covers over my head and finally began to feel a tiny measure of comfort and relief. Exhausted, I drifted off to sleep. When I awoke, my mother was home from the office. She was putting the red leather outfit onto a padded hanger.

"You didn't go out like this, did you?" she asked.

"No," I said—yet I couldn't give up my defiance. "But I think it's beautiful."

"Well, then . . . perhaps you'll save it for another time," she said. I almost detected sadness for me in her voice. She walked toward the bed, and I remembered that I still had on the necklace, so I pulled the covers high so that she wouldn't see it. She sat down next to me.

"Baby," she said, as if offering a treasure that she felt had spared her unnecessary heartache, hoping to spare me the same. "Some things are just too dangerous to play with."

And in my heart I knew she was right . . . but I couldn't let her know that, and neither could I allow myself to see it. I had wrestled free, ever so slightly, and I wanted so much to be in control of my own life.

Slowly, our lives developed a rhythm. Our time together was divided between New York, the place we both called our home; Los Angeles, where I worked; and Las Vegas, where he was training. We indulged ourselves a bit less. The late nights were not as late and there was a little less champagne.

Michael was just a little difficult to get into training camp, and he spoke just a little more frequently about enjoying fighting less, about his weariness with the sport. He had accomplished so much at such a young age, but somehow it wasn't as satisfying as he'd thought it would be. He still missed Cus, his mentor, his trainer, his confidant, the person who could impose the discipline he so badly needed. Cus hadn't lived to see Michael crowned heavyweight champion of the world, but I think Michael always felt he owed Cus that title . . . owed a debt to the man who had saved his life and encouraged him to make more of it than anyone else—including Michael—had imagined or dreamed was possible. But now, with the debt paid and the dream fulfilled, it seemed difficult to muster the motivation. There was still one more mountain to climb . . . one more goal to be achieved . . . one more dream to be realized. Cus had believed that Michael could not only become heavyweight champion, but also break Rocky Marciano's record. But that would take hard work, focus, determination, dedication, persistence . . . just doing the same thing one more time, over and over and over again. Achieving that goal would require discipline, and when discipline isn't self-imposed, it must be imposed from the outside. Oh, how Michael missed Cus.

Now, "Team Tyson," as it was called, was assembled in Las Vegas to train for the next fight. The team consisted of Michael's manager Jim, his trainer Kevin, and his best friend Rory, the person who was to stick with him "closer than a brother," as Jim always said, watch his every move, and keep him out of trouble. That was a tall order for any young man, and all of Team Tyson knew it.

I had promised Michael I'd take care of him, though I had made no such commitment to the team. But then Kevin called me and said, "Robin, Michael's left camp. I'm sure he's on his way to you. Bring him back and be prepared to stay yourself." That's when I knew I'd become a member of Team Tyson.

It couldn't have been more than an hour later when Michael arrived on the Warner Bros. lot in Los Angeles. We were rehearsing a musical number as he walked through the stage door and took a seat on the stairs where the audience would sit during tapings.

What I was doing here as Darlene Merriman in *Head of the Class* seemed insignificant and almost silly compared to what Team Tyson was attempting to accomplish. I became a little bit self-conscious and very uncomfortable as Michael watched me. Finally, the director called out.

"What's wrong, Robin?"

"Nothing," I answered, a bit embarrassed.

"Take a break and get yourself together," he said. And I walked away from the set and toward Michael. I threw my arms around him, giving him the big hug we both needed.

"What are you doing here?" I could barely get the words out he was squeezing me so tightly.

"I had to see you," he said.

"But you're supposed to be at camp."

"I know," he said, his head resting on my shoulder. "I'm lonely there without you, and I don't feel like boxing."

"Look, we'll go back together after the taping is done. Okay?"

"Okay," he said. "That's great. Now go back to work." As I turned away, he called me back. "And Robin, don't ever be embarrassed in front of me. I love you and everything about you." Never had I felt so loved, so comfortable, so complete . . . so at home. I felt so filled up, with my soul longing for nothing.

As lovely as this moment was, it marked the beginning of what would become an ever-occurring conflict. My work always seemed to get in the way of what Team Tyson was trying to do, and I was always expected to drop everything and come running. "You have a very important job to do here with us now, Robin," Jim would tell me. "We need you." Michael would add, "You have me now. You don't have to work."

But acting wasn't just a job. It was what I *wanted* to do, had longed to do for as long as I could remember. I had fought for the chance to do it, and that in itself was a tremendous accomplishment. I couldn't imagine just giving up and walking away from all my hopes and dreams, my victory. And I think that despite his protests, Michael liked my independence. We lived in my house when we were in Los Angeles and we drove my cars. My housekeeper cooked his breakfast and washed his clothes. Something about that made me feel safe and on even ground with him.

Training camp became a special, if hectic, time for us. Sometimes Michael would work extra hard on his roadwork and sparring, and then take a break from camp, join me on a flight, and sit patiently for hours, watching me work. Other times I'd leave him at camp and go off to work alone, always promising to return as quickly as I could.

For Michael, training could be healing and peaceful, or it could be turbulent. When he trusted his "gift" and believed in his ability, things went well. But there were also times when he wrestled with the authenticity of his talent and with the reality of his demons . . . demons that, I suppose, resembled to a greater or lesser degree the ones we all have. I guess that's what was behind the sudden urges to leave camp, to escape.

I became the team member; Michael openly and in many ways easily shared his fear and anxiety with me. By then I had become not only his woman but his friend and he was not only my man but I felt in so many ways he was the person who understood me best . . . he knew my vulnerability. This was a precious trust for Michael. But nonetheless, I trusted Michael.

Fear was quite a factor in all our lives. Cus had given him a way to fight his fear, something he could wrap his mind and heart and soul around, a way to transform that fear into fire . . . a way to transcend his fear and become a valiant warrior in fearful times.

"Fear," Cus told Michael, "is your best friend or your worst enemy. It's like fire. If you can control fire, it can cook for you, it can keep you warm. If you can't control it, it will burn down everything around you and destroy you with it. If you can control your fear, it makes you more alert, as graceful as a deer coming across the lawn." Cus had given Michael this gift, but sometimes Michael's faith in it wavered. Cus was now gone. Michael had his team leader, but the person he relied on to reassure him the gift was his—that person was his woman . . . that person was now me.

───◦◦◦───

Early on, these days in training were the happiest times of our lives together. These were the sane, sound, sensible times, manageable times. Clubs and dancing were replaced by video games and movies on videotape. Egg whites and ice cubes replaced sausage links and pancakes. I think the indulgence Michael missed most was champagne and caviar. Certainly I did; every so often I'd secretly slip away while he was sparring for a bit of beluga and Cristal. But once Michael had completely committed himself to training, he never faltered and, obviously, he never failed. Actually, his discipline was extraordinary . . . exemplary.

The pounds would simply roll off, taking with them all of the indulgences we had permitted ourselves and leaving in their place the kind of physique most of us could never dream of having. I could see the difference between leaving him on a Monday and returning late Friday night.

"Wow, you look handsome," I told him. And he did, with that wonderfully muscled body ripped and sculpted. He smiled and said, "It's only gonna get better," as I let my hands join my eyes in examining the work that he had put in. Michael was very disciplined about training. Fortunately, of all the many rules in training camp, "not making love" was not one of them.

It was easy to love the man that Michael became during this time, the man who could dominate his desire, leash his mind, and control his fear. There was a calm about him, and a caring. He was focused on connecting with the "Absolute," with the "All and All," "All Powerful and All Mighty." He knew this was the source of his power, and it was clear that it was important to him that he be deserving of that power. These were times when you could count on Michael being "good," and I was simply amazed by his focus and concentration.

Team Tyson kicked into gear as well, with a singleness of purpose and resolve. And once Michael was truly on board and committed, a magical, mystical force seemed to take over. One could not help but be awed by the beauty of this creation . . . and the fight that would finally culminate in the creation of this fine art would only serve to put this masterpiece on full display.

The team leader was Jim Jacobs. If Cus had been Michael's father, Jim was his big brother. Jim knew Michael and loved him, not just the fighter but the man Michael was capable of being. Cus had always protected Michael from outside influences and from his own demons, and now Jim was continuing his work. Perhaps they both understood better than anyone that no one and nothing was a greater threat to Michael than Michael himself. I suppose having a good trainer, a good coach, a good parent means having someone always one step ahead . . . someone who knows what we, with the grace of God, will one day learn about our sport, our gift . . . about ourselves.

Jim liked me because Michael loved me, and Jim had a sense that I could be good for Michael and therefore good for Team Tyson. Now that Michael had indeed become the youngest heavyweight champion, the focus was not only on retaining the title but also breaking Rocky Marciano's record. There was a lot resting on the shoulders of such a young man, still hardly more than a boy . . . someone who had lost the shoulders on which he once stood. Cus had been a man of strong character and indominatable vision, and losing him was a dreadful blow for Michael. But Jim was a loving man who had also learned well from Cus . . . if someone had to step into the master's shoes, certainly Jim was the best man for it.

So I was glad when Jim's love and protection extended to me. He'd sit me down for long talks about my own dreams, which was something new for me. Though my mother, Stephanie, and I had always been a team too, my dream to be an actress had been resisted by our team captain. Jim seemed to understand this, and he seemed to understand her resistance to Michael as well. He listened so well that it was as if he could feel what I was feeling, that he agreed and was simply on my side, and by the time he offered advice, I was prepared to hear it.

So I became part of the team, a fixture in the training camp. We'd order in Chinese food and watch hours of old boxing footage, or a film of Michael's next opponent. Michael and Jim studied boxing and I'd study right along with them. And I listened eagerly when they shared old Cus stories. There was a peace about Michael whenever Jim was around, so I was at peace. You just knew that he was in control and had our best interests at heart.

At the apartment in New York, Jim was never far away. He and his wife, Loriane, lived upstairs because, as Jim told me once, he wanted

Michael to have his independence, but he wanted to be able to keep an eye on him too.

One evening, Michael and I were in the kitchen. I was washing dishes and Jim had just gone upstairs.

Michael sat at the table, head down.

"Before Cus died, I'd just gotten in trouble again . . ." *Oh, no.* I could sense the guilt rising up inside of him and the fear stirring up too, and I could feel the darkness that fear and guilt bring with them. "We had so many rules and sometimes I was good about living by the rules and sometimes I just wanted to be in my old neighborhood, with my old friends . . . Robin, they were part of me too, and I was part of them. We argued about it, me and Cus, because when I went to Brownsville I always seemed to get in trouble. Right before he went into the hospital, he told me that he was going to wash his hands of me if I kept going back there . . . if I kept defying him. But I went back anyway and I did get in trouble. When I went to visit Cus in the hospital, he told me he was finished with me. He said, 'Get out of the house before I get home.' Cus died later that night. He never got home. And Jim doesn't know that Cus had washed his hands of me. He doesn't know that Cus wanted me out of the house . . . that he'd given up on me."

Michael buried his face in his hands as though to cover his shame. Then he put his head down on the table as if the guilt was too much to bear.

"No, Michael," I said. "Cus didn't mean it. That is what a parent tells a child when they are trying to get you to do the right thing. It's like my mother putting my bags in the hallway. She wasn't really putting me out. She was trying to bring me to my senses."

"No. He said that he realized that deep inside I was no good and would never be any good."

"Michael, stop it. Stop torturing yourself. People say a lot of things in anger, things they don't really mean. Cus loved you, loved you more than you love yourself, and that's what parents do. He just wanted you to be everything you're capable of being. You were so blessed to have him . . . I only wish I had a father who cared like Cus. I am just sorry that this was the last thing you shared."

Finally Michael lifted his head and met my eyes.

"The one thing Cus wanted me to do was break Marciano's record. And I'm going to. It's the only reason I'm still fighting. I'm gonna break the record . . . for Cus. Then I'm done."

If Jim was one lifeline, my mother was becoming another. As much as she'd objected to Michael, she seemed worn down by our determination to be together. Or perhaps she had resigned herself to the fact that we would and she thought she would have more control as someone inside the "camp." But once she joined the fold, we were left like sheep without a shepherd . . . we lost an important source of perspective from the outside world.

But Mom was sincerely impressed by Michael's discipline, and she began more and more to let down her guard as she discovered some of the things that were so endearing about him. What really made the difference is when he started calling her "Ma." My mother had always wanted a son, and suddenly her mind and her heart seemed to be opening to this very vulnerable, often gentlemanly, tough guy. Surely in the back of my mind, I wondered if my mother, with a compulsion for control, was indeed weakening, or using yet another maneuver to manage our lives . . . a more passive one . . . though I suppose the two were not mutually exclusive.

There would be no more demands to stop seeing him. No more threats to withdraw her love or support. He was one of us now and that meant she would defend him to the death and love him like her own to the end. She would sacrifice everything for him, because that was simply the way she "mothered." Without a doubt, my mother was self-sacrificing, because that is what mothers do. But there is no sacrifice without a price to be paid, something to be forfeited.

Things seemed good—busy, but good. We had our lives down to a little bit of a system and everyone seemed to adjust, knowing that whatever we did, we were going to do it together. When I was on the set, chances were he was somewhere close by, and if he had a press conference, I was there. Jim knew that if he wanted Michael to show up, he'd make sure I was coming. So I usually got the call from Jim even before Michael did. He trusted me to make sure Michael was there. Jim took care of business and I was taking care of Michael.

And now that it felt like my mom had surrendered, room was made for Michael not only in her heart but at our apartment. When we were both in New York he laid claim to the love seat that was in the bedroom Stephanie and I shared. He said it gave him the best night's sleep, and we all laughed about that because we knew it couldn't really be comfortable. We played the Centipede arcade game my sister had given me for my birthday, and I always beat him. We'd stay up watching TV and Mom would yell from her room, "Turn that thing off! It's too late to be watching TV." We were a family and we did what families do. He loved it and we loved having him there . . . by now, all of us loved having him as part of the family.

Later that spring, we were all in L.A. together, and Michael organized a night out for us. We'd go to a rap concert at the Hollywood Bowl to see Run-DMC and the Beastie Boys. My mom and I weren't sure we wanted to go, but Michael and Stephanie were so excited about it, it was impossible not to join in the fun and the excitement. We all piled into the long black limousine, wearing whatever each of us thought fitting for this outing . . . plus big smiles. Stephanie and I thought it was hysterical, taking our mother to a rap concert. When we got to our seats, we clapped and sang along and danced, and Mom watched and actually admitted she was having a fun time.

Suddenly Michael excused himself to go to the bathroom. Looking at him, I noticed he was drenched in sweat. "Are you sick?" I asked. He shook his head, and I told him to hurry back.

I don't know how much time passed, but suddenly several very large men and a couple of police officers approached us.

"You need to follow us," the largest one said.

"What's wrong?" I asked, but I didn't get an answer.

We were escorted through the large, excited crowd and out to the parking lot. To my surprise, Michael was out in the lot, looking even sweatier than he'd been when he'd left us. He had a strange expression on his face; he appeared to be in a panic. He grabbed me by the arm, saying, "Get in the car, Rob."

By now, there was a crowd swarming around us, with police holding them back and photographers snapping away.

"What happened?" my mother asked.

"Just get in the car, Ma."

The mood in the car was exactly the opposite of what it had been when, only a short while ago, we had come. No one spoke a word. Michael was still sweating, and finally Stephanie grabbed a napkin from under one of the glasses. Slowly and perhaps a bit apprehensively she passed it to Michael. "Thanks, Steph. Can I have a few more?" She passed him more, and then said, "Are you okay, Michael?" She asked the question in only the way that she could, soft and gentle and nonjudgmental.

"I was in the parking lot, and this girl just went crazy."

"Why were you in the parking lot?" I asked. "I thought you said you were going to the bathroom."

I never got a straight answer from Michael. Then, when we got home, there was a call from Jim. I kept asking him what was going on, but all he'd say was, "Don't worry about it, Robin."

I wouldn't get any answers until almost two weeks later. By that time, Michael was back in training camp. When I walked into the kitchen one morning, Mom was sitting at the table. I had never quite seen the look she had on her face that morning. She seemed confused and bewildered . . . dejected and maybe just plain old sad. I poured myself a cup of coffee and joined her at the table, and my mother pushed the copy of the *Los Angeles Times* toward me. My eye zoomed straight to the headline. That's how I found out that Michael had been charged with assault and battery.

"Oh, my God, no!" I said. Now I understood the look on her face a little better. She was indeed bothered and bewildered, but she was also defiant . . . the kind of bold resolve that a mother gets when she has a child in trouble. "We have to get through this."

We got through that. Jim made sure of it. Jim skillfully fought the battles outside of the ring while Michael skillfully fought the ones inside.

Chapter Twenty-Seven

Rather quickly, we became both a team and a family. For Michael, that was not unusual; his team had always been his family. It wasn't unusual for me, either; my family had always been my team. So when Michael asked that it be made official, it all seemed very natural. It seemed like something that was simply destined to be.

Both of us wore sweats: After all, we were hard at work, training in Las Vegas for yet another fight. His big, strong hand engulfed my own, and as we strolled into the restaurant, he kissed my hand and held it to his chest, and once again, I could feel the pounding of his heart. We went to the quiet little corner table that was always ours. Our usual warm and friendly waiter seemed unusually excited to see us. He pulled out my chair and his broad smile grew wider.

"Thank you for joining us," he told me, as if I could now be included in their plans.

I hardly had the chance to accept the seat he offered before Michael began speaking. And the waiter hardly had time to step away from the table, now all smiles.

"You know we're gonna get married, don't you, Robin?"

"Yes." I said. I did know it. I could feel some force moving us in that direction.

"Then let's do it!" he said. Suddenly he was holding a black velvet box, and inside was a large diamond ring that simply glistened. He placed the ring on my finger. All he said was, "Okay?" And I said, "Okay" too. By now the smile on my face nearly matched the brilliance of my ring as I held my hand out, admiring it and loving him. Michael was beaming too, with pride. The waiters gathered round the table applauding and each one shook Michael's hand. They were excited, we simply knew it was inevitable.

When we told Jim, he gave me a hug and said, "It's a beautiful ring, isn't it, Robin? It should be. It took him hours to pick it out." Michael blushed a bit, and I suppose I did too.

Even my mother seemed . . . well, perhaps not altogether happy about our engagement, but certainly resigned. I think she eased any angst she may have felt by accepting the challenge of this new project, a new person she would mold. Work eases the angst of many; hard work can sedate the soul of an anxious man or woman. And certainly, freeing Michael from his pain, bringing light to his darkness, and loving him like a member of the family would be hard work. And since this was a battle she realized she could not win one way, she had wholeheartedly committed to dealing with it in another.

Stephanie, on the other hand, surprised me. One afternoon, I was in our bedroom in New York, playing on my video game. She came into the room and, without even taking the time to say hello, said, "Don't marry him, Robin. I can't tell you how I know that you can't, but don't marry him." Engrossed with shooting down the spaceships, I barely looked up at her. "I know you love him," she continued. "We're like a family. I understand that, but I'm telling you: Please, let's just keep it like this. Don't marry him!"

I let out an exasperated sigh without looking up. "If we're already a family what's wrong with me marrying him?" I said, still fighting the ships that were trying to destroy me. The machine went black, and I looked up to see my sister holding the plug she'd pulled from the wall.

"You're not listening to me. I can't tell you how I know. I just do. Don't marry him, Robin. Don't do it!" And now I could see tears beginning to fill her beautiful brown eyes. Her words were as quiet as they had always been, yet they seemed foreboding and filled with urgency. "Don't do it, Robin," she repeated. "Don't marry him."

I could hear the urgency in her voice and it startled me . . . but then I brushed away her words and the feelings they created in me. She was my baby sister, and in many ways she was still trying to find her way. But there was one achievement, the one thing that truly stood out as hers: she was so comfortable, so at ease, so at peace. She was simply okay being Stephanie.

"Don't worry so much about me, sweet Stephanie," I said, kissing her cheek. "I love him and he loves me, and besides, what's the worst that can happen?"

Choices are the keys to life—they unlock doors. Choices are the shackles of life—they encumber us, bind us, weigh us down. We are freed by them and enslaved by them. Through the awesome power of choice, we create the issues of our lives. Or, as my sister warned me that afternoon: "You remember what Nanny always says, Robin?" She answered the question for me. "When you make your bed, you'll have to lie in it."

And now I had a starring role on a popular TV show and was engaged to be married to a man I loved. Everything was so right I couldn't imagine anything going wrong. I was immature enough to believe that this is the way my life simply would be.

I appeared on *The Tonight Show* with Joan Rivers hosting, and showed off my utter bliss along with my dazzling ring. My grandmother was thrilled; nothing excited her more than *The Tonight Show*, although she was a bit disappointed that Johnny Carson himself hadn't been hosting. Soon after that, *People* magazine voted me a "break-out star."

I remembered the fuss my mother had made when I said I wanted to be an actress. "It's not a stable life!" she'd insisted. It might be years before I became successful—if I ever did. Now, on a warm February day, driving along Sunset Boulevard, I felt rather smug for having proved her wrong. Then I recalled a dinner with Mindy Marin, the casting director who'd hired me. It was the night before the first episode of *Head of the Class* aired. After congratulating me, Mindy said, "Enjoy your last day of anonymity. Because once it's gone, you'll never get it back." She seemed to put a strange weight on the words, as if they were a kind of fairy-tale curse. For a brief moment, I wondered if my mother had somehow gotten Mindy to frighten me, and I laughed to myself at the possibility.

When I got home from the taping, Michael was there, pacing anxiously. "Let's go shopping," he said. "You need to pick out a dress. I want you to have something special for the All-Star Game." We had tickets to the basketball game in Chicago the next day.

We headed to Alaïa on Rodeo Drive. Michael had introduced me to the store and Alaïa had quickly become my favorite designer. I picked out a long black dress—just a bit clingy, of course. Everything they had was clingy. Then we stopped by the Beverly Hills Hotel. In the past, Michael had stayed there often and become friends with the jeweler there, who had the most unusual treasures in his shop. He loved not only shopping in the store, but just spending time exchanging stories. We often left with beautiful little trinkets, but when we climbed back in the car that day, Michael had a large velvet box. He held the box out in front of me and opened it. I couldn't believe my eyes.

It was something like Audrey Hepburn would have worn in *Breakfast at Tiffany's*. It was a seven . . . eight . . . maybe ten-tier diamond necklace with matching earrings, all fire and dazzle, a lovely golden glow unlike anything I'd ever seen. I hadn't felt quite this much like royalty since my grandfather had called me "Princess."

"Do you like it?" he asked softly. "It's beautiful!" I said, equally softly. I think we both felt that this beautiful ornament deserved our reverence and respect. Or perhaps we spoke softly because it just took our breath away.

He carefully took the necklace out of the box and placed it around my neck. It didn't seem to go with my jeans and cashmere sweater, and for a moment I felt silly. But when I looked at Michael's face, that feeling faded fast. He was so proud of himself, so proud of his accomplishments, so proud that he could give the woman he loved something so precious. I knew it because I could see it in his eyes. I could feel it.

Michael insisted I wear my new jewelry on that night's flight to Chicago.

⸺∽∾∾∿⸺

At the basketball game, I think we watched each other more than the action on the court. All of the stars of the time were playing, and the stands were even more star-studded. By now, I'd become so used to my new jewels that I had forgotten that I was wearing them until Oprah and I greeted each other. "Wow!" she said, gazing at my necklace. "That's beautiful, Robin!" Michael smiled proudly.

After the game, Michael said there was someplace he'd like to take me. I was happy to go wherever he wanted, even though I was a tad bit curious.

When we got in the car, he said, "There's someone I'd love for you to meet. He's very important to me."

"Okay," I answered, wondering why he was suddenly so serious.

"You know I love you very much, don't you, Robin?"

"Yes." I said. "I know that. And I love you."

He gazed deep into my eyes. "I'm gonna make everything I've

done wrong right by having you in my life and loving you." Michael seemed on a mission, a well-considered, deliberately planned, precisely executed mission.

I found myself at a church after the game. Michael held my hand tightly and knocked on the rectory door with the other. For a split second I wondered if I was properly dressed for this visit, and I tugged at my tight dress. But it seemed that as soon as the thought occurred to me, a man appeared at the door, with a crisp white collar and a warm and welcoming smile.

"Hello, Robin," the priest said, as he extended his hand to greet me. "I've heard so much about you." He draped an arm around Michael's shoulder, and the three of us walked into the rectory.

"I was so glad when Michael asked that I marry you," the priest said. "What a pleasure that will be. I've known Michael for a very long time."

Oh, this must be the priest that Jim spoke of, I thought. *The one he described as such a dear friend.* So I told him, "That will be wonderful! I can't wait to begin making wedding plans."

"I was thinking we'd get married now," Michael said.

Now, this was a surprise.

"You mean you didn't tell her?" said the priest, who seemed a bit surprised now himself.

Michael looked a little sheepish. "I thought it would be nice if it was a surprise," he said. "And I had never heard of a surprise wedding."

Yet his plan went on . . . Our premarital counseling took all of ten minutes. The priest asked a bit about our hopes and dreams. Then he said, "It's clear you two love each other. I can feel it and I don't think I have ever seen Michael happier."

Like so many other girls, I always dreamed of a wedding with a long white gown and bridesmaids and lots of friends and family in attendance. And the dream danced in my mind's eye at that moment. *But who would give me away?* And then I thought, "I don't really have anyone to give me away" . . . and I gave my consent to the plan.

"Yes, we do love each other very much," I said. And, after all, if I were married, I'd be a woman for sure. I would finally be free, and I would have a man who loved me.

We left the rectory a married couple. Well, anyway, we had a marriage ceremony.

We returned to our hotel—both of us terribly excited and happy, and both of us slightly, secretly nervous. Each of us was unsure of how to behave, now that we were husband and wife. Why wouldn't we be unsure? Neither of us had seen up close a marriage we could imitate, so we were left to our own improvisations and fantasies. We had placed ourselves in these roles we had idealized, and now we would fabricate behavior that we had never seen up close and in person, the kind of up close and in person example provided by parents.

I went to the bedroom of our suite and removed my black wedding dress and jewels. I needed time to fix my new role in my mind. I wanted to be a wonderful wife, and I know Michael wanted to be the perfect husband. But what a wonderful wife said or did, I surely did not know, and Michael had no point of reference for his role, either.

So I decided to take a bath. Whenever I felt unhappy or confused or unsettled, I took a bath. As I ran the water and added just enough bath gel to ensure the right amount of bubbles for my mood, or this level of confusion, I could hear Michael dialing the phone in the other room, and I wondered who he was calling.

"Robin! I'm calling Ma. Do you want to tell her or do you want me to tell her?" I bolted to the other room and took the receiver from his hand. The phone rang three or four times, then Stephanie answered.

"Hi, Steph," I said sheepishly. A pause, and then she asked, "So did you do it?" I wondered how she knew.

"Yes, we got married."

"I knew it!" she said. Michael was so close that he could hear our conversation. "Tell her to put Ma on the phone," he said anxiously. Stephanie called Mom, saying—with not a hint of enthusiasm for the idea—"Well, they're married!"

Mom took the phone. "Is it true?" she asked. But there is no way I could describe the pain and disappointment in her voice. I didn't have time to say more than "Yes," before Michael grabbed the phone.

"Ma! We got married!" While he told her the entire story of the day, I took my bath. When I got out of the tub they were still on the phone. The only thing that interrupted their conversation was a call from Jim on another line. "I gotta go, Ma. I'll call you right back. I gotta tell Jim we got married."

Michael shared with Jim the details of our day, and then Jim asked to speak with me. I grabbed the phone and placed it under my chin so I could still continue to smooth lotion on my body. Michael went past me to the bathroom, mumbling something under his breath that I couldn't quite make out.

"Robin," Jim said in a low calm voice, "you two are not married. You've had the ceremony, but it's not legal because you did not get a marriage license."

Before I could say a word or move a muscle, Michael took the phone from me, and hung up on Jim. He seemed genuinely disturbed that his plan hadn't gone the way he'd expected, and I tried my best to soothe him. Since he had to be in New York City for a press conference the next day, Jim set up all the arrangements for us to have a civil ceremony at City Hall in Manhattan. Although it still bothered Michael that his romantic plan had a little glitch, I felt great that Jim seemed to need me as much as I needed him. Michael, Jim, and I had worked together to both honor Michael's commitments (the press conference) and make our union completely legal. We decided to go out on the town to celebrate.

As we left the hotel, the doorman greeted us. "Hey, Mike! Good evening, Miss Givens." Mike grinned and said, "She's *Mrs. Tyson* now.

We just got married." I loved seeing him so happy, and I loved feeling so much happiness myself.

When we got in the cab, the driver asked, "Where you two headed?" We just looked at each other and laughed. The truth was, we hadn't a clue. We told the driver to look for someplace romantic and intimate, someplace open this late on a Sunday night. Finally, we stumbled upon a little jazz bar. When we walked in, we realized that it was simply perfect.

There were a lot of empty seats to choose from, and we chose a table near the stage, but not too close. Michael called over to the waiter. "Bring us the best bottle of champagne you have. We got married today." And I smiled too, mostly because I realized this waiter didn't care one little bit that we had just gotten married, and he didn't even care that the heavyweight boxing champion had just walked into his club. His indifference was quite rare, and refreshing.

We gave each other our full attention as we held hands. Every so often, he held my hands to his lips and kissed first one and then the other.

All of a sudden, Michael seemed to get another bright idea and left the table. He ran to the stage and whispered in the ear of the man who'd been standing behind the microphone singing. I don't know what he said, but in an instant Michael was the one standing onstage, singing into the microphone. "This next song is dedicated to my new wife," Michael announced. "I love her so much and I'm gonna shout it to the world." I looked around the room, and there wasn't much of "the world" in it. My embarrassment quickly turned to amusement . . . it was absolutely the most flattered I had ever been, and it was absolutely the funniest sight I had ever seen.

So I relaxed and enjoyed the best gift he'd ever given me. He began to recite words in time with the music the band played, and as he spoke, his feet did their best impression of The Temptations. "The moment I met her, I knew she'd be my wife. She's one of a kind and I love her more than anything in the world." And without a care for

what anyone else may have thought, without the slightest bit of trepidation, Michael began to sing "My Girl." The back-up guys, whom
he'd met only moments ago, harmonized with him so easily, so
smoothly, so lovingly. It was like nothing my heart could've ever
imagined. It was beautiful to behold and irresistible to experience.
His movements were awkward, and he hardly carried the tune, but
he sang the song as if he had written it for me . . . with pure and perfect love, and I adored him. His sweetness and innocence at this moment . . . the way he tuned out the world and just focused on me
helped transform this magical moment and this magical place into
a mystical experience.

We went back home to New York as I had promised Jim we would,
and Jim had kept his promise too. He'd arranged for us to go to City
Hall first thing the very next morning. They opened the doors knowing that we were waiting. We were married once again, legally this
time, by a man whose face I cannot recall. And Michael, though I
knew he was grateful to Jim for keeping everything in order, found this
all quite annoying and a bit of a nuisance. We left the building and
walked down the steps of City Hall officially a married couple.
Michael and Jim shook hands and hugged and Jim hugged me and
gave me a kiss on the cheek before he whispered in my ear, "Please
make sure he's there for the press conference later." I nodded and then
we were in the car off to see Mom at her office.

Tom was the first to greet us. He hugged me and patted Michael on
the back. Olga jumped out of her seat with hugs and kisses for me and
Michael that seemed to go on forever. "Congratulations!" she said. "I
can't believe you did it. But no one's surprised. I think your mom's a

little upset that she wasn't there, but don't tell her I told you. It doesn't matter, though. We're going to throw you a wonderful reception." Olga was so excited, she was out of breath.

We walked into Mom's office together. My mother sat behind her desk, talking on the phone. Stephanie stood near her, apparently awaiting our arrival. She held Michael by his shoulders and kissed him on his cheek. "I guess it's official now. You're my brother." And then she came over to me and squeezed me tight. She whispered in my ear, "I knew you were going to do it anyway," she said. "I love you, and I'm always here for you."

"I know, Steph," I said. And finally she let me go.

She smiled. "Mom and Olga have been planning the reception all morning. You know you've given Olga her favorite thing to do . . . throw a party! She's in heaven."

Just then, Mom hung up the phone and ran to us. She gave us both a big hug and kiss and then called for Olga to bring in the champagne. In an instant, Olga was pouring out the Cristal, and they were toasting our new marriage. We had come a long way in a very short time, and no one had come further than my mother. What a change of heart! Michael was family now. All of it seemed easy and natural and intimate, the kind of easy intimacy that a true family shares. But I could only imagine the mix of emotions she must have experienced. Ease and peace and order were paramount to her. How did she ever believe she could maintain order in what was inherently a mess? Then my mother got right to the business of our reception.

Though today she was proud that she was in a position to choose the Helmsley Palace, pleased that Michael was so warm and caring toward her and even more pleased that he treated me so well, as far as she knew—yet had she had her way, had she been able to choose for me . . . certainly this would not have been the man she chose. But Mom was going to make the best of my choice and my decision.

People behaved as if I'd married royalty, and I suppose he was a king with an international domain, and far-reaching powers. He ruled the ring and had great authority over his subjects, those for whom he was generating great sums of money. And they in turn ruled the news, tabloids, and TV.

What in the world had I gotten myself into?

<hr />

On Valentine's Day 1988, a hundred friends and loved ones gathered to celebrate our wedding. Michael invited some of his old friends from Catskill and a few from Brownsville. His sister, Denise, was his only blood relative there, but his boxing family was present in full force. My grandfather flew in from Lexington and shared a table at the reception with Nan. He smiled at her and gave her a peck on the cheek that she offered reluctantly. Her forgiveness she appeared to withhold completely. Though she had forgiven him long ago, she would never let him know. All that tension . . . one would have thought that she still had a soft spot in her heart for him. And judging by the way he looked at her the spot in his heart was even softer.

"You sure do look good, Grace," he said. "You've hardly changed a bit. And you still have those pretty legs."

Nan rolled her eyes. "Newby, it seems you haven't changed a bit either and I would venture to say you never will."

My mom gave him a big hug, saying, "Oh, Daddy, I'm so glad you're here!" As for my Aunt Peggy . . . well, her reaction was indescribable. She sat next to him like a little girl who refused to let her daddy out of her sight. This otherwise reserved woman, who never had much to say, talked up a blue streak all night long. She was little-girl giddy.

My Uncle Stormy and my Uncle Mike and Pep and all of my cousins were there. And they all hugged Michael and kissed Michael and welcomed him more than into our family, but into our hearts and he seemed so very glad to hold that place. There were old, old friends from my early childhood and friends from New Rochelle Academy and of course from Sarah Lawrence. From Brownsville to Bronxville, from Lexington Avenue to Lexington, Kentucky—we had quite the gathering. No matter what we did or did not have in common, that night together, we all had a ball celebrating our marriage.

On the surface, the marriage didn't change our relationship much. I returned to Los Angeles to tape *Head of the Class*, while Michael remained in New York to prepare for his next fight. This might have seemed odd for most newlyweds, but it had become the normal pattern of our busy lives. It would not take long for the differences marriage made to present themselves.

My agent called with great news: I'd been asked to audition for *The Women of Brewster Place*, a TV miniseries based on a novel by Gloria Naylor. I had read the book and loved it, and when I was told that Oprah was both producing and starring in the miniseries I became even more excited about the opportunity. But it just kept getting better. Lynn Whitfield and Jackée Harry had just been cast, and Cicely Tyson was already attached to the project too. The possibility of working with an icon and my idol was absolutely thrilling. It just didn't get any better than this . . . at least not to me.

The only problem was that the audition was scheduled for the same day I was supposed to join Michael on the trip to Japan for his fight with Tony Tubbs.

I called Michael to explain. Surely he'd understand why I needed to stay. "I love the part, Michael!" I said, excitedly. "I'll be on the very first flight right after the audition" I assured him.

"Why do you want to still do that stuff?" he asked, sounding sullen. "You're married now."

"Michael, this is a great role. And besides, acting is what I *do*. You know that. It's just one day."

"I don't understand you, Robin. Women do that stuff until they get a husband. And you've got one now, so it's time to stop. Don't you think I can take care of you?"

"Of course I do, but that's not the point, Michael, you know that. Look, I'm staying for the audition. You can stay too, if you want, or I'll be right behind you." The click I heard made his feelings clear, and I wondered for a quick moment if I'd made the right decision. But then my excitement about the audition returned and I put everything else out of my mind, thinking, *Oh, he'll come around . . . he'll understand how important this is to me and he'll surely come around and be happy too.*

The day of my audition, I nailed it—I could just tell. The excitement I felt after the audition only magnified my excitement about the project, as I thought, *I've got a real chance at this.* I jumped into my red Suzuki jeep to head for the airport. I zoomed down the street completely exhilarated. I knew that even if I didn't get the part, I could be proud of myself for doing such a terrific job in the audition. There was simply no way I would get that job . . . that would be just too good to be true . . . but I could be proud of myself for trying. The fact that I was a new bride was the furthest thing from my mind—until I stopped at a light and two men in the car next to me spoke as if they had known us for years. "Hey! How ya doin', Mrs. Tyson," one said and the other chimed in, "Congratulations and be sure to congratulate your husband for me." I smiled and waved, touched and a little surprised. That was the moment I realized how exposed my life had become, how much Michael and I were considered public property. And it was also the moment I realized there just might be a conflict between my new role as wife and the thing I loved doing so much.

The plane to Japan was huge and rather crowded, but I was ushered up a circular staircase to an area that seemed quite private.

"Hello, Mrs. Tyson!" The heavily accented voice was pure as a bell, and I turned to find a woman with the delicate beauty of a classical Japanese painting. She gave me a robe and slippers and settled me into my seat, chatting all the while. She didn't always choose the right words and some of the words she chose required a bit of imagination to interpret. And I suppose she knew she was a bit difficult to understand, because after some of her comments she would place her hand over her mouth, wrinkle her face, and giggle. It seemed only to add to her femininity and grace, and I giggled right along with her. "I'm sorry. I am still practicing my English. It is not very good."

"Well, your English is much better than my Japanese." She bowed and I returned the gesture. For that moment she became very serious. "Thank you, Mrs. Tyson!" she said, then moved away.

I settled in my seat and took a long, deep breath. *Mrs. Tyson.* Suddenly I felt a strange twinge of anxiety. It was as if I'd hopped into the front car of the Cyclone at Coney Island and the steel bar had just clicked down, locking me into my seat. No turning back now! I was in for every twist and turn, every slow trek up the hill, every stomach-flipping plunge down.

"Mrs. Tyson, this is for you." The lovely flight attendant was back, this time with a perfectly chilled bottle of Dom Perignon. She poured a glass and then brought a tray of delicacies: smoked salmon, caviar, truffles. The plane began taxiing toward the runway and as I sipped the champagne, I decided to ignore that flutter of uneasiness. All I could do now was try to enjoy the ride.

———— ✖ ————

The last time I'd seen my sister before the trip to Japan, she gave me a book, telling me, "Rob, this is perfect for you." She recounted a story that she'd read in the book about a woman who, in search of wisdom, consulted a guru, moved to a cave, and surrounded herself with books. Every day her guru would come to ask if she had accomplished her goal, and every day she would say, "No," and he would strike her, then leave to return the next day. This went on day after day, until one day, the woman finally resisted the blow. She had more than accomplished her goal . . . she had discovered all that she needed to know. She had discovered how to stop the pain. Stephanie told me, "The only thing that is going to stop the pain is a change . . . a change in you. Because that is all you have the power to change. And that, Robin, is the most difficult change of all."

Though I was unclear what my sister was talking about, I knew my sister knew me so well . . . I settled back in the seat and opened *Codependent No More* by Melody Beattie.

After a long while I finally drifted off to sleep, and was awakened by the jolt of the plane landing in Tokyo. I felt a sudden wave of panic, although I wasn't quite sure why. I went to the restroom to gather myself, unaware of what I was feeling, or why. I brushed my teeth and scrubbed my face as clean as I could get it. And I stared in the mirror, searching for help from the girl who stared back at me. For the moment, this small bathroom felt like a safe place to be. I pulled my hair in a tight ponytail, and then I washed my face again, even though I had just washed it. The knock at the door made me realize that I had been in the bathroom for quite some time.

"Mrs. Tyson?" the familiar, soft voice said. "So sorry to disturb you, but it is time to go." I unlocked the door and slid it open. "Are you okay?" the flight attendant asked. I nodded unconvincingly, not quite sure myself. I noticed that I was the last one on the plane, and the entire crew had been waiting for me.

I walked off the plane, still feeling uneasy, still not sure why. And then I arrived at customs, and was confronted with more cameras, more microphones, more flashing lights and shouting voices than I'd ever experienced or witnessed in my entire life.

This is where it all seemed to begin. I'm sure it had already begun, but . . . it was as if I had awakened somewhere strange, in the middle of something unfamiliar, and I thought if only I could go back to sleep and turn back the hands of time. I suppose awakening, like most things, is a process. This was the first time I realized I was in something I wasn't prepared for, and in deep. There was no possible way I could navigate the waters and no way I could control the current. I seemed simply to be swept up in the current and had no control over its direction. And for the first time I sensed that I was in over my head. All I could do was hold on. I was officially out of control.

I checked my clothes and wished I had on a better outfit. I ran my fingers across my clean face and wished I had on some makeup. I pulled my backpack closer and clutched the book Stephanie had given me, holding it tight to my chest as if it could comfort me. Finally, through the mob fighting to get a quote from me, through the flashing bulbs, through the police who were there to protect me, I saw Michael. As happy as I was to see him, I wondered why he hadn't warned me. He grabbed me and hugged me and ignored all that was happening around us as if it weren't happening at all.

"I missed you," he said. He grabbed my backpack and put his arms around me. "Move!" he said to one of the photographers, faking anger, then bursting into laughter. "These people are crazy here!"

I hadn't brought any luggage, so we went straight to the waiting car. After a long ride we arrived at the hotel and went up to our suite, which was basically the top floor of the hotel. The next few days were filled with everything that I loved about training camp. Our time together was calm and peaceful. When Michael wasn't busy, we watched Japanese TV or played tag in the hallways. Michael took early morning jogs and I slept. He worked out and I read. I was part of every bit of his training, except for sparring. That was the only thing I wasn't allowed to be part of or to witness. I didn't question it. It was just the way it was and would be.

And then my agent called: I'd been offered the role of Kiswana in *The Women of Brewster Place*. I can't begin to describe how happy I was, how thrilled at the chance to work on such a great movie with such a wonderful cast. I was certain that Michael would be thrilled too. But I was wrong about that.

"Why do you continue with this bullshit?" he said, throwing a wet towel down on the bed and pulling off his sweats. He'd just come back from a run. "I thought this shit would end when we got married!" Oddly enough, his words reminded me of my mother—as if this were something I could simply turn off or grow out of, as if it were not important at all. And there was no care at all that it was important to me.

His anger was cold but quiet, so he caught me completely off guard when he grabbed me by my hair and yanked me to the floor.

"I'm telling you, I don't want to hear about this anymore!"

"Let go of me!" I screamed. I felt him wrap my hair around one fist, as the other hand wrapped itself around my neck, tighter and tighter until he squeezed the tears from me, tears I desperately didn't want to cry.

"Please stop, Michael! Please! I can't breathe!" I struggled to remove his hand from my throat, and then there were no more words, no more tears, just my pleading, terrified eyes. He let go of my hair first and then my neck, and I gasped for air.

"Oh, don't be such a baby," he said. "You're fine. I don't care. Go do whatever you want."

By the time he got out of the shower, he was back to the loving husband he had been. Over the next couple of days, I was quiet and withdrawn, confused and wondering what I should do—what *could* I do?

"How long are you gonna be acting like this, Rob?" he finally said. "You're okay. You're not hurt." And he was right. I wasn't hurt . . . but

I felt hurt. And that in and of itself became difficult and confusing for me. I was fine, but I was not fine, and when Michael and I climbed in bed at night, he could feel my confusion and distance. When he made love to me, I searched for the answers in my confused mind. The incident was over, but it was not gone. "Stop acting like this," he said as he lay on top of me. Little did he know that everything in me was trying to forget, but my soul just couldn't.

The next day, I attended Michael's press conference. By this time, I was familiar with the script: Michael's opponent promised to be the first to take him down, and Michael, looking humble and mostly bored, listened. Today was a little different, because he never took his eyes off me. I attributed it to what had gone on between us, what was still going on.

Once Michael left the podium, he announced to a reporter, as others listened on, that his wife had just gotten a role in a miniseries with Oprah Winfrey. "It's based on a book. What's the book, Rob?" he asked, as he placed his arms around me.

"*The Women of Brewster Place*," I answered. What was this about?

"I'm so proud of her," he said to the reporters. He repeated it as we entered our room. "I am really proud of you. And I'm very happy for you." This was the reaction that I'd wanted. This was the reaction of a man who loved me. It was a couple of days late, and it followed a lot of baffling, upsetting behavior, but it was here. And we made love that night as if nothing bad had ever happened between us.

※

Jim had not been feeling well. But still the fight went according to plan, obviously with a victory for Michael. Shortly after the fight, Michael and I lay in bed, stunned and sobbing, too grief-stricken to move. Jim had died, and his death was a shock. Little did we know, as we lay there grieving, all hell was about to break loose. We headed back home sad and stunned.

Don King was on the same plane back to the United States. Michael knew him, of course; King was one of the most successful, and notorious, boxing promoters in the world. Jim, and Cus before him, had warned Michael time and time again to stay away from Don King.

Bill Cayton, Jim's partner, was also on the flight, but Michael wanted nothing to do with him. We ended spending most of the long flight with Don.

Don was charming and smart and entertaining, and he seemed to lighten the sadness that we were all feeling. He also was definitely interested in Michael, and no matter what Michael had been told about Don, Michael was just as interested in him. Perhaps because Jim was gone now. Perhaps because the very fact that he'd been warned so much, so often, made him curious. Whatever the reason, I heard Michael say, "My wife just picked a house. We're going to see it when we land. Why don't you come with us?"

I wasn't sure what Michael was doing. I'd been there when Jim was teaching him the ins and outs of the world, and would remind him of the dos and don'ts. This was the biggest don't, and the biggest pitfall.

Toward the end of the flight, Bill came and sat next to us, and told Michael that he wanted to get to "know him better." Michael just shook his head and smiled. And when Bill left, Michael snuggled his face in my lap like a child and said, "Please promise me that you won't let anyone hurt me or take advantage of me. Promise me that you'll protect me!" His words and his face were serious, even grave. All I said, all I could say, was, "I promise!" I promised, but just what was it he expected me to do?

∽∾∾∽

Michael had asked my mom to pick out our new house, a house fit for the king . . . and his bride. She had narrowed down the choices for us, and then during training, I made a quick trip back from Tokyo to make the final selection . . . a beautiful mansion in New Jersey. I brought pictures back with me when I returned to Tokyo and

Michael could not believe his eyes, nor could he wait to see the house. All the way from the airport to Bernardsville, Michael fidgeted and stared out the window, asking "How far away are we?" and "Are we there yet?" every two minutes. He was like a child in his eagerness, and it was a pleasure to witness this side of him. He'd worked hard and this home would be his crowning glory.

"You're not gonna believe this house!" he told Don. "Wait till you see it!" And I felt proud that he trusted me so.

When we pulled into the driveway, the house seemed even bigger than I remembered it. Perhaps the house itself was eager to welcome its king. Michael's eyes widened like I'd never seen before, and his smile stretched across his whole face. It was obvious that he was more than pleased.

We took the long drive down the road to the house and he squeezed my hand tight. When the car stopped, all he said was, "Come on, man! Let me show you around!" Off he and the promoter went, but not before Michael rushed back and kissed me and said, "Thank you!"

My mother arrived a few minutes later. "Does he like it?" she asked nervously.

"He loves it!" I said, as I watched him give a tour of his new house. I was so happy that he was happy, and I said to my mother, in turn, "Thank you."

From that day on, the infamous boxing promoter was a fixture in our lives. Plenty of people on Team Tyson objected—including me—but it didn't matter.

At first, I didn't have many complaints, because I honestly didn't see what was wrong with it . . . or what was wrong with Don, for that matter. I didn't understand everyone's warnings, their absolute distrust of this man. He was funny, he was entertaining, he spoke of his family with such love and devotion that you could not help but envy his children for having a father with such commitment. "I've got fifty acres and I built a house for each one of my kids where they'll always have a home," he boasted. You could not help but understand Michael's attraction to the man, there was something quite fatherly about him, as if he were the ultimate protector.

At first, I was willing to give him the benefit of the doubt because the rest of the team criticized me just for allowing Don to be around Michael. It was as if I'd stopped doing my part, or was even orchestrating Michael's demise. But they overestimated my power over Michael. I didn't control whom Michael spoke to and entertained in our home, whom he spent time with outside our home. I tried to please them, to make everything the way they wanted it to be, but the fact is that I just didn't understand the situation, what was at stake, or how much our lives were about to change, after Jim's death. I just didn't understand.

Michael, who understood perhaps just a little better, assured me he could handle his newfound relationship with this man. "When you're in the room with a snake," Michael would tell me, "all you have to do is keep the light on."

⸺∞⸺

Team Tyson decided to have dinner all together with Jim's wife, Loriane, at their apartment.

I was apprehensive about going. I knew that Bill would be there, and everything about him made me feel uncomfortable, mostly because I knew how Michael felt about him. But Michael always masked his feelings better than I could. Whatever I was feeling was usually written all over my face. I had serious second thoughts about going, but Michael wouldn't hear of it.

"I need you," he said. "I need you to be my wife. And what about what you promised me on the plane? You said you'd protect me." He smiled that smile that warmed my heart and I wanted to live up to every promise that I'd ever made him, and every promise that anyone had ever made to him.

Everyone else was already at the apartment, eating take-out Chinese. No one seemed to be talking to each other. Michael and I sat alone at a small table off the kitchen. As we ate, we both wondered why we were there, what this dinner was all about. We weren't a part of whatever was being discussed—not that we minded.

Then Bill walked over and informed us that we'd be leaving for Los Angeles in the morning; Jim's funeral would be held there the following day. We were supposed to close on the house in Bernardsville on the same day. So I thought to myself, we'll have to change our closing date. Michael didn't seem concerned. He offered a solution. "I'll go to the funeral and you take care of the house," he said.

"Let's change the date of the closing," I said. "I want to be there."

"No! We're not changing a thing. You're staying." He was adamant and that seemed fine.

Without another word spoken, we arrived back at our apartment. But I wasn't very pleased with his plan. We settled in to watch a tape of an old Rocky Marciano match, which was something that Michael had loved to do with Jim.

Each time the bell clanged at the end of a round, the sound echoed in the silent apartment. I left the lonely chair I had been sitting in and sat next to Michael. As much as I wanted to comfort him, I needed to be comforted too.

And he sensed that. "Rob, I know you want to be there," he said, his voice gentle. "But that house means a lot to me. I don't want to wait a day longer than we have to. That house is our future." He wrapped his arm around me and kissed my forehead, and I felt safe and loved.

The phone rang several times. It was on my side of the sofa, but I ignored it, not wanting to disturb the moment. It stopped and started again, so many times that we couldn't pretend it away.

I picked up the phone, still holding Michael's hand.

"Hello, Robin." I recognized the priest's buttery voice right away. "Is Michael there?"

"Yes, he's right here," I said. But before I could pass the phone, Father said, "Actually, Robin, I called to speak with you." I settled in to listen.

"Robin," he said, "You know Jim and I were very close, but the one thing I never understood about Jim was his relationship to Bill. And I believe in my heart that if Michael wasn't in the position he was in, he'd have nothing to do with Cayton. But it is as if Michael has been willed to him like chattel. Do you understand?"

"Not really. I'm sorry."

"Robin, Michael deserves to be with someone who truly cares about him and really understands him. You want what's best for him, don't you?"

"Of course, Father!"

"Then you'll help me, won't you?"

"Of course, Father!"

And he said good-bye. I simply told Michael that Father was sorry for his loss.

Michael went to the funeral and I closed on our house. We moved in right after Michael got back . . . I think all we had was a bed and a kitchen table and chairs. But we were happy, oh, so happy. Michael decided that he was going to be in charge of the decorating. That was fine with me because it all seemed overwhelming and I was set to begin shooting *The Women of Brewster Place*. He walked me from one room to another, telling me what he planned: "This one's gonna be all white, and this one is gonna have gilding all over the ceiling."

I loved seeing him so excited. The phone rang, and I ran to what would be Michael's office to answer it. It was Bill.

"I'll get Michael for you." I said.

"I don't need to speak to Mike. I need to speak to you."

"Me?"

"Yes, you! I just want you to know that I know what you're try-ing to pull, and I'm going to do everything in my power to make your life miserable."

"Fine. I'll let you tell my husband that." I yelled for Michael to come to the phone, and heard a click.

"Who is it?" he said.

"It was Bill, but he hung up," I said.

"Forget Bill. I wanna show you what I want to do."

He was like a kid, and this was the part of him that I got to see and know and love. People didn't see him the way I saw him. They didn't know him the way I knew him. And there were times when I felt so blessed. I am sure that every woman who has ever been in a roller-coaster ride of a relationship has felt and maybe even said, "They don't know him like I know him."

Working on *Women* was more amazing than I could have imagined. Lynn Whitfield, Jackée, Oprah—and Cicely Tyson, a woman I'd ad-mired my whole life. I was in awe, and deliriously happy. Donna Deitch was a warm director, and everyone was incredibly supportive, we quickly became close . . . as if we had been and would be friends forever. We all felt that we were doing something that would be re-membered for a long time, and we were pleased to be there and be part of it.

Maybe I seemed too happy, too independent, because Michael began acting more and more suspicious, jealous, and possessive.

He hated what I wore to work. Though it was by no means se-ductive, it was also not my typical sweats. These women were all such ladies, and I simply wanted to be one of them. The happier I became, the more jealous and possessive he grew. But it was such a wonder-ful opportunity for me that it was nearly impossible to temper my en-thusiasm. When the AD phoned with my call time, Michael would accuse me of sleeping with him: "Have him call here again and I'm gonna come down to that set and kick his ass." Michael stayed up later and later, and got mad that I wouldn't stay up with him. He started drinking more than usual and when he'd come home from being out he'd throw things around the house.

"Michael, stop it!"

"Stop what? This?" And he put his foot through the television screen.

I yelled again, "Michael, stop it!" hoping to bring him to his senses.

Now he was pulling food from the refrigerator and throwing it at Lucy as she ran from the kitchen to her room.

Finally, he fell to the kitchen floor in utter despair and regret.

And I spent the night on the kitchen floor, with Michael, calming him down.

The next morning Lucy crept in, while Michael was still asleep.

"Are you okay, Ms. Robin?" Lucy asked.

I nodded and stood up, stiff and sore. "I'm so sorry, Lucy," I said, as the tears streamed down my face.

"It's not your fault, Ms. Robin. Don't cry." And she hugged me for a long time.

—————

I decided that the best way to assure Michael that nothing was going on between me and anyone on the set was to include him in what we were doing. I went to the director and asked if Michael could do something on the movie, and she was kind enough to find a part for him. The rest of the cast and crew were excited, and being a part of things seemed to ease whatever fear or insecurity Michael was feeling. He went to wardrobe and makeup and was very nice to everyone. He took it all seriously and really did his best.

"How am I? Am I okay?" he asked me.

"You're doing great, Michael."

"You know I love you, right?"

"Yes, I know, Michael. I love you too."

He seemed disappointed when the shooting for his scene was finished.

One night when we were shooting a very important scene, Michael showed up completely drunk. Embarrassed, I tried to keep him out of everyone's way.

"Just go wait for me in my room, Michael," I said. It was late, and all night we had been shooting a scene that took place in the rain. We were all tired, cold, and wet.

"I wanna know who you're f——in'!" he said, back to the same old thing.

"Please, wait for me in the room. Maybe you should try to sleep." He grabbed me by my braids and pulled me close to him.

"You're not going anywhere till you tell me who you're sleeping with, and then I'm gonna kick his ass." He grabbed me by my throat and threw me against the divider between my room and Lynn's.

"Please don't, Michael!"

"Shut up, bitch," he said as he slapped me over and over again. "Get up, bitch, I'm not hurting you. If I wanted to hurt you, believe me, you'd be hurt."

He picked me up by my throat till my feet were dangling in the air and then threw me into the divider again. All the wind was knocked out of me, but all I could do was think, "Thank God that Lynn isn't in her room." I was so embarrassed I wouldn't have known how to explain.

"I'm not gonna be there when you get home tonight, bitch!" And he left the room. I gathered myself and joined the rest of the cast.

"Where's Mike?" someone said as I left my room. "Did he go home?"

I nodded.

"What's wrong? You okay?"

"Just a little tired."

We finished in the wee hours of the morning. I went home and found Michael sprawled out in the bed sleeping. I packed a small bag and drove myself to the airport and flew home to New York.

I think my mother had an inkling that something was going on, but she thought her acceptance could help control things. She was with us every opportunity she had, and most of all I suppose she believed her vigilance could prevent anything serious from happening. Yet I think she knew all along what could happen . . . what had happened . . . what was bound to happen. *That's why she didn't want this relationship in the first place*, I told myself during the flight to New York.

But now I had a commitment to Michael, and I had gotten everyone else to commit too. I suppose my mother had a sense of what he might be capable of, though she had never really witnessed any indication of how serious this lack of control could be at times. Jim had talked to her about Michael learning to control his impulses, and how there was no better discipline than the ring, and so Michael should fight, and fight often. But Michael was expressing less and less interest in boxing and now Jim wasn't here to motivate him or help control him.

"Are you okay?" my mother asked.

"Yes," I answered. "I just needed to come home."

I curled up in my bed, and soon after, the phone rang. I could hear my mother speaking to Michael, and I wondered what he was telling her. She passed the phone to me without saying a word.

"Michael, this is too hard for me," I said. "I can't live like this. It's just too hard."

"Just come home!" he said. "Either you come home or I'm coming there." I was silent knowing that he would, in fact, come. "I'm sorry!" he said. "I'll do anything you want, just come home."

I got out of bed, grabbed the bag that I'd come with, that had yet to be opened, and headed out the door.

"You just got here, Robin! What's going on? This just feels like a bunch of chaos to me . . . stay for a little while. Don't go back now."

I shook my head. "I have to go to work in a couple of days anyway. I might as well go back now. Besides, he'll just come and get me if I don't."

Mom gave me a long look. I told her I just needed some space.

"This is crazy," she told me. And she didn't even know how right she was. To some degree, we were all out of control. "Chaos is just a way to distract yourself," she said.

I headed back to the airport and boarded the next flight back to L.A.

Chaos is not something around us . . . it is something in us. Any chaos around us is simply a manifestation of the chaos within. That is why chaos follows some people wherever they go. They can't leave it behind because wherever they find themselves, that's where they are and there the chaos is as well. And so it was with me.

Life began moving so quickly that it was hard to keep up with it. Flying 3,000 miles and then turning around and flying back—that seemed normal. I'd begun to live somewhere out of my body and started watching the girl that everyone called by my name, unable to direct her, unable to advise her, unable to help her at all. I just watched her experience her circumstance with not as much compassion for her as certainly I should have had, because in order for her to go through it, to a great degree I had to detach myself . . . from myself.

When I got home, Michael was waiting for me with a velvet box.

Inside was a gorgeous ring, an emerald surrounded by diamonds, and a matching necklace. It was beautiful, but I'd begun to associate these gifts with difficult times. They always seemed to arrive when he felt guilty.

"I'll be better, you'll see," he said. I just shook my head and walked back to our bedroom. I put the ring and necklace with all the other "peace offerings."

I remember my grandmother talking about the nights her straying husband hadn't come home. "I would walk the floor all night with 'the headache,' waiting for Newby to get home. I'd grip the palms of my hands with my teeth to relieve the pain in my head, conjuring up in my mind all the many things that could have happened to him. Sometimes I'd bite my hands so hard they bled. I always kept BC Powder. But BC didn't work on those nights . . . 'cause BC doesn't work on that kind of headache."

When I was a child, I didn't really understand the story, didn't understand the terror of these imaginings that a woman might conjure up, or all of the images that can go through the mind of a woman. But the first night Michael didn't come home, I heard her words all over again and understood them for the first time. No wonder BC Powder didn't work on "the headache" that wasn't really a headache at all. It was a heartache, the pain of disappointment and betrayal, and no pill or powder can really relieve that.

That night, I paced the floor as I phoned everyone we knew, every place he might be. I told myself that he was fine; if something had happened, someone would have called me, I would have heard by now. That left only one thing. I didn't bite my palms until they bled, but I could almost feel the sorrow pour from my broken heart.

We were supposed to meet a journalist and his camera crew at our house in Bernardsville. Not long after *Head of the Class* debuted,

James Grant had done a story on me for *TV Guide*. Now he'd been assigned to write a cover article about us for *Life* magazine.

James had always made me feel comfortable, which was not an easy feat considering the many stories that less scrupulous journalists had concocted . . . with help, I am sure. After all hadn't I been warned that my life would be made miserable? But James was a journalist I felt I could trust. Over the past few weeks, he'd spent a lot of time with both of us. He spent time with us in L.A., he had gone to a fight with us in Atlantic City, and this weekend in Bernardsville he would complete the story he was writing. Michael and I were supposed to drive up early in the morning from NYC—and now it *was* early in the morning, very early, and I hadn't seen him since yesterday.

I fell asleep on the couch, curled up around the phone. Its ringing woke me, and I opened my eyes to the dawn of another day. It was Michael.

"Come on downstairs. I'm waiting out front."

I climbed up on the back of the sofa to peer out the window—and suddenly remembered that Christmas so long ago, when I'd peered out the window waiting for the man who never showed up . . . waiting for my father. But, once again, Michael *had* shown up. I saw Michael's car, and confusion throbbed in my head. I was relieved, furious, hurt, exhausted, a thousand different emotions bursting for release. All I could say was, "Where the hell have you been?"

He didn't answer. "Come on down. We're gonna be late."

I struggled to get some control of myself, my feelings, this whole mess. I didn't answer; I just hung up and ran to get ready.

"Where in the hell have you been?" I asked again, climbing into the limo, as we pulled away.

"What do you mean?"

"Tell me where you were last night," I demanded, wiping away the salty tears. I leaned forward to get a tissue from the box next to him on the seat. And that's when I saw it.

He was wearing a white velour warm-up suit and smeared in the most unimaginable places was red lipstick.

"Stop the car!" I screamed. Michael just laughed. Finally he answered my question with a cold and cruel honesty that makes you wish that you'd been lied to . . . that calls into question how much integrity you really have . . . that calls into question who you are, and how much you are willing to concede.

"You know I love you, Rob," Michael said. "Who you love don't have nothin' to do with who you—" but he caught himself before he had the chance to admit the ugly truth.

I suppose he should get some credit for honesty, if nothing else. And while I understood how terrifying real love and real intimacy were for him . . . while I understood him, I didn't understand myself at all nor did I really recognize myself. I could not comprehend how I came to be sitting there and why on earth I would allow myself to continue to remain there. I was devastated and furious, but at that moment the rage I felt could take no other form but a flood of tears. Why did I feel so helpless?

By the time we got to the house in Bernardsville, the *Life* magazine crew was already there, and James Grant greeted us at our own front door.

Michael worked extra hard to charm me that morning, and slowly I thawed a bit, and a bit more. By the time we took the cover shot, my eyes were still swollen from tears shed and unshed but, as he draped his strong arms around me, for a moment—just a brief moment—I felt safe . . . and then I sobered and wondered, *Now who is going to protect me from you?*

"I'm so sorry," he said quietly. "I don't know what gets into me sometimes. I'll never do it again. As God is my witness I will never do it again." That was a first . . . he was calling on God to witness his vow of fidelity. *Maybe we've had a breakthrough*, I thought. All I could do was pray . . . it was as if I was drowning and I had come up for the third time.

I am not quite sure how I managed the smile that made the cover of *Life* magazine, because had the camera captured the truth, it would have shown me engulfed in the deep dark waters of desperation. For the first time in my life, I had no one to turn to and absolutely no idea what to do. I recalled how Nanny would, out of nowhere, utter "Lord have mercy!" That seemed like a fitting prayer for me . . . Lord have mercy!

Things were better for a while. He showered me with love and attention. He gave me the most precious gift of all: his time. And the public grew increasingly fascinated with us as a couple, though certainly that was a double-edged sword. We were invited to the White House, asked to present at the Emmys, and I felt like a princess. We were asked to do a Pepsi commercial, and the day we shot it was particularly wonderful. All the extras on the set were thrilled to meet us, and Michael was especially warm and charming. Lisa Bonet and her new husband, Lenny Kravitz, visited the set. We'd become friends when I was on *The Cosby Show,* and I was excited to meet Lenny. They were a gorgeous couple, and as beautiful as Lisa had always been, she was even more stunning with her big belly. I was excited for them— and for myself and Michael too, because we had just discovered we were pregnant. Everyone told me how lucky I was, and I felt like a princess . . . for that day, at least.

It was after shooting a commercial for Japanese TV that something occurred that made a true difference in our relationship. It had been an early call and we were famished, so I suggested breakfast at the Pink Teacup. Both Michael and I loved their breakfasts: salmon croquettes, hot sausages, grits, eggs, and biscuits. My mouth was already water-

ing as I changed out of the clothes from wardrobe. We thanked everyone, Michael signed some autographs, and we piled into Michael's new
cream-colored Bentley. I thought it was a little showy and didn't particularly like driving around in it but Michael loved it more than I'd
ever seen him love any car.

I was so tired that I fell asleep for a moment on the ride to the
restaurant, with my head resting on Michael's shoulder. As we
pulled up at the Pink Teacup, he kissed my forehead and stroked
my cheek.

"Do you want me to carry you in?" he asked.

I stretched and smiled, thinking about how tender and loving he
had been recently, and how much I loved him. "No, I'm awake."

He climbed out and held out a hand for me.

"Come on, Mrs. Tyson." And I smiled again. It was a bit chilly
and he wrapped himself around me, warming me with his tenderness.

Mom met us there. Once we'd ordered, Michael and I went back
to cuddling. I couldn't recall when I had felt more at peace or more
happy. I wrapped one arm around my husband's shoulder and attempted to slide my other hand into his pocket for a bit of warmth.
Suddenly he stiffened up and placed his hand over his pocket as if he
were hiding something from me.

I forced my hand inside and pulled out a handful of condoms—
three or four packages. I was almost blinded by rage and betrayal. I
grabbed the car keys from the table and ran outside. I climbed in the
driver's seat of the Bentley, sobbing hysterically. The thoughts that
swirled around in my head were as out of control as my tears.

My mother opened the door and got in the backseat. "Calm
down, Robin. Please." Her voice helped sober me from my anger, but
then Michael climbed in the car with a smirk on his face that only
the devil himself could wear.

Why did he love seeing me in pain? How did he always manage to
do this so perfectly? Get me to relax, get me to feel at peace, get me to
feel that we'd made some progress and that our lives could be normal,

get me to trust him . . . to lower my guard again—only to knock the wind once again. How was it possible to go from loving someone to hating them in just an instant? I don't know but I did. I started the car and pulled away from the curb. I had no idea where I was headed. I struggled to gain control of my emotions, but I was losing the battle.

"You shameless son of a bitch!" I was crying, angrier than ever before.

I had trusted him with my heart, and he had done his best to devour me. I had trusted him with my family, and he was destroying them as well. How could my best friend also be my fiercest antagonist? Full of rage and pain, I wanted to hurt him the way he'd hurt me, crush him the way he'd crushed me. Whether blinded by my own rage or blinded by my need for revenge, I plowed into a parked car sitting in the direction his Bentley was pointed. Obviously I was out of control and nearly out of my mind. It never even occurred to me that there would be anyone in the other car—but there was. By the grace of God, he wasn't hurt. He and Michael climbed out of the cars at the same time, and Michael pulled out a wad of cash, hundreds and fifties and twenties. Without counting it, he placed them all in the man's hand. I don't think the man said anything. I just remember him staring down at all the bills, then getting back in his car and driving away.

By now, a small crowd had gathered, and one of New York's finest appeared. I wasn't blinded with rage anymore, but I was still furious and hurt, and I began to walk away. Michael started to explain to the policeman what had happened but he said he was driving and he took all of the blame for the "accident," then finally he just said, "Excuse me, officer, I've gotta go." As he turned to follow me, he tossed the keys to the policeman. "Keep the car."

The press loved the Bentley story, and the public was entertained by it. Day after day there was a new episode of the Bentley story and in the painful drama that was our lives. Michael stuck to his version, that he was the one driving instead of me. Maybe his conscience prompted him to accept some measure of blame. Confusion was

now the master of our lives and confusion reigned supreme in me
. . . I longed for his love and at the same time I wished I had never
met him. I yearned for his protection and I desperately wanted protection from him.

More and more our lives were spinning out of control. *I* was spinning out of control. Michael would stay out all night or stay up all
night, and I would try to keep up. My mother tried to comfort me,
but now she was fearful of his behavior and anxious about mine—
perhaps I wasn't fearful enough of either. Michael become more and
more erratic and unpredictable, kind and gentle one minute, and the
next . . . well, God only knew.

I'd lost the ability to feel fear, to feel anxiety . . . pretty much to
feel anything at all. By now I was numbed by the madness, my feelings deadened by the bedlam, pure and utter bedlam. I felt it was
coming at me from all sides: from Michael, from the media, from inside myself. It was just too much to take in, absolutely too much to
experience, and I was overwhelmed and exhausted.

That morning, I ran away as fast as I could. I ran and ran and ran,
and as I ran, I experienced feelings that were so foreign and thoughts
that were so unfamiliar. I just wanted to die. That was the only solution to my problems that I could imagine.

Not long after this episode, Michael and I paid a visit to a doctor, the
kind of doctor who heals the wounds of the broken-hearted . . . who
repairs broken relationships . . . who convinces you that dying is not
the only solution. He was also the kind of doctor who can help take
the bitter out of love, and help you love the one you love . . . and most
of all, help you love yourself. Without a doubt both Michael and I
needed a course of treatment, some plan for each of us to heal the
hurt—both the hurt that we experienced as a couple and the hurt that
we each brought to the marriage. But we came to the doctor's office

begging help for Michael . . . I suppose because Michael's pain was more apparent.

There we sat, in the doctor's consulting room on Central Park West. It was a dark office, but I suppose that set the mood for baring your soul. The walls were paneled in mahogany, with a mahogany bookshelf stuffed with books on one wall and diplomas lining another. Another wall told the story of the doctor's family through photographs, and the fourth demonstrated his artistic taste: African art and portraits of rhythm and blues singers. The doctor sat in a brown leather chair.

He wasn't an old man, but he seemed to have the warmth and wisdom of one. We'd gotten the referral, oddly enough, from a publicist who had worked hard to discourage a journalist from writing a mean-spirited story that involved the two of us, one of many that bore little resemblance to the truth of what was really happening in our lives. I have experienced how painfully destructive this can be, and it seems odd to me that there is no real punishment for assaulting someone's reputation, no punishment for battering a person's good name. But reputation is what people think of you, and that can be manipulated. Character is what God knows of you, which is the truth . . . and the truth is everlasting. The rest may have entertainment value, but it has no significance for the improvement of mankind or the advancement of humanity . . . it only serves to distract us from our own concerns. No one is ever better for it, and many are deeply hurt because of it.

This publicist knew the doctor well and had firsthand experience attesting to his competency. He told us a little bit about the man he called the good doctor, including the fact that he'd grown up poor in rural Texas. Obviously he'd come a long way since then, and I think that was one reason why Michael trusted him.

At that first visit, Michael sat down in a brown leather chair and, after looking at the many diplomas and certificates that graced one of the walls, he got right to the point: "How did a country nigga like you get to Stanford Medical School?"

The doctor laughed and in a deep baritone voice said, "It wasn't easy. Just like it wasn't easy for you to become heavyweight champion of the world."

"No, but I bet it was easier than becoming a doctor." Now they were both laughing, and Michael was more relaxed than I'd seen him in a long time.

From that first visit, I believed in my heart that everything could be made okay, that this good doctor could fix whatever was wrong. During our sessions, Michael and I both shared our fears and anxieties, and the doctor helped us deal with them. For all the pain these sessions stirred up, our time with the doctor was also filled with laughter and hopefulness. Unfortunately, there were too many demands on our time and too much opposition from the other members of Team Tyson, who feared these visits might just stir up something that interfered with business. So we started seeing the doctor less and less often, and finally stopped seeing him altogether.

———⁂———

But our short-lived experience seemed to have helped us a bit, and my pregnancy seemed to make things more hopeful. We were so thrilled, and Michael seemed more at peace and less unpredictable. It appeared that we'd weathered a few storms; our life together seemed smooth and steadfast and it looked as if we were stronger as a couple.

We were in New Jersey when the bleeding started. Michael and I, along with his trainer, Kevin, rushed to the emergency room. Both Michael and I were terrified. Then Kevin almost fainted when they took my blood. Who'd have thought this tough guy would be so sensitive? But I think that is what helped make Kevin truly tough.

The doctor in the emergency room gave us what seemed to be

good news. Basically, I should not be alarmed by the bleeding, my cervix was closed and my pregnancy was "viable," as he put it. I knew what the word viable meant but for the life of me I wondered how a doctor could use the term with an expectant mother when describing the condition of her baby.

The following day Michael and I saw our own obstetrician in Manhattan, a kind and gentle healer. We had known one another for a very long time, because he had been my mother's doctor too. He took loads of time with me in the examining room and with us in the consultation room. He was encouraging . . . but I wondered if he was optimistic. "We're going to have to keep an eye on you, Robin," he told me. "I'm going to have to see you every other day for the next few weeks."

Michael headed to training camp in New Jersey and I remained with my mother at the apartment. I had no choice but to stay; neither Michael nor I could handle what could possibly happen with our baby. I had never seen such sadness in Michael as when he kissed me goodbye and assured me the baby would be fine and I would be fine . . . "Robin, we're going to be just fine," he said.

And indeed everything was fine for a few weeks, but then my hormone levels leveled out, and then started dropping. Then one day I visited the doctor's office and the sonogram showed that my pregnancy was not "viable" after all. I saw such sorrow in this healer's eyes.

He tried to console me before he spoke the words he knew would be the most painful of all to hear. "Robin, you're going to be a wonderful mother and you'll have the opportunity to have many children . . ." Certainly I had come to realize the power of the word by now. There was a time when I could speak the words and bring my dreams into my lived experiences. But by this time in my life, words in the form of deadly gossip and scandalous lies had been used to inflict near-mortal wounds upon me . . . the words this healer spoke at this very moment cut so deep into my soul that all its sorrow erupted. ". . . but this pregnancy will not go to term," he said. Sorrow burst loose from my weeping soul. I was flooded with shame as

I searched my heart to discover what I had done to deserve this. My heart was caught in the deluge and I was submerged in mourning of my past. All I had ever really wanted was my father's love . . . all I longed for now was a man who truly loved me . . . all I hoped for was the chance to offer my own child the love that I had never had—a father's love. But in spite of all the grief, all the mourning, all my pain . . . I never shed a tear. I simply said to this kind and gentle man, "I guess it wasn't viable after all."

Michael was with me in the hospital room. A nurse gave me an injection I barely felt and told me, "This will make you woozy." She put up the bed's railings, and I gripped them hard, as if I could hang on to everything that was leaving me. Michael placed his warm hand over mine, leaned over that cold steel railing, and whispered, "Don't be afraid, sweetheart." He kissed my cheek through the tears that were now pouring down. The nurses stood next to the bed and I watched the ceiling ripple like ocean waves. Michael stood alongside me, smoothing my hair, kissing me, whispering over and over, "I love you. Don't be afraid."

"You have to wait outside, Michael," the nurse turned to him and said. "This procedure takes only a short while. Robin will be just fine." Procedure . . . she was a warm woman with an uncaring choice in words. *Yet she's a woman,* I thought, *and deep inside she must know what a loss this is to me and to my husband.* This procedure would mark the end of this chapter in our lives, and it would be added to our story of pain and suffering. "Michael," she said sternly, reprimanding him when he stood there, refusing to move. "You'll see Robin again soon." She spoke our names so casually, so easily, as if the three of us were all friends. That shows the power of the media. Between the tabloids and television, Michael and I had spent so much time with people in their living rooms, at their breakfast tables, that they knew—or thought they knew—all about us. "But you don't know us!" I wanted to protest. "You don't know what we're going through!" But my mouth was so dry I couldn't form the words. Michael kissed me again and blew one last kiss as he finally left the room. *This is such a tender man*, I remember thinking. As I recall, that was to be perhaps the last tender moment we would share.

My mother told me later that she walked down Park Avenue on her way home that afternoon, sobbing uncontrollably. This was the same woman who was so private and whom I had seen cry on so very few occasions. But on that day she mourned not only the loss of her first grandchild but an accumulation of losses. She had left an abusive husband and survived, even thrived. But, I think Mom wondered if she could survive my marriage. Certainly, this very private woman had great difficulty having a daughter who was so public. In those circumstances, the things that most people are allowed to do in the sanctity of their privacy can become fodder that fuels public interest and entertainment. All too often that entertainment is at the expense of a dignity that has been hard-fought and hard-won, as in the case of my mother. She later said the Bible was the only thing that brought her comfort during this time, and she found answers there to every question she had.

Mom almost appeared more pained than I was about the miscarriage, but I guess some people are just more in touch with their feelings.

It was difficult not to completely trust a priest. It was hard to imagine that he might not be honest with us, harder to imagine that he might not have Michael's best interests at heart. So when he told me what to do, I did it. When he told me who was good and who was bad, I accepted his judgment, and when he told me who was trustworthy and who was not, I believed him. I didn't think twice about anything he said. He'd visit with us, walk with us, and talk with us, and together Michael and I freely gave him every opportunity to guide us . . . perhaps in the wrong direction.

I never knew that this priest was friends with Don as well. And even that did not trouble me right away . . . it was easy to like Don. I'm not sure who it was that revealed to me that the priest might have been working on behalf of Don and against Bill, Jim's partner. Or maybe it just began to reveal itself . . . so much was going on at the time. But even that didn't seem so bad.

Bill was a cold man who made boxing seem all business . . . but then I suppose it was. Jim, on the other hand, at least had made it family business and I think Michael felt that Don did that too. Don spoke dismissively of Bill taking over Jim's place in Michael's life. "What do they think that boy is?" Don asked. "He ain't no horse or cow that you can just will to somebody. That boy's got to be with someone that understands him, and there's no way in the world that man can understand that boy. No, it's time for that boy to be with his own kind." Don was entertaining, and in an odd way—in his own way—he seemed to make a bit of sense . . . or maybe it was just that he was so darn amusing and so damned distracting.

The priest would talk to me and at first I would convey his words to Michael . . . I just began to understand, actually to feel more than to know, that something was awry, and I felt that to continue would betray my promise to Michael that I would protect him. I knew I'd angered this promoter when I suggested that yet another Don would be a good choice to advise Michael about business . . . that there would be no better Don to help handle money than the Don that was named Trump.

If hell had been quaking, it threatened to break loose then. I had no ties to the man, and I hardly even knew him, but he had obviously proven that he could be fiscally responsible and maybe he could teach my husband the same. The very thought of this Don having a foothold in boxing must have ruffled the feathers of some mighty big birds. The stage was set for all-out war . . . enemy camps were set to do battle and I was caught, along with my family, in the cross fire. And truth be told, unbeknownst to him, so was Michael. Oh, he thought he was in control and he hoped to use this war to control me. But in some ways, he was as ill-prepared for combat as I was . . . in some ways, we were both casualties of war. I was seriously wounded but he would be taken hostage and held as a prisoner of war. Michael would eventually be promoted and managed by this same Don who thought it was time for him to be with his own kind.

And it was that simple. By introducing another option, another Don, I became the enemy of powerful people.

The day of the Spinks fight, we must have made love for what seemed like hours. Afterward, as he held me in his arms, he said, "I know it's been bothering you, what the papers are saying." And it was true. I'd started becoming something other than the champion's wife—something worse. I was a distraction; I was interfering with his career; I was softening up Iron Mike. I didn't talk to Michael about it much, but he knew me well enough to know that I hated it.

He kissed me and said, "I'm gonna make this fight short and sweet, just to answer them. I'm gonna do it that way, just for you."

Barely an hour had passed since we reluctantly let each other go when I got a call at the salon where I was having my nails done.

I had no idea who it was . . . and of course it was Michael. "Are you okay?" he asked.

"I'm fine," I said, smiling. "I'm the one who should be worried about you."

"I know you're worrying," he said. "Don't! Tonight will be very simple, I promise! Just make sure you look beautiful. I love you!"

Then, a short time later, Michael climbed into the ring and gave me a wink. The fight began, and ninety-one seconds later, it was over. Short and sweet, just like Michael had promised.

My mom and Olga put together an intimate post-fight cele-bration. Everyone was trying to get in to see the champion, so it was quite hectic outside, but inside it was celebratory and quiet all at the same time. It was filled with lots of family and close friends who had become like family. I was talking to the woman who booked me on my very first acting job, and I glanced over to see Michael's sister, Denise, taking pictures with Oprah. It felt like all the threads of my life were beginning to weave themselves together into quite an eclectic tapestry, and I loved it because that spoke of who I truly am. While the world is comfortable putting each of us in a box that they can easily characterize, none of us is quite that simple. Yet, I think sometimes we find it comfortable to do the same and place ourselves in a certain box. But when we know ourselves better and we come to accept what we know, then we begin to love the many tints and textures that make us who we are, God's wonderful creations.

But far from being festive, Michael was in a somber mood. "What's wrong?" I asked him repeatedly, but all he would say was, "Nothing!"

Finally, he said, "Let's get out of here. Shelly gave me a cheesecake and I can't wait to eat it!" Shelly was yet another boxing manager who had his heart set on having Michael to manage. I was beginning to realize that while Michael loved being champion, there was a big part of him that hated all of this attention.

We said our good-byes, and Michael and I went back to the apartment. While all of Atlantic City partied, we shared an entire cheese-cake that had been intended to entice. And nothing made me happier than having my husband all to myself.

––––––⬡––––––

Bernardsville, New Jersey, is one of the most beautiful towns in the Northeast, and Michael and I loved the place and the home we'd bought there. The townspeople were especially warm and welcoming. After Michael won the Spinks fight, the town's mayor announced they were honoring him with a parade. Many of our new neighbors had been at the after-fight party and I think they wanted to show their gratitude for us welcoming them into our lives as well.

The morning of the big parade dawned bright and sunny. We had traveled from Atlantic City and when we reached the house in Bernardsville, Michael dropped me off and said he'd be back soon. We had invited some friends to enjoy the celebration with us, and it felt like a housewarming party. Oprah and Stedman were the first guests to arrive—which was somehow fitting, since the lovely linens she'd picked out had been our first housewarming present. I showed her around the house and the grounds. While we were walking through the garden, she said, "This is beautiful!"

Several other guests arrived, including Don King, who was by then a constant presence. Michael still was nowhere to be found, and I was getting worried. I thought, *What in the world am I going to tell the people who organized the parade? Where is he?* I watched Don tell jokes I'd heard a dozen times before, at the same time picturing the townspeople lined up on either side of the street, eagerly awaiting their champion's arrival. I imagined their excitement draining away, replaced by disappointment, even anger.

I was worried sick, but Don seemed completely cool. You knew better than to like him, but it was hard not to. No one was more charismatic, and in many respects, no one was wiser. He was *beyond* shrewd. He lived in two worlds, equally comfortable in both. Like Michael, he'd been raised on the meanest of mean streets, but Don was also comfortable among Ivy Leaguers and head honchos in corporate America. . . . "Only in America," he would say of all the opportunities he had been given and the opportunities that he seized. He knew the rules of both worlds and, more dangerous, knew how to use the rules of one world within and against the other. Finally, Don told his favorite riddle, one I had already heard so many times. "What's the one thing that niggas and white folks have in common?" he asked. As always, before you had the chance to answer or to even ponder the question, he answered it himself, with a laugh that seemed to rise up from his big belly and erupt to fill the room. "They both hate niggas!" He could befriend you and disarm you, even when you knew full well you must protect yourself from him. Smart as you are, he's smarter. I stared at this man with that towering shock of graying hair, and I wondered for a moment just how he'd gone from intruder to welcome guest. I prayed that as Jim looked down on us, he understood and was not too angry.

The hours ticked by, and Michael did not arrive. I tried to seem casual and unconcerned but inside I was sick with anxiety. Oprah noticed and said simply, "Relax." I appreciated the support, but at the same time, I couldn't help but think, *Easy for her to say!*

The mayor of Bernardsville was the only one who seemed to share my anxiety. The plan was that he'd take Michael down to the fire station and then Michael would lead the parade on a fire truck. The parade's start time came and went, and now everyone was watching the clock and counting the minutes. No Michael.

The mayor murmured something about the people waiting for the parade. There was a beat, maybe two, and then Oprah leaped to her feet and said, "Well, what are we waiting for? Let's go to town!" Oprah climbed up on the fire truck and reached for my hand to join her. And the parade began, as we waved and greeted the people who were so excited about this unexpected treat. Then, in the distance, I saw a long black limo and soon Michael's car pulled up. He climbed out sheepishly and joined the parade. The excitement grew; everyone was more than happy. In the end they had gotten more than they could have imagined. They had gotten their champion *and* their idol.

⊶⊷

We all returned to the house relieved and a bit exhausted. And we gathered in the library and began chatting about the parade, snacking on refreshments, so relieved that everything had gone well. Michael, feeling defensive, was full of bad attitude. He walked past us all and went straight upstairs. No apology, no explanation, not a word. I excused myself to go talk to him.

He was in our room, with his back to me. "What's the matter with you? Where were you?" I said. He whirled around and slapped my face, then grabbed me by the throat and held me against the door. "Don't ask me any questions. Don't talk to me. Just go leave me alone!"

I went into the bathroom and dampened a towel to hold against my stinging cheek. I tried my best not to cry; swollen red eyes would surely be a giveaway . . . and more than anything, I did not want to be embarrassed. It seemed as if the slaps were becoming more and more frequent . . . it is amazing what someone can get used to. I would almost describe it like a parent who believes in corporal punishment as if they have the right, and it was simply no big deal. But that is not true completely . . . because it was meant to devalue.

I felt I had no choice but to go downstairs and face our guests. I tried to put on a little makeup; I went to the wine cellar and grabbed a very good bottle of wine. Carrying it into the library, I put on a smile, hoping no one would notice. What I did not notice then, what I would not realize until later, was how quickly Michael's behavior was spiraling down into chaos and unpredictability.

If I had thought there was hope, that hope now seemed more and more to be waning. Now, the drama seemed only to increase at our home in Bernardsville; our home was turning into a house of horror. Toward the end of that summer, Michael went through a period where he hardly ever slept. He'd stay up for days at a time, usually drinking, and if he was up, he expected to have company. My mother, Olga, and I took turns staying up with him and entertaining him. Every so often, Stephanie would come to help, but she was getting frustrated with him and with us for humoring him. Still, it was always a relief when she was there because she seemed to be the only person who could get him to behave.

At the end of that summer my mother, Olga, and Stephanie all were in Bernardsville, keeping an eye on Michael. I was in Los Angeles, taping *Head of the Class*. Stephanie was actually looking forward to being at the house now, since I had invited Martina Navratilova to stay and train for the U.S. Open using our court at the house. Martina came with her coach, Tim Gullickson, and Lori McNeil, our good friend who had now become like family, would be there training with her coach too. Stephanie had actually met Lori at the first professional women's event in history where two black women would be in the final. Lori and Zina Garrison were fierce competitors on the court and like loving sisters off it, and now all of us were friends. My mother organized a formal dinner to celebrate Martina and Lori's arrival, and that evening everyone gathered in the kitchen as they waited for dinner to be served. Everyone in the group enjoyed one another's company and had been friends since joining the tour either as competitor or as coach. Martina had the most adorable little yappy dog that went with her everywhere. When Stephanie called me in L.A., I could just picture the scene, and we laughed about Martina's noisy baby.

But soon the mood seemed to darken. Once again, an event was held up to give Michael time to show up, and once again he kept everyone waiting for hours.

This time, Michael was in Harlem, at Dapper Dan's, an all-night clothing store. It would have been hard for me to imagine how anyone could get in so much trouble simply buying warmup suits, but Michael did. He ran into an old boxing opponent, Mitch Green, and they got into a fight. Mitch's eye was swollen shut, and Michael broke a bone in his hand. I raced back from L.A. to make sure Michael got the care he needed.

Of course, the tabloids ate up this story and feasted on the public interest in it.

———— ∞ ————

Michael's behavior had grown more and more erratic. He was staying up for days at a time, which meant that nobody got any rest—not my mother, not Olga, and certainly not me.

In early September, he drank and played the piano for hours and hours, all through the night. Actually, he wasn't playing the piano at all. Neither of us could play the piano. Instead, he spent all night pounding away on that beautiful grand piano. I begged him to stop and come to bed, and when he refused, I went upstairs and tried to sleep. His antics had stopped being funny a long time ago. Finally, I marched downstairs and said, "Michael, you're making too much noise and you've had enough to drink . . ." Before I could finish my words, once again—*pow!*—he hit me.

"Don't you ever tell me what to do in my house!"

I ran to the den, grabbed my keys from the desk, and jumped in my car. I didn't even get dressed. I just drove, and I didn't stop until I was in Manhattan. When I got to our apartment in the city, I went straight to bed, but I was so exhausted I couldn't even sleep.

Michael called the next afternoon.

"I'm up in Catskill. I want you to come here," he told me.

"No," I said, "I'm not coming!"

"Please, Robin, I need you!"

"Michael, I just can't listen to you right now. I'm not coming."

I could tell he'd been crying, but I was tired of his tears, tired of his anger, tired of the roller coaster of living with him. I was just plain tired.

I had no idea what to do anymore. My feelings for Michael were at war with my fear of being manipulated.

"Michael, I'm angry and I'm tired and I'm confused, and I just need some time to think. Please call the doctor."

"No! I need you, not a doctor. Please come." Now he was crying.

"Michael, you must be exhausted. I think if you just got some sleep—"

"I need you and you're gonna leave me. You're gonna leave me like everybody else leaves me."

My head was pounding. "Stop it, Michael!"

"If you don't come here, I promise you I'll kill myself."

I couldn't think clearly and it was hard for me to stick up for him and protect him and to stick up for myself and protect myself at the same time. There was silence for a long while, except for his sobbing.

"I'll do it, Robin. I swear I will."

"Stop talking like that," I said. Now I was crying too.

"Are you gonna come, Robin?"

I felt trapped and manipulated and lost. What was the right thing to do for him? For me? And if they conflicted, how did I choose?

"I'm losing it, Michael," I whispered.

My life, like my tears, had become uncontrollable. Every day, I read things about myself that made me unrecognizable to myself. But I recall Nan telling me that God knows us and he knows our tears. Our relationship had become entertainment. Now, just imagine your problems and your pain were being used for the amusement of others . . . and you can never say what you would do unless you walk a mile in a man's shoes or in a woman's for that matter. After a lifetime of doing things right, of being an overachiever, I was doing everything wrong. And the thing that was most important to me, the thing I wanted to do most, I was failing at. "Take care of me," Michael had always said. "Stand up for me. Don't let anyone take advantage of me." I was happy to do that for him, and I thought he'd surely do the same for me. But now, I was so worn out that I could no longer keep my promise to him, and I was becoming more and more frightened that he couldn't keep that promise he'd made, when we left Vail together and he swore he would love and protect me always.

"No, Michael," I said. "I'm not coming up there."

There was a pause, then: "Good-bye, Robin. I wish I'd been better to you. I love you."

And he hung up. I called back but no matter how long I let the phone ring, there was no answer. I called Rory, Michael's best friend, who lived nearby. I knew Michael had been talking about buying guns and since I refused to have them in the house, I was afraid he'd already bought some, and taken them to Camille's.

"Rory, does Michael have any guns?"

"No, not that I know of." Yet I could hear the panic in this otherwise calm and deeply quiet young man's voice. "What's going on?"

I told him about Michael's call and begged him to go over to Camille's right away. Rory was the perfect friend for Michael to have chosen, which is not altogether surprising, because sometimes Michael knew himself and knew what he needed. Michael and I had often compared Rory to Stephanie, an old soul in the body of a young person. Like Stephanie, Rory had a wisdom far beyond his years. He had insight and perception, and I think he liked and respected me every bit as much as I liked and respected him. I suppose the thing we respected most about each other was just how challenging the role of friend or wife to Michael could be. The challenge for Michael lay somewhere between knowing better and doing better. It was this void that threatened to swallow him up . . . this same dark abyss that could also devour a friend or a wife, and destroy everything around it. That is the place where Michael struggled—not in the ring, which he had mastered. It was that shadowy place that lies in each of us . . . to a lesser or greater degree . . . for some it is like dawn and for others it has the darkness of midnight.

"I'll meet you there," I told him. And we both hurried off the phone.

But who doesn't want to banish the darkness in favor of the noon-day sun? In many ways, Michael was no different than me or Rory— or you, for that matter. The biggest difference is that his darkness was perhaps a more formidable challenge.

Before I could make it out of the house, Rory called back. An ambulance was on its way to get Michael. He'd crashed his car into a tree, and he was unconscious.

We had failed . . . both his friend and his wife. I don't know how Rory felt because he, like Stephanie, spoke such few words. But by now, I just longed for noonday.

⚬⚬⚬

I called the good doctor . . . the doctor that we had stopped seeing prematurely. I was convinced that had we seen him on a regular basis, he could have helped us *not* reach this point. Maybe he could help now . . . maybe it still wasn't too late. But to heal, one has to make a commitment to healing, and refuse to give in to those who do not understand or care . . . those who surely have an agenda that does not include your being whole, healed, and genuinely strong. Even iron can be eaten away and even iron can corrode and crumble . . . and the man-child they called the Iron Man would be proof of that.

The good doctor met us at the local hospital, then recommended that Michael be transferred to a hospital in Manhattan, where the doctor was on staff. It seemed Michael had a concussion.

Of course the press was there to greet us, as the stretcher was wheeled out of the ambulance and I climbed out after him. The press

always managed to find out where we'd be, and I wondered what tomorrow's eye-catching headline would be in our real-life drama today. Certainly the truth was horrible enough. I tried to block
Michael's face with my body so he couldn't be photographed. I wished
so very much that we could be left alone to live our lives . . . to work
out our problems . . . to make mistakes, to learn and to grow. I often
wondered why they could not find the true story. When I see young
people the age I was then, they seem like such children to me. We
were two young people trying desperately to find our way. And the
"public" is only made up of individuals who are trying to do the same.
So if we were truly public people, why was there not more compassion from our fellow public for us?

At the hospital in Manhattan, it was confirmed that Michael indeed had a concussion. But still the good doctor ordered a battery of
tests, and afterwards told Michael to rest in his room.

I washed my face, straightened the covers, and climbed into bed
next to Michael. And I thought of that old adage Stephanie had
quoted . . ." If you make your bed, you'll have to lie in it." And I wondered how both Stephanie and my grandmother knew so much. He'd
been given some sort of sedative, I suppose, because I spent much of
the evening watching him sleep more soundly and rest more peacefully than I'd seen in a long time.

I pulled up the covers to make sure he was warm enough, and
then I rested my head on his shoulder and wrapped an arm around
him because I too needed some comfort. I was so relieved that he
wasn't seriously injured, but I was furious that he had put both of
us—all of us—through such emotional pain. I desperately wanted
him to get better, but I was becoming more and more exhausted with
trying to help. He was my husband, he was my lover, he was my
friend, but he was also the person who caused me great torment. How
odd to crave comfort from the person who in many ways I was beginning to find most threatening . . . and I wasn't sure what he threatened most. The physical threat that I experienced at times was only

part of it . . . there was also a looming threat to my very being. So much so that I was tempted to give in and just let it happen . . . let what would be, be.

I suspect those distorted, twisted, and confused feelings are not rare and are probably quite common in some relationships . . . unhealthy relationships, that is. But by that point in our relationship, I had little energy to invest in saving myself. What inner resources I had were going into protecting him the best I could.

Those next few days were often more like a party than a time to recover. People came and went just to get a look at Michael, and some even asked for autographs. At times he seemed to enjoy the attention, and at other times he was quite annoyed by it. It all seemed so odd to me . . . *This has to be taken seriously*, I thought. And I seemed to be the only one doing that.

Finally, perhaps on the third day, the good doctor eased through the door. He didn't look grim yet he had a look of concern on his face. "Have a seat, Robin," he told me. And I did, right on the bed where Michael lay. The good doctor stood near the bed and spoke to us both. "Michael, I think I have an explanation for what's been going on, the unpredictability, the uncontrollable impulses . . . I also think that if you make a commitment to being well, you and everyone you love can live a better quality of life."

"What the f—— does that mean?" Michael asked, in his blunt way.

But, he went right on, completely unfazed by Michael. "There have been many brilliant artists and thinkers who have struggled similarly," and he recounted a few, such as Vincent Van Gogh and Edgar Allan Poe. Even Theodore Roosevelt was faced with a similar challenge.

Then, this good and kind doctor turned to me and said, "I know it has been difficult for you too." That is what happens when people suffer; the ones they love suffer with them. That is why being well is a family commitment . . . otherwise, being unwell will become a family suffering.

"But you can get a handle on this rather than it having control of you," the doctor said. "There are some medications that can be tremendously helpful."

"How the f—— am I going to fight?" Michael asked. "Not that I give a shit about fighting."

Still, this kind and gentle man wasn't disturbed, and now he spoke prophetically. "Well, Michael, I will tell you this. If you don't get this under control, there will come a time when you won't be able to fight. Your life will spiral out of control and you will wish you had taken the steps I'm suggesting now."

Then he started to list the various medication options but before he could get a whole sentence out, Michael burst out, "Just no thorazine! It makes me way too out of it." I was shocked listening to their conversation—mainly because Michael didn't really seem surprised by any of this. I realized that this was nothing new to him. All I could think was, *I wish when Jim was counseling me, he had counseled me about this.*

⬤

Even now, twenty years later, there are illnesses that embarrass people. While it is still perfectly acceptable to say, "I am a diabetic" or "I was born with . . ." most any congenital disease, some illnesses are still thought of as a weakness of morals or character, rather than something from which to be healed. And twenty years ago, people were even less sensitive. It is no wonder that someone bearing such a burden would feel some shame because of it . . . shame that they didn't deserve, because they were simply sick. Don King perhaps captured the general sentiment when he said, "I'd rather be a sonofabitch than be sick." The treatment for someone sick is to get help; while the treatment for a sonofabitch is, all too often, a revolving door in and out of prison. And all too often the sonofabitch will try to treat him- or herself—to self-medicate, as I believe it's called—only to find themselves caught in the quagmire of addiction.

Michael felt relieved to have this doctor who, like him, had come from a humble background, give explanation to all that he had felt and much of what he had experienced and we as a couple had dealt with. The good doctor at last shed some light on why Michael behaved the way he did and why he could not control himself. Maybe this better quality of life the doctor described really was possible after all.

—∞∞∞—

We decided to handle this as a family. We went to my mom's apartment and had a family meeting, new family that we were: Michael and me; my wise young sister; my mother; her trusted assistant, Olga; and Rory, Michael's best friend. We'd use this as an opportunity to help dispel the myths about this kind of illness, to reduce the shame that this kind of illness adds to its suffering. As my mother said, "All you need is just one person to stand up, like Betty Ford!" I had to smile at that—it was so *Mom*. By the time we'd talked through everything, we all felt tremendously positive and hopeful, especially Michael.

He also felt relieved. Ever since he was a boy, he'd been accused of being bad at times, even evil. Cus had done the greatest thing for Michael by providing him a disciplined environment for channeling his aggression—the ring was one of the best places Michael could have been as a young man growing up, when Cus took him from a situation that would never have reformed him. Yet the ring had not been the complete answer, and now Michael almost wished the good doctor had been there from the beginning.

When it was time to leave Mom's apartment, we knew there'd be tons of press people waiting outside and we decided to have some fun with them. Rory disguised himself as Michael and Steph dressed up in one of my outfits, and they ran out of the lobby and jumped into Michael's limo. While the press chased them, Michael and I slipped out another entrance and took another car to the airport. I was returning to Los Angeles to prepare for the special *Head of the Class* episode that we were going to shoot in Russia, and Michael was going with me.

⚬⚬⚬

Michael started taking his medication, just as prescribed, and at first he was full of hope and determination. Unfortunately, that didn't last. The doctor had described the side effects but encouraged him to stick with it. "They will diminish and the benefits far outweigh any of those effects you might feel." But so many who could benefit also say they don't like the way medication makes them feel and too many will not stick with it. If taking your medication makes you feel *worse* in the short term, it's hard to keep taking it, especially when so many people around you are telling you that you don't need to take it at all.

And there were plenty of people willing to talk to reporters, doubting any diagnosis, and declaring that Michael would never retain his championship while he was taking medication. Of course, I was blamed, directly or indirectly, for this new blow to the Iron Man.

⚬⚬⚬

The next few days were tremendously busy as we got ready for our trip to Russia. Most of the cast members brought along family members eager to make the trip, and Michael and my mother both wanted to come along . . . though I am sure my mother thought of herself as not so much a tourist as a guardian. Even though I had faith in the course of action the good doctor had prescribed, I knew that healing is part of a process and that this was not an immediate fix. I had been looking for my own assistant, someone who could do for me what Olga had done for my mother—which was, simply, everything. Someone whom I could trust like my mother trusted Olga—implicitly. Someone who, like Olga did for my mother, could be me when I was busy being me somewhere or with something else. I found Phyllis, and she seemed perfect. She was the same age as Michael and me, and her perky, enthusiastic personality and her willingness to take on anything and everything made her an ideal assistant. Plus, there was just something about Phyllis that I trusted. I thought this trip to Russia just might be the perfect time for her to start, since my mother and I both surely could use the help.

I explained the situation to Phyllis, and she was understanding and supportive. Her entire job on the trip was to entertain Michael, and to make sure he stayed out of trouble and took his medicine . . . all of the things that I would do if I had not been working. In mid-September, Michael, Phyllis, and I flew to Russia, while my mother, relieved that I was not alone, was scheduled to join us in a few days.

We'd been warned that there might be a shortage of food, so we were encouraged to bring staples—canned tuna, crackers, peanut butter—for our two-week stay. The collapse of the Berlin Wall was a year away. Still, it seemed very strange to me that a country powerful enough to threaten the world would have so much trouble providing the very basics of sustaining life. The visit made us grateful for the comforts we had taken for granted at home.

Even so, Russia was a lot of fun. My mother arrived with plenty of food to share with the rest of the cast. Michael seemed relaxed and happy, calling the doctor every day just as he had asked so that Michael could let him know how we all were progressing. Phyllis was enjoying her trip and doing a great job at the same time. And I was happy to have my own assistant, yet another step in my independence. Phyllis and Michael usually visited me on the set early in the day and then spent the afternoon sightseeing.

Our last night in Moscow, the American base nearby invited us over for hamburgers and hot dogs, and by that time we were practically drooling at the thought. We had a wonderful time with the troops, and Michael was as happy as I'd ever seen him. He talked and told jokes, played cards and threw darts.

But then . . . that thing happened, when suddenly everything that was fun and funny about Michael turned frightening and became threatening.

We had an early flight back to the United States, and we still had to pack and get ready to leave. When I suggested heading back to the hotel, Michael wanted to stay at the base and hang out with a few of the guys.

"But, Michael, I'll be too worried about you to sleep."

"Rob, I'll be fine. I'm a grown man."

"Don't worry so much," one of the guys said. "We're just gonna show him around town on his last night. And we can give you a ride to the airport."

I knew I wouldn't be able to stop Michael from going, so I took him aside and reminded him that he wasn't supposed to be drinking when he was taking his medication.

"I can take care of myself, Robin," he said.

"I know that, honey," I said. "But please be careful."

So I went back to the hotel and packed our bags, then climbed into bed to get some sleep. I was awakened by someone banging on the door.

I looked at the clock—it was a little after four in the morning. Still groggy, I walked to the door.

"Michael, is that you?"

"Of course it's me! Are you expecting another man?" He was slurring his words and was obviously drunk—but there was a strange edge to his voice I'd never heard before.

I cracked the door open and he threw all his weight against it, slamming it to the wall. "What are you checkin' for? Don't you know my voice?" He stumbled into the room, scattering the suitcases.

I got back into bed and turned off the light, but even in the darkness it was easy to see trouble brewing. He climbed on top of me and began kissing me.

"Stop it, Michael! You're drunk and I'm tired." He didn't stop. "*Stop it, Michael! I mean it!*" He just peeled back the covers and pushed harder against me. The stubble on his face burned as it scraped my skin, and his breath was hot and heavy with booze. I began to gasp for air as he continued to kiss my face and neck and lips, sloppy kisses with no love in them at all. "Stop it! I don't want to do this right now," I said as he moved his hands between my legs.

He sat up and straddled me. "You don't want to do this?" he yelled. "I'm your husband! What do you mean, you don't want to do this? Maybe you were expecting somebody else! Tell me, you stupid bitch! Were you expecting somebody else?" As he had on so many other occasions, he grabbed me by my throat.

"Michael, stop it!" I managed to say. He let go of my throat and then grabbed at my pajama top, ripping it open with one quick and brutal motion. I tried to cover myself with the shredded fabric, and this angered him even more.

"What are you doing, you stupid bitch? You're my wife!"

I reached for the phone to call my mother's room but he knocked the phone away.

"I'm your husband! Who are you calling? I'm your husband." He climbed on top of me again and pinned my hands above my head.

"Please don't do this, Michael!" Now I was crying. Still holding my wrists with one hand, he pulled my pajama pants down with the other. It felt like I was fighting for my life, and I hated him for making me feel that way. I begged him to stop as he undid his pants and began to shove himself in me. I cried, and I stopped fighting, just waiting for him to finish. I was lying there hating his skin next to mine, hating his sweat dripping on me.

Finally he got up and went into the bathroom. I wiped my face and attempted to gather myself together. I pulled sweats and a t-shirt from my bag and slipped them on. I shoved my torn pajamas in the trash and climbed back in bed, trying not to cry. *This can't be what God intended for my life.*

Then I heard loud banging and crashing noises from the bathroom. I climbed out of bed and walked to the bathroom door. I tried to turn the knob, but it was locked.

"Michael, please open the door," I said, trying to sound calm and capable in the midst of my own unraveling.

"Go away," he said. "You don't love me. I want to die. Just let me die!"

I ran to the phone and called both my mother and Phyllis, asking them to come to my room. And then I headed back to the bathroom door. I could hear the silence inside and wondered what he was doing. I banged on the bathroom door.

"Open this door right now, Michael. You're scaring me!" I heard the door click, and I turned the knob and opened the door. There he sat, clutching a bottle of vodka, shoving pills in his mouth. He turned the bottle up and took a big gulp. There were empty prescription bottles scattered all over the floor.

"What are you doing?" I screamed. "Stop it!"

"I want to die," he kept saying, tears streaming down his face. I tried to wrestle the pills from his hand and knocked most of them to the floor. "Look what you did," he said, and then he started crawling on the floor, trying to retrieve the pills.

There was a tentative knock at the door and I ran to answer it. It was my mother and Phyllis, both still in their pajamas. "He's taking all of his pills, I don't know how many he's taken," I said, almost too panicked to speak. Then Michael burst through the door, almost knocking Phyllis to the floor. All three of us chased him down the hall and begged him to come back to the room.

"No!" he yelled. There was a security guard seated at the other end of the hall, but he didn't move a muscle at the sight of a huge, sobbing man and three frightened women running down the hallway. Then Michael was on the elevator, heading downstairs. My mother had disappeared, and I couldn't imagine where she had gone. I begged Phyllis to come help me. She was clearly terrified, and I had to almost drag her onto the elevator.

"We just have to get him in the room," I said on the ride down. "I have to call the doctor. Maybe we'll have to take him to the hospital." Thoughts were swirling around my head, and I could tell by the look on her face that she wondered what she'd gotten herself into. The elevator door opened, and there was my mother already here trying to talk Michael into coming upstairs.

"Leave me the f——k alone!" he yelled, and then he turned toward the elevator. He dragged Phyllis off the elevator and into the lobby, and then started chasing us, one by one. He gave us each our turn as he chased us through the lobby.

"Please call the doctor, call someone!" I kept shouting. My mother made it back on the elevator, just as Michael grabbed Phyllis and then threw her to the floor. It was so strange to see it happen to someone else, to know exactly what it felt like, and I kept thinking, *I'm so sorry, Phyllis. I'm so sorry.* I tried to pull him away from her, screaming at him to stop, until finally he did stop and walked back to the elevator.

Phyllis was huddled in a ball, crying, and I helped her to her feet. We walked to the elevator, and as we waited for it, I could see the man at the front desk staring at us. I hated him for not doing anything. Phyllis and I rode up to our floor without saying anything, just crying.

As we turned the corner from the elevator bank into the hallway, I could hear Michael's drunken shouting, although I wasn't sure what he was saying. As we got closer to the atrium, I could see he was hanging over the railing by his fingertips.

I screamed, "Phyllis, please go find my mother!" As if my mother could actually do something. And then I ran to Michael. The cold marble floor of the lobby was eighteen floors beneath. He kept mumbling, slurring, "I wanna make a comeback!" he said, over and over again. "I'm gonna make a comeback . . . I'm gonna make a comeback." What was he talking about? *What* comeback?

"Michael," I said, as calmly as I could, "you are the heavyweight champion of the world. Everybody knows that, honey. Please, let's just go back to our room." But he just kept mumbling, and as I begged him to climb over the railing to safety, I watched him dangling there, holding on by one arm and then the other, moving with no panic and no hesitation, with the grace of the athlete he was. Was he toying with life, both his and mine? I felt both fear and dread, but most of all I worried that my own grip on sanity had become more precarious than Michael's grip on that railing. I started to scream, and I couldn't stop.

Finally, Michael hoisted himself up over the railing. I ran to him and wrapped my arms around him in a desperate, angry embrace. As we stumbled toward our room, I glimpsed the guard at the far end of the hall. He still hadn't moved.

As soon as we reached the room, Michael raced to the bathroom and threw up everything he'd put in his stomach over the past hours. It was as if the angels were camped 'round about him and made sure he would be safe. There is not a soul that God would not seriously grieve the loss of—not yours, not mine, not Michael's. And He gives us all the opportunity to be saved. Sometimes those angels 'round about us that are sent to save us are hardly recognizable . . . certainly we would not consider them helpmates of the Lord. Sometimes our relationships with them are blissful and sometimes they are painful. But what can possibly be bad, be wrong, be a mistake . . . if it leads you to Him. No, He cannot bear the loss of one single soul. And I am sure that those of us who seem the most lost . . . who appear the most forsaken . . . those are the same ones who give Him cause to stomp His feet, clap His hands, and welcome us home with great celebration.

I cleaned Michael up and helped him to bed. By now, every bit of emotion, every tear had been drained from my body. I wasn't afraid, I wasn't upset, I wasn't angry. I was empty. I knocked on my mother's door, but there was no answer. I walked toward Phyllis's room and heard sobbing. The door was slightly ajar, and I saw my mother on the floor holding and rocking a hysterical Phyllis.

I didn't go into the room. I watched Phyllis sob, but I could not find words to tell her how sorry I was, how much I regretted involving her in this disaster. I saw the bedside clock.

"We have to get ready to leave soon," I said in the doorway.

"I'm not going anywhere with you and him!" Phyllis whimpered.

And I completely understood. If I'd had a choice, I wouldn't go anywhere with the two of us, either.

I went back to our room and finished getting our things together. I showered and dressed, had our luggage brought downstairs, and checked us out at the front desk. I left extra money to cover the damage to the room. Then I waited in the lobby, not talking, not thinking. I had somehow developed a way of going through the motions . . . going on doing what I had to do . . . but feeling very little and often not feeling anything at all.

When the guys from the base arrived, I got them to help me get Michael up and dressed and into the van. My mother had convinced Phyllis that we all needed to leave together, so she was in the van too, still crying.

We weren't a talkative group. Michael spent most of the ride at the side of the road throwing up, but the rest of us didn't say much either. At the airport, we sat waiting for the flight, still not talking. I was surprised, and worried, that Michael wasn't sorry. After all his other outbursts, he was always very contrite, and somehow I always ended up consoling him. That morning, he was quiet but he seemed angry, very angry.

"Are you okay?" I finally asked.

"I'm fine. Just shut up."

I did as he asked because I had little fight left in me.

As we boarded the plane, everyone was, as usual, very happy to see him. "Hello, Mr. Tyson," the flight attendant said, with a huge smile.

I had a window seat, with Michael next to me. My mother and Phyllis were seated ahead of us, on the other side of the aisle. My mother never turned to look back at me. I wondered what she was thinking. I wondered if she knew how sorry I felt. In fact, sorrow was the only feeling I had left.

"Can I get you anything?" the flight attendant asked.

"Champagne," Michael said.

"I don't think you should have anything else to drink," I said.

"Don't tell me what to do. Just sit there and shut up!"

I sat, and I shut up.

She returned and poured him a glass of champagne.

"Leave the bottle," he said.

I told Michael I was going to the rest room. Instead, I went to the flight attendant and asked her not to serve Michael anything else to drink. She looked me straight in the eye, with not a hint of a smile.

"If you think that I'm going to jeopardize myself and everybody on this plane by not giving him whatever he wants, then you're crazy."

I didn't answer. I just turned and went back to my seat. I began to recall a memory that I so desperately wanted to forget and I was filled with a chill of fear realizing that perhaps this was no idle threat . . . It was not long after we were married that I awakened with the cold blade of a knife at my throat. "I'll kill you," Michael whispered in my ear. "It would be so easy to kill you." The tip of the blade pressed just a bit more into my flesh.

I didn't move. What had I done to upset him? And then I realized that I hadn't done anything except witness his embarrassment, and love him anyway. At that moment, he hated me for that. He hated that I loved him, because he felt he didn't deserve to be loved. I lay there actually rather calmly with a knife pressed against my throat, wondering if my loving him and understanding him would actually be the death of me.

He put his face close to mine and continued to whisper his threats. I could feel the sweat beaded on his face and the pounding of his heart, and despite my outward calm I could feel the frantic pounding of my own heart too. They almost seemed to pound in rhythm. Maybe it was the sound of a heart that never feels it's good enough, never feels it's worthy . . . the heartbeat of an overachiever, a perfectionist trying to feel precious enough to be loved. I took his hand and lowered the knife, and he gave in and dropped it. I held him and offered him comfort, though by now I was the one who was trembling. And as quickly as he'd come to the room, he got up and left. I followed him to the door. Part of me felt that I should call out for him to stay, but the bigger part of me was still very afraid, was relieved as I saw him walking away down the hall.

I turned on all the lights in the room, trying to banish the darkness. I checked under the bed, behind the curtains, unsure of what, exactly, I was looking for. I opened the closet door . . . and found it. Every single thing of mine had been cut into tiny pieces. Every dress, every pair of shoes, the fabric of my clothes, I suppose it seems unbelievable but I wondered how long—and with what determination—it had taken him to shred the leather of my shoes.

I thought of the pain he must be in and the danger I might be in, and I felt alone and frightened. This was like nothing I'd ever experienced, ever even heard of. Who could I talk to about this?

I crawled back into bed and lay shivering under the covers. *He actually didn't hurt me*, I told myself. *And he's been under so much pressure. Things will be better now that this fight is over. I love him, and my love will help heal him.* That's the thought I clung to as I drifted off to uneasy sleep. *Things will get better.*

The plane took off, and after we broke through the clouds, I stared down at them, wishing they could carry me away to a better place. I wished they could comfort me and hold me and fill the empty spaces in me.

"Look at me," Michael said. I turned to meet his eyes and was jolted by how empty they seemed. "I could kill you and get away with it. People love me. I could kill you and no one would care." Then he whispered to me, in such a sinister way, "So that's what I've decided to do."

I searched his eyes, trying to tell if he was serious.

"What, you don't think I can do it?"

"No, I think you could do it, but why would you want to?" I tried not to show that I was alarmed. Tried not to believe him.

"Because you make me sick, that's why. I don't know how I'm gonna do it yet, but I'm going to."

I'm not sure that fear best describes what I was feeling. I was hurt and confused, because I knew that Michael loved me. I knew that because we had talked and could talk about anything, share anything, and now he was sharing his plans for my death and in a bizarre way, I felt this conversation proved how close we were. How intimately we were connected. But still I cried . . . cried tears I didn't even believe I still had.

He stopped the stewardess in the aisle. "Can you please bring my beautiful wife a glass? She needs some champagne to cheer her up. Besides, we're celebrating."

After she left to fetch the glass, he leaned close to whisper in my ear.

"Do you know what we're celebrating, honey? My being free from you." He kissed me on the forehead. "Ma and I are going to be happy when you're gone. She'll be sad at first, but don't worry, I'll take good care of her. She'll miss you for a little while, but me and Ma will have lots of fun."

How could he be so cruel? I wondered. *How could I have married this man?*

"Wipe your tears away, Rob. Don't worry, it won't hurt. You'll never see it coming."

I tried to tell myself that he was just kidding, that it was all the alcohol talking, plus whatever was left of the pills. But the truth was that I was very afraid.

I looked at my mother and thought of her life without me around. *Michael is probably right*, I thought. *She'd miss me for a while, but then she'd be okay.* I wondered if Stephanie would miss me. I turned and looked out the window again and pictured myself sitting on the clouds, and it felt like I was gone already.

Norman Brokaw had big plans for Michael. He was confident that Michael could make the transition from the ring to the screen. He and Barbara Walters were friends, I believe, and he thought her show would give us the ideal opportunity to address and clean up some of the issues that swirled around us.

The interview was scheduled for the day after we returned from Russia. Her crew was already there lighting when we walked through the door. My mother thought that under the circumstances we should cancel the interview. We were tired and we had been through quite a trauma. But, Michael really wanted to show the world his house.

I walked into the room that had become my safe haven, the laundry off the kitchen that was also the sanctuary for our beloved Rottweiler puppies, Jessie and Sam. Though Olga and Mom were in the house, still I didn't want to be upstairs with Michael. I stayed up as late as I could holding and stroking my puppies in an effort to soothe myself and finally I fell asleep. Michael must have been exhausted because he slept through the night.

The next morning, I walked to the kitchen and poured a cup of coffee. Michael appeared and wrapped his arms around me. "Get dressed, Rob, Barbara Walters is coming." He spoke as if the last twenty-four hours had not happened—as if we had come from a week of bliss.

I looked at him and he seemed happy, without a care in the world.

Actually, he seemed to be in heaven. After all the things he had said to me, after all the pain he had caused. How would I ever face Phyllis again? How had I been able to face my mother? How would I ever be able to live with myself? I was confused. I was confused and angry.

My mother walked into the kitchen. "I don't think you should do the interview," she said, trying once more to avert something she sensed coming.

"But, I want to show her what I've done," Michael said. He loved that house so much.

"You can show her another time, Michael," Mom told him.

Then finally I spoke to Michael for the first time that morning, actually for the first time since we got home from Russia, "I think we should talk to the doctor and tell him what happened."

Michael nodded his head as if in agreement. "I'll talk to him if you do the interview. Now, go get dressed."

Against my mother's better judgment and I think even against my own, I walked upstairs where the hair and make-up people had set up shop.

Barbara encouraged us tell the truth, to be honest about our predicament. She thought it would be important and powerful and would help so many people. We believed her.

We all went to dinner after the taping and celebrated having accomplished something so difficult and so significant. Norman called to say how pleased he was that we had accomplished our goal and how pleased Barbara was with the way things had been handled.

I am not completely sure of how something that had been so celebrated spun so out of control. But I can imagine in whose interest it was for Michael not to get help, for him not to be healed. But in the spinning of this piece, an opportunity was missed to raise awareness for so many who likewise struggled to be inspired to heal.

Chapter Twenty-Eight

I knew before I said "I do" that I shouldn't, that the wisest thing would be to say, "No, I don't." There is a great power in saying no. "No" can be the barricade that blocks out so much heartache, while a simple "yes" can open the floodgate. We have to be oh, so careful of what we say yes to. I suppose we awaken the moment we understand the cosmic law that simply cannot be broken, the law of cause and effect. After all, every choice has a consequence. I suppose that is what Aunt Ruth meant when she told my mother, "Some men can take your looks"—the wrong choices suck the life out of you, wear you down. And sometimes, a wrong choice requires God's mercy and His grace to survive.

There were signs, red flags that were raised along the road to disaster. But I permitted the fantasy of what could be to outweigh the signs, and I allowed those same fantasies to soothe the healthy anxiety I was experiencing. In many ways, I felt Michael was the most caring man I had ever known, the one who understood me, and accepted me, and loved me. He knew me so well and therefore, most of all, best of all, in spite of all . . . he always showed up.

Despite how brief our time together was and in spite of all the chaos that ensued, my husband was my best friend. In the deepest of ways . . . at the core of my very soul . . . Michael will always be that. I love T. S. Eliot, and it was he who said, "Fortunate the man who, at the right moment, meets the right friend; fortunate also the man who at the right moment meets the right enemy." I am simply blessed for meeting Michael, for knowing him. I live a richer, fuller, more blessed life because I knew Michael.

It's tempting to demonize the people who have hurt us, especially those we have loved. But once we can find the good in the relationship, we can accept goodness in ourselves. Not all relationships should be kept intact. On the contrary, some relationships feed the unhealthy aspects of our personalities, and create a ravenous delight in the unhealthy aspects of our beloved. These relationships bring out the worst in us, reveal the dark recesses of hidden secrets and lies that fester. They expose all that we want to hide from the world, all that we want to conceal from ourselves. Yet . . . "If this is an enemy, surely he has done for me a service no friend would dare."

None of us is pure good or pure evil. No one can force us to become someone we truly aren't; no one can bring out something that isn't there in the first place. For so long—too long—we dress up the pain and cover up the damage. We fight against acknowledging the truth. But if we are blessed, there comes a time when we can no longer carry that burden. We have to surrender and find a new way forward.

It's thirst that makes a cool drink so refreshing, hunger that makes a warm meal so satisfying, exhaustion that makes sleep so welcome, the dread of darkness that makes light such relief. One must know chaos before peace becomes a dire necessity and know the bitter agony of life in order to truly cherish its sweet joy. Being lost is what makes coming home such a miracle. It's true that God works in mysterious ways, and in so many ways I thank God for Michael. It was through knowing Michael that I came to know God.

On one particular day, like too many other days, Michael drank him-self into a rage, shouting at us, throwing around dishes and furni-ture and anything else he could lift. On this day, he'd singled out poor, loyal Olga for special abuse, following her around, muttering "Stupid bitch" over and over again.

One by one, Olga, Stephanie, Mom, and I took refuge with the puppies in the laundry room. Mom would be the first to tell you that, by trying to control my relationship, by trying to change Michael, to mold him . . . into joining the fold, we had become sheep without a shepherd.

I could hear my mother and Olga murmuring to each other. Then I glanced over at Steph.

This wasn't the first time we'd been trapped together by Michael's rage—far from it. But for the first time, she wasn't look-ing at me with her usual softness. She didn't offer me the expected comfort or compassion. She didn't look at me at all. For the first time, she was lost in her own pain. I watched the tears spill from her beautiful eyes, down the lovely face she kept turned away from me. Time slowed, and I could almost feel each tear piercing my heart like a needle. The room seemed cramped and crowded and it was hot, but my sister was shivering. I watched her tremble and weep in utter exasperation and abject desperation . . . and I under-stood. It was so very simple: She wanted her life the way it had al-ways been. For as long as I could remember, my baby sister was always there with her clear mind and sober judgment, with tremen-dous love and selfless generosity. She never, ever made anything in our lives about her.

So there we were, the four of us. In this huge, beautiful house, filled with the finest things money could buy, and we were barricaded in the laundry room, the only room where we felt safe.

Michael started banging on the door, bellowing at us to open up. The door vibrated with the pounding of his fists, and his screams echoed through the empty rooms. I looked over at Stephanie, and suddenly everything else seemed to grow dim. Olga's whispered Spanish, my mother's panicked pacing, the eager, confused puppies all seemed to fade from my sight. My vision became tunneled—all I could see was my sister, my sweet, sweet sister, still weeping. She and I were all that was left in the room. I wished her tears could drown me and put me out of my own pain.

"Stephanie?" Slowly she lifted her head. Her eyes met mine, and for the first time ever I saw weariness in her gaze.

"How long are you going to do this?" she asked. She sounded genuinely curious. "I just want to know how long you're going to put us all through this."

I remembered that afternoon she'd begged me not to marry Michael. Her warning was now a reprimand, and her simple yet harsh question cut through the fog of uncertainty that was paralyzing me.

Guilt rose up inside me, and it was bitter, oh, so bitter. I wanted to go to her, wrap my arms around her, tell her how truly sorry I was. I wanted to tell her that I hadn't meant to drag her into this, any of this. I wanted her to forgive me for thinking of myself—always thinking only of myself—always insisting that my whole family think of me too. I wanted to tell them how sorry I was for putting myself in this horrible situation and, worse, dragging everyone else who loved me right along with me.

But I didn't move. I couldn't, not yet. I bottled up the words I wanted to say, the guilt and the shame that I felt. And like guilt and shame will, they found their hiding place, a place deep inside of me where they could fester. And a festering dose of guilt and shame breeds an elixir of numbness that we can sip from in measured amounts every time we feel pain.

So many times over the past few months, I had simply shut down, stopped feeling anything at all. How else could I have survived? Chaos had become normal. This day, in this room, I had to trust Stephanie's tears, because I had none left of my own. Witnessing her pain was as close as I could get to feeling my own.

Michael was still banging on the door and hollering at me. I could hear that his anger was winding down, and he was reaching the point where he would want me to reassure him, comfort him, love him. "Come on out, Robin. I'm sorry . . . let's get out of here."

I listened to the voice of the man who filled and satisfied every sick part of me, every lonely part of me. The man who seemed to love most the very things I feared were unlovable about me. I was tempted, so tempted, to open the door, to begin the process of reconciliation and reconnection. And then I looked at my sister. Her eyes were willing me to understand how much she believed in me, how much I needed to understand that I was worth more than this, that I deserved more than this. Those eyes said, "I love you. *You* may not love you, but I do."

I heard the banging and I heard Michael's pleas. It was as if I were an addict and my drug was calling out to me, begging me to give in. I didn't care if this moment was part of a greater cycle of destruction . . . it had the power to satisfy me . . . or if not to satisfy me, to fill me . . . if not to fill me, then to offer an instant of relief.

I looked at Stephanie and I loved her so much. She was everything I had always wanted to be—she had the courage simply to "be." That was all the satisfaction she needed. She hadn't accepted the burden of fulfilling my mother's hopes and dreams. She just was who she was. And I didn't want to disappoint her. I wanted to return her to her normal, natural, easy way of being in the world.

Her tears were the only thing that had penetrated my confusion and fog for a very long time, and that's how I knew I could trust them. "No," I shouted to Michael, without taking my eyes off Stephanie's. "I am not coming with you." I spoke with all the conviction I could muster, but it was as much a question as it was a statement, and I waited for her to tell me that I was doing the right thing. Her eyes gave me all the encouragement I needed. "I can't do this anymore,

Michael," I said. "I don't know where you want me to go, but I'm not going. I'm not going anywhere with you anymore."

I heard the loud thump of something heavy—a chair?—hitting the door. I walked to my sister and she held me. Her tears washed over me like a baptism. At that moment I glimpsed what it would be like to be whole and healed and new. I held her close and wiped her tears, but just as I never cried that day, I never uttered the words "I am sorry." Both the tears and the words would come later. But, in my heart, I believe that was the day I began to heal and I began my journey to wholeness . . . the day I took the first step to becoming who I am and had always been intended to be . . . the day I would head home. Though surely I took a circuitous route.

———⊗⊗⊗———

I left our house in New Jersey that afternoon, and I didn't look back for fear that I would not go on—could not go on. Michael made a scene, of course, threatening and throwing things, but I left anyway. With my knees shaking, unsure and uncertain of what I was doing or where I was going, I left. I didn't take anything that belonged to me. Not a car, not a piece of clothing, not a fur coat, not a piece of jewelry or a pair of shoes, or a pair of panties for that matter. I just left. I felt I had no other choice. If I wanted to ever have the chance to live—to feel, laugh, love—there was no other choice. Something simply compelled me, something much wiser than I, something a lot stronger than I.

I did not move on my own accord. I drew on the strength of all the strong women who had come before me, women of vision and courage, women of pride and purpose, women striving for perfection. No, these women were not perfect by any means, but in striving to be the best they could be, they found the courage to go on. Standing on the shoulders of these women, I was being lifted beyond my circumstance and above what I could see in front of me. It must have been my heart that glimpsed a better future, the very thing that had inspired and motivated them, the very thing they wanted and believed in for me.

My grandmother, my mother, and now me . . . I had been unaware of what it took for the women who came before me to simply stand. But then standing isn't so simple. I did not realize the challenges that they had faced simply to go on. But going on is not that simple, either. Experiences are the only things that can make appreciation and compassion part of our very essence. Through our own experiences we come to appreciate all that it took for others to survive. And through our own experiences we grow in compassion for others. And the only reason I even had the opportunity to stand tall was because of them. If I did not pull myself up and accept the challenge, if I were to sink into despair and destruction, I would not be worthy of their defiance and their courage.

I had to leave his abuse and the abuse of myself in an effort to claim the strength that was my heritage and the courage that was my inheritance, to realize the blessings that awaited me. Most of all, I needed to understand why I would deny myself the richness and fullness of a blessed life in favor of a destructive relationship. Then maybe I would be able to stand on my own—not like window dressing for the enjoyment of others, like a Macy's window during the Christmas season, but with formidable shoulders on which others might stand.

Without the painful and devastating experience of my marriage to Michael, I don't know how strong my shoulders would have been. But, surely, this was not of my own accord; recovering, healing, being whole is a blessed experience. I would need God's grace if I would become all that I was meant to be, all He had created me to be.

There had always been a seamlessness, an inevitability about the way my life unfolded. I suppose when a train is securely on track it can move smoothly. When a Mercedes-Benz travels the autobahn with no speed limits, the engine purrs and it can move effortlessly. But what happens when it hits a bump in the road, or when the train comes off the track? What happens when a wounded little girl grows up to be a fragile young lady who hides her wounds, from the world and from herself? What happens when she meets a wounded young man just as eager not to experience his pain? What happens when they meet in the spotlight? In my case, disaster happened. But without it I may not have had the opportunity to grow in grace, so I cannot regret the experience.

There was no longer the ease that my life had once had. I could say, "If only I'd seen it ahead of time, if only I'd realized . . ." but I lacked the vision. Vision is seeing something that you haven't experienced. Vision is seeing something that no one else quite sees, seeing something that no one else believes in. Vision is wisdom, and vision is given us by the grace of God alone.

Grace—now, that is something just between you and God. I've come to believe that you can have just as much of it as you are willing to accept. Sometimes, to be in a position to accept it, you have to be flat on your back, with all your strength depleted, when you simply have no resources of your own. I had no idea about the difficulties that would result from the choice that I was making. I did not realize that I'd have to become more confused before I was clear, experience more darkness before I could see the light, and be more lost and farther from home before I would find myself and truly come home.

I flew to L.A. with my mom and Olga. Stephanie kissed me good-bye at the airport. "I'll be here if you need me, but I'm staying home!" she said. I was expected back at work on the set of *Head of the Class*, and I was determined not to let Michael take everything from me, rob me of my self. I was fighting for the truth of who I was.

Olga sat next to me on the plane, with my mother across the aisle. We hit a patch of turbulence on the flight. The plane seemed to drop, and the pilot would steady it when all of a sudden it would drop again. The pilot's voice came on the intercom: "Ladies and gentlemen, please return to your seats and make sure your seat belts are securely fastened.

We're just going through a rough patch, but it will clear up shortly. We are still on schedule, and we will arrive at our destination right on time." He basically described my life, right then and there. Olga had her own brand of wisdom to offer for the occasion. She told me, "My mother always says, *Dios hace camino rectos con pautas y torcidas . . .* God makes a straight path from crooked roads and pauses." My mother chuckled a bit; I think she was warmed by the universality of mother wit. I was wondering what Olga's remark had to do with our current turbulent trip, and Mom answered my unasked question. "God will work it out," she said. "He certainly does make a straight path to Him."

I craved the sweetness and simplicity of the time when Michael and I first met, and perhaps I thought that by returning to the set and my house in L.A. I could turn the clock back to when we were so very happy. But also, I needed to hang on with grim determination to the things that made me *me*. If I left the job I loved, I would have no chance of holding on to any sense of myself.

Michael bombarded me with phone calls, insisting I come home to our house in New Jersey and insisting I leave my job. His persistence felt more and more threatening. But I knew better than to give up my job. When he called, his tone vacillated between hurt and anger, his words between pleas and threats. My emotions vacillated too. I missed him. And there was a big part of me that just wanted to go back to him. I didn't feel as noble and strong as everyone wanted me to be. The truth was that I didn't know what to do without him. When the phone rang, I felt relieved. It didn't matter whether he was crying or cursing, begging me to come back or telling me how he was going to destroy me with the press as his ally. So much of what was written about me bore little or no resemblance to the truth of who I was or what was actually happening in our lives.

One night, in the middle of a tirade, he announced, "I'm tired of fighting. I'm retired from the ring, as of now."

It wasn't the first time he had talked about quitting boxing. He was the youngest heavyweight champion in boxing history, and it proved to be a heavyweight burden to bear. And he seemed to have a strange sort of boredom replete with fear as he prepared for every battle. But for now, this pronouncement was purely to taunt me. I recalled the good doctor warning him that unless he took being well seriously, there would come a time when he would not be able to fight. This, however, was not that time.

Michael went on with his threat: "I'm only going to fight you." It was obvious that the prospect of this fight excited him.

"Remember I said I was gonna kill you? Don't worry, I've changed my mind. I'm not going to kill you. I'm going to make your life so miserable, you're going to cut your own throat!"

"Please don't," I begged, as if I were helpless, as if he really had the power to do it.

"It's too late! You've made your decision, and I'm gonna love every minute watching you go down."

The most bitter irony was that Michael was the only one who could comfort me. He understood better than anyone my love for him and my intentions, yet he permitted me to be held captive by never coming to my defense. It was as if my captor were also my comforter . . . the one who held my lifeline also held the link to my destruction. I am sad for the little girl I was then, so wounded, so needy, so conflicted. Yet there would come a time when I would celebrate her survival.

My mother seemed to be gaining a renewed strength, and a renewed understanding of her role and responsibility. Not long before, I had seen her in her most weakened condition ever, but in the most recent days, that exhaustion seemed to be transformed somehow.

She explained it when she came and sat at the foot of my bed, after several weeks of this miserable limbo of indecision. Terrible as it was, there was also something familiar and therefore comforting about all the chaos. It was as if the two of us, Michael and I, had made some morbid pact that everyone who loved me was asking me to break, but I was paralyzed, absolutely exhausted from trying to figure it out.

I was tucked under the covers, waiting for Michael to call again, when my mother smoothed the covers just a little tighter and sat down.

"You know, Robin, I have had the strength to hold on because of the words that resonate in my mind: 'When I am weak, He is strong.' This situation is very hard for you, I know. And if you don't go back, maybe it will become even harder. I know you are confused, and I can tell that you haven't really made up your mind." She took my face in her hands and peered into my eyes, attempting to blot out every other thought that might be distracting me. "But I just want you to know that you can have a life. You can have a wonderful life. But I'm sorry to tell you that as much as you want it, you will never have a life with this man. I realize it has been difficult for you. I know just how hard it has been, and I don't know how you have done it. You have an indomitable strength, one that I have never had." I was shocked by her admission, but nearly floored that she thought I was strong. My mother went on: "God must love you an awful lot, and His is the love that never falters and never fails. The rest of us are merely human. He will give you the grace you will need to get through this, and my mother always said, 'God's grace has a way of glorifying the past, validating the present, and bringing us into a marvelous future.'"

My mother had never spoken to me this way before. For the first time it was as though she were speaking to me as one woman to another. . . . certainly she had never acknowledged my strength. I had always thought that I had to try a little harder and be a little more for her, and I always wondered, could I ever be enough. I think as hard as it had been for her too, Michael's presence had brought blessings.

Now my mother leaned forward, making sure she had my full attention. "There are some things that even your mother cannot do for you, things that are just between you and God." She hugged me, and she left the room.

Grace comes in many forms. I think all you have to do is be open to it, and I know that there can come a time when you *have* to be open to it . . . a time when you realize there is no possible way you can go forward of your own accord.

I felt so sorry for causing her so much hurt. And I felt so sorry for wanting Michael still. I felt so much grief for not listening to her initially, and heartbroken that I had ever agreed to talk to him. And yet I loved him, or craved him, still. I had no strength of my own, no resolve of my own, no dignity of my own, but I knew that she loved me and that I could trust in her love for me. I had to, because I had no love for myself.

I filed for divorce the next day.

Now, the quaking hell that had broken loose would find its way on earth—the tabloids became more of a nightmare.

One afternoon, I was in my bedroom but I could hear my mother as she spoke on the phone. Her words were sharp, cold, so deliberate—like the scalpel of a surgeon. "Reuben, you've never given her a thing. I can't imagine that you would ask her for something now, no matter how dire your circumstances." There was a pause, in which he must have said something because she said, "You couldn't afford to give her time either?" She paused again, and then said, "So now let me finally understand. Not having a job is what kept you from loving your children? Well, if that's the case, if I were you I would damn sure have found some work somewhere. I'll let you talk to Robin now and you can ask her yourself."

I was reluctant to really have a conversation with him, but I took the receiver and said, "Hello?"

"How are you?" he asked. It was the first time, since that day he last appeared when I was in college, that I'd heard his voice. And before I had the chance to answer, he said, "I keep getting calls from those tabloid newspapers. They keep asking me about you, and they even offer me money. I could sure use the money . . . but I thought I would just ask you for it instead."

My answer was almost as stunned as my mother's had been. "Well, that's good," I said. "Because you don't know anything about me." I handed Olga the phone. "Would you send him a check?" I asked her.

With far less emotion than I'd ever felt towards him, I realized how pathetic he really was. He could not be nearly as broke as his spirit, which must be broken beyond repair. He may have fathered me but he had little to do with me beyond that. I think that is when I began to stop wanting his love, or expecting him one day to love me. I was no more his daughter than he was my father.

Chapter Twenty-Nine

Oprah once told me, "If we knew better, we'd do better." Without a doubt! And knowing is not completely an intellectual knowing; it is more often the deepest purest knowing where we experience the consciousness of the "all-knowing," when our understanding is in harmony with the Truth. Our realization is in accord with the Almighty. Then our will, our ways, and our words are filled with wisdom. Now this Power surely has wisdom greater than ours. And this Power has a plan that we would not have the imagination to dream or the audacity to put in place.

I longed for the truth, to immerse myself in it and know that it does matter. When acting is done well, it is filled with truth, and I craved truth. When acting is done well, nothing is more satisfying for an actor. The Cicely Tyson kind of acting, the Meryl Streep kind of acting—to me, they epitomized truth.

I could hide in other characters, and I felt safe enough to explore the truth of what I was feeling through those different characters. So I wanted to lose myself in my craft and decided to enroll in a good acting class. I knew it would give me the occasion to explore myself, and if that became too challenging, it would give me the chance to hide from myself.

When I saw Brad on the first day of class, the word that came to mind was "beautiful." He was lovely to look at, but the real joy was watching him search for the truth in his sincere, open, vulnerable way. That had a greater impact on me, and impressed me more, than his obvious good looks. It was impossible not to notice him. And it was a pleasure to find myself paying attention to another man even in passing. I never expected that.

I also never expected to be working with him within a week. But then I walked onto the *Head of the Class* set, and there he was. The producer introduced this young actor, Brad Pitt, to the cast, and he called each of us by name. We smiled at each other, and it was like coming into the sunshine from a gloomy, cold place. I needed him in my life. He was heaven-sent. He was kind and gentle and understanding, with a playful sense of humor. The time I spent with Brad was such a wonderful respite from all I'd been through—he was so comforting, encouraging of all my career aspirations, never dominating, never controlling. I just basked in the lighthearted fun and deep sincerity that surrounded him.

But even in this new, sweet relationship, public opinion intruded. When we'd walk hand in hand on the street, guys would say "Don't give up on the brothers yet, Robin!" Brad would laugh in that easy way of his, never taking it seriously. Though we were fellow Sagitarians we were opposites, he and I. I was wound tight enough for the both of us, and he was so laid-back. Not even hostility from the world heavyweight champion bothered him.

One evening, we had just come back from dinner when Michael came up behind us. I quickly ushered Brad into the house, afraid of what Michael might do. He yelled in my face, "I know you don't want that white boy!" But Brad wasn't fazed at all.

On occasion, Michael would call in the wee hours of the night threatening to come over. Most of the time, we would hurriedly leave my house for fear that Michael would make good on his threat. Brad seemed to take it all in stride, and he never made me feel guilty. Instead, he'd hold me in a quiet, consoling way.

It was difficult to accept his easy, quiet, generous love when I'd been so used to something else, and I still had too much healing to do to accept anything genuine from anyone. I had too much to learn still, but it was nice to have a glimpse of the way things could be—*should* be. But I knew that this heavenly man, much like my sister, shouldn't be drawn into the hellish experience that was still my daily reality.

I began coping with my fear and anxiety by running away, though I told him I had discovered a new sense of adventure in myself. It was Brad who put me on a plane to Paris. He gave me a silver bracelet that he took right off his arm. I cherished it more than any diamond that had been given to me to make amends, because this man who was oh, so free, meant it as a symbol of freedom for me. He kissed me good-bye and I knew that he hoped I could finally find the freedom to be free.

Traveling became my means of escape. I ran to historic places, romantic places, exotic places . . . I just kept running, to some of the most remote and foreign places on the face of the earth. I only stopped when I was offered a job, such as the role of Imabelle in *A Rage in Harlem.*

What a wonderful cast and a magnificent project! And for a moment making this film stirred my excitement and reminded me of the pleasure life can offer. Director Bill Duke was so patient with me, such an advocate for my talent. He taught me so much.

What a privilege it was to work with Forest Whitaker. He's both a consummate professional and a wonderful person, an old soul. But I was awestruck to be working with Gregory Hines. He was the greatest tap dancer of his generation, a crucial figure in the evolution of dance, but also guardian of its heritage and tradition. That generation seemed to be full of folks who knew they had a job, accepted that they had a purpose, and were simply in sync, it seemed, with God's plan . . . and then us colored folks, even as children, willingly accepted the struggle but not as a burden, but as a privilege.

Gregory Hines was an inspiration to my mother in her early years in Harlem. In fact, he was an inspiration to the whole neighborhood . . . he set them all on fire with hope and it wasn't long before little Gregory was seen and loved by all America.

But if he was an inspirational icon for my mother, my grandmother's interest was a little more basic. One day when I called Nan from the set, she joked, "Don't try to take my man, now!"

"Nan, he's married and anyway he's much too young for you," I teased.

"Oh, Robin! Don't be such a Miss Priss." She always thought I was a bit of a stick-in-the-mud.

But before long sadness and guilt would creep back in, anxiety and fear would rise up in me like morning sickness, and I would struggle to fake it, wondering if there would ever come a time when I could truly make it.

Miramax Films produced *Rage*, and Harvey Weinstein became a good friend. One night, the phone rang, and before I could even say hello, Harvey was booming, "We've been nominated for the Palme d'Or! We're going to Cannes!"

This was a time when I immersed myself in my work, and allow myself to become absorbed in what I loved to do. I felt willing but I did not feel able. Even my mother, who had not exactly embraced my choice of career, urged me to keep my nose to the grindstone. "Acting is what you do. It's what you love, it's who you are." She'd finally realized—and accepted—why I hadn't wanted to go to med school. Yet still—what I once loved, what once gave me such satisfaction required so much more effort and provided so much less pleasure.

On the heels of *Rage*, I jumped right into *Boomerang* with my old friend Eddie.

There was a time when this was all I had dreamed of, and all that I could have wanted. But it was so hard to simply go on when the people that I loved had been so hurt by my choices . . . those same people who had rescued me felt their job was not complete, and they still kept watch over me. I had absorbed the time, attention, and love of a lot of good people. The guilt was overwhelming. But my guilt, my fear, my anxiety, like so much else, had little to do with reality.

Mom seemed somehow to be more focused on herself. She took a sabbatical from work and studied formative spirituality at Duquesne University. Leave it to Mom to make lemons out of lemonade. She said she knew there was a miracle to be had in the midst of our family crisis, and she was going to discover it.

I suppose my guilt hid from me the reality of what was occurring, but more and more I felt guilty and I punished myself and beat myself up for being so selfish. The only choice they'd made was to love and support me, and it had been so costly to them—at least, in my perception. Losing your privacy can be tantamount to losing your life, or at least the life you had always lived. There is almost nothing that can prepare you for the loss involved in becoming a public person. But what I didn't know then, what I would have to experience for myself, is the fact that sometimes we have to be shaken loose from a life we know in order to live a life of purpose.

I spent so much of my time and energy attempting not to live in the moment, trying to fix the past, which only added to my sadness because my here and now was a dream come true.

My relationship with my husband brought me to a place where I had to get help if I was ever going to be whole. I found myself in the same doctor's office, the doctor I had seen with Michael. I just knew the good doctor understood me then, and I was confident he would understand me now. It was a relief not to have to start from the beginning with a stranger. We talked a little about my marriage, but only a little. We mostly talked about my life. He helped me to recall who I'd always been and who I was intended to be—the true me, the essence of me that could not be destroyed by a neglectful parent or an abusive spouse.

I talked to him about the time I'd gone to visit my father in Kentucky and what had happened, and I talked about just how painful that was. I talked about the conversation with my mom when I returned home. And I know that my face must have lit up when I talked about what it had felt like to have my grandfather call me "Princess" over and over again. And I wondered why my father hadn't felt that I was a princess. For a moment I wondered to myself, but then had the courage to voice my wondering . . . what had I done wrong? I listened to that kind doctor when occasionally he would respond, and with every response it was as if he would give me a key and just a little bit of courage to unlock my pain. With each door set ajar and each wall torn down, I became daring enough to approach yet another. And he gave me the gentle assurance that I was indeed becoming who I had always been intended to be.

We talked about my grandmother having had the courage to leave everything that was familiar; to leave with two little girls must have taken more courage than I knew . . . at least more than I knew then. And as unsure as she might have been, as afraid as she must have been . . . she found the courage for a new beginning . . . and found herself in a new place, in spite of all she had been through. There she was in a new home and with a new beginning, and she would be the first to tell you it was by grace.

I never knew what she meant then, but I knew there must have been something that she clung to and counted on. I knew that "Grace" was not only who she was . . . for me and Stephanie and Melanie and Jason too, all of her grandchildren, grace was *what* she was. When things got tough, too tough even for her, she'd cast her gaze upward. "Not by my might," she would say, her fists clenched and pointed toward heaven, as if she could inject the heavenly power into her circumstances. We never asked a lot of questions. We just accepted that Nanny had a special relationship with God, and he was as real to her as any one of us were.

I talked about my mother and all that she had shared with me and I thought about all that she had chosen not to share with me, and for the first time, I thought of her as a woman, separate from being a mother . . . *my* mother. For the first time, I could think of her simply as a woman and all that being a woman alone demands.

My thoughts took on words, and the words rolled off my tongue so easily with this man, the doctor. He said very little. He seemed to know there was little need for him to talk. Slowly, I began to replace my regret with gratitude. And I did feel oh, so grateful, as if I had been awakened from a deep sleep . . . as if I had come out of a bad dream.

I don't know if every therapist helps make you aware of God's presence in your life, and I don't know if every counselor makes the grace of God in one's life so apparent, but this one surely did. The good doctor somehow even revealed to me the grace in my marriage and the gift my husband had given me. One day he leaned forward in his seat and said, "If you ever have fallen on your knees in utter helplessness and cried out to God for the strength to get up . . ." And he leaned just a little bit closer, making sure I didn't miss a word. "You have to thank whoever put you on your knees and made the introduction." And he reared back in his seat and let out that warm, infectious, baritone laugh. And I couldn't help but laugh right along with him. In spite of the overwhelming pain and wretched darkness that had brought me here. In spite of feeling my only recourse was to die. In spite of those thoughts of death bringing me my only relief.

My mother once put it, quite eloquently, in a note she wrote to me while she was in Pittsburgh, studying at Duquesne:

> *There are times in our lives when we fall into darkness.*
> *The lonely weight of sinking stillness, of isolation, cleverly fools*
> *us into believing the agony is not only unique to us, but is ours*

to bear alone. Surely we are not alone. There exists a universal truth in the confusion of uncontrollable change, in the fear of uncertainty, in the torture of sleeplessness, in the "dark night" of our souls. We are certainly not alone. It is a time when we are joined by millions of others who suffer this modern day plague, commonly known as depression, and above all else, it is the time when we are sought by God . . . who since the beginning of time has used this "dark night" to bring souls to Him. All God wants is for us to grow . . . to grow in love, to grow in wisdom, to grow in faith, to grow in joy . . . to grow in grace. The growth and maturity of the human spirit is a lived experience; it cannot be taught and is not told. The realization of God's love and mercy is one that we live into as we experience the living parables of our lives, endure the sufferings of our lives, and cherish every miracle of our lives . . .

She had been determined and she had indeed discovered the miracle in our crisis. And it seemed that I had finally fallen into my pain after so very many years of denying it—long before I ever met Michael.

God would not let my story end in my own self-destruction. God let me live to tell my story of redemption and my long journey home.

Chapter Thirty

When we were a bit further along in our process, when my tears were not so bitter and my laughter a bit more sweet, the good doctor asked, "If you are not inspired by the realization of a dream, could it be that your dreams are changing?" Maybe there really is something to that biological clock after all.

I wanted nothing more than a child of my own. Now, surely that is a dream inspired by God. All of the work, all of the effort, all of the love that goes into rearing and raising a child . . . since it is more work and effort and love than is humanly imaginable, surely motherhood must be God-inspired. And that is what I dreamed of, what I prayed for . . . all I wanted. In October 1993, God answered my pleas with a token of mercy and love for me: a beautiful baby boy.

Certainly I learned from my family that becoming a public person should be a matter of choice. I will not make that choice for my children. It's my responsibility to protect them as best I can. What I am willing to share about them is how precious they are to me, proof that God is merciful and forgiving. My time with the good doctor helped ease my anxiety, relieve my guilt, and prepare me for my new dream and my greatest gift. . . . God is good!

I named my son Buddy, because in all of its sweet simplicity, the name meant so very much to me. It simply said "friend," and there is no greater compliment that can be given than to declare someone a "friend" . . . there is no deeper expression of gratitude that can be given than "friend" . . . there is no greater love than the love of a true friend. The word promises loyalty and commitment and a love that is binding. I would have him and he would have me as we faced all of the joys of the world and all of its sorrow. Buddy—I loved him so, with his big chestnut-colored eyes and his round, bald head, and his crooked toothless smile that set my broken heart afire. It wasn't until he turned that serene infant gaze on me that I realized how much of my heart was intact and ready to love. It wasn't until I saw his smile that I realized I could be happy again. Healing is just that simple; though it is a process, it seems to happen in an instant. Buddy made life worth living. Buddy made life better than good; somehow he made me feel safe. Loving him was so safe, and his love for me just felt like the love of God, like being showered in the love of God.

Seeing the world through his innocent, almond-shaped eyes, I began to trust in the world again. He restored the honesty and purity that had been such a part of my life. I decided I didn't want to work, at least not yet. I would use this as an opportunity to immerse myself in healing, to understand what had happened to me and what I was feeling, to decide how I would grow and go on. Maybe I too could find the miracle in my crisis. And, anyway, I just wanted to be with Buddy and I wanted him to be with me. I decided I wouldn't take on another project, not just yet. I was determined to be the best mother I could possibly be.

In the spring of 1994, I found the most charming house on one of the most charming islands in America, if not the world. I had been there on many occasions for the annual tennis tournament. It seemed so peaceful and so ideal for my beautiful little boy and me. Buddy and

I moved from Los Angeles to a small town in South Carolina. I would focus on loving him, on accepting all the love he had to give me.

"We're going to be very happy here," I told him. I lifted him from the car seat and placed him on my hip, which I called his saddle. He fit so comfortably there. The house was fun and full of light—perfect. We sat in his new room for hours, trying to decide just the right color for the walls. We painted it the perfect baby blue, and we hung giant letters on the wall: Buddy's World.

We were very relaxed, me in my beloved sweats and Buddy in just his diaper. Never ever did he wear shoes. Those precious, plump, little feet were as wide as they were long; they seemed to reject shoes, and I never insisted. It was fine with me—they were much easier to cover with kisses that way.

We'd wake up early in the morning and go to the beach to feed the seagulls. I'd write during his naps, searching for the words to explain to myself what had happened, what I had gone through, and why. I did a lot of cooking—well, at least my idea of cooking. I come from a family of absolutely incredible cooks, and I have no idea why I didn't inherit the gift. Everyone has always teased me about my food. But my Buddy didn't mind. His favorite was a special ratatouille just filled with vegetables. He gobbled it up, and I made it for him nearly every day. It felt good to say, "I'm making your favorite!" and watch his eyes light up.

In those early months, when Buddy sat in his baby seat cooing and gurgling away, I began to see the world again, but in a completely different way. Through Buddy's eyes everything was spectacular . . . awesome and filled with love. The white moon ball in the big black sky—amazing. Buddy chasing our furry Persian cat, Blue, crawling around the house and begging Blue to play—awesome. Putting Buddy to bed in that baby blue room that told us every night it was "Buddy's World"—pure love. Most incredible of all was the realization that God had indeed forgiven me, given me another chance to see the world through the eyes of a child . . . my child.

Buddy was beginning to walk when I got a call from a producer everyone respected named Ed. Weinberger. He'd produced many episodes of *The Mary Tyler Moore Show, Taxi, The Cosby Show*, and other hits, and he wanted me to join a new show he was doing called *Sparks*. I watched Buddy as I toyed with the idea of returning to work. *Are you ready?* I asked myself as Ed. pled his case. Could I face my doubts with Buddy on my hip? No doubt about it—yes!

So the two of us, along with Blue, boarded a flight to L.A. My Buddy and I were beginning to see the world together.

Sparks was everything that Ed. had promised. I'll never forget the day that Buddy and I walked into what I thought was my dressing room. Instead, the wonderful crew had turned it into a playland paradise filled with stuffed animals and toys. I don't know who was happier, me or Buddy. My castmates Miguel Nuñez and Terrence Howard were more than fun. We cut up like kids on the set for the entire run of the series. Kym Whitley lit up the set not only with her indescribable beauty but with her lightning sense of humor. I made friends for life on that set. It was a blessing in every possible way—the perfect way to reenter the world.

Sometimes we rush and take matters into our own hands. Sometimes we don't pray for the guidance we need. But the little missteps along the way only serve to reinforce our dependency on the Lord. The good doctor's prescription for healing included keeping a journal and reading healing texts. "You'll notice that when you read the words of a person who has healed, it will encourage your own healing," he said. "There is a common language spoken of the broken heart that has healed." Melody Beattie was someone who spoke a language I understood right off the bat, and certainly Marianne Williamson's writings spoke deeply to my soul.

The stories I'd heard my whole life suddenly took on new meaning. It was almost as if, generation after generation, the same person was reborn, with an opportunity to heal wounds, strengthen the spirit, live life anew . . . as if it were simply God's plan for perfecting His people. My respect for the strong women who came before me grew, and I began to realize that many of my strengths were gifted by them. It was as though I was being given the opportunity to apply their strengths, their character, their courage in the light of newfound freedom today. And I cherished all they had given me. I had always thought that my grandmother hadn't lived much because my memory of her was in the home: cooking, cleaning, taking care of us. But I realize now that Nanny lived more than most because she loved more than most. I realize that loving is the very heart of living. It waters the wilted flower or the wilted spirit. It smoothes the wrinkles from a dress or from a brow furrowed with fear. Love can take a few blows, but most of all, it protects us from the blows that are surely to come.

Even in my new and improving life, a life wherein I felt worthy and I felt loved, my past occasionally intruded. In the summer of 1997, Buddy and I were in England for Wimbledon. One morning, the phone rang: It was Stephanie.

"Michael fought last night. And he sort of . . . lost it." My first thought was that he'd been hurt, and I was grateful that she'd been the one to call to break the news.

"What happened?" I asked. She took a deep breath.

"He was fighting Evander Holyfield, and I don't know . . . I think he must not have been doing so well because . . ." She had a hard time choosing her words. "It was painful to see, Robin." I guess he was afraid he was going to lose . . ." She trailed off.

The good doctor's words echoed in my mind: "Michael, if you don't take getting well seriously, there will come a time when you won't be able to fight." I hoped that time had not come.

Stephanie said, "I wanted you to hear it from someone who loves you, before the press finds you." My eyes filled with tears. After all this time, I still felt I had not found the words to apologize enough for all I'd put her through. But in that moment I had the right words . . . Love, it is said, covers a multitude of sins.

"I love you so much, Stephanie! So, so much! And . . . thank you. Thank you."

"For what? For being your sister? For being your friend? I love you, Robin. All I've ever wanted was for you to be happy."

"Thank you," I whispered once more.

There was one more thing I needed to say to my sister.

"Steph, how did you know?" Only my sister, the truest friend of my heart, could have known exactly what I was talking about—that afternoon she begged me not to marry Michael.

"I *didn't* know, Robin. Not really. No one could've known exactly what would happen. I just knew you deserved better than you thought you deserved. I knew you were worth more than you realized. And I just wanted you to know it too."

I was silent, trying to absorb her words.

"Try to forgive yourself, Robin. Really!"

My little sister's words gave me the strength to face the day.

In 1999 my family became truly complete with my second son, Billy, and my heart simply overflowed with love.

Buddy wanted me to name him "Spike" after his pet hamster, and I considered it. *Buddy and Spike—yeah, that'll work*, I thought. But when I told my Aunt Peggy what I was considering, she was appalled.

Even though she was already weak from the cancer that would soon take her life, she was the same forceful personality she'd always been. "Robin, you can't name your son Spike," she told me in no uncertain terms. "And you sure can't name him after a *hamster*." We all laughed—Steph and Buddy and Jason and Melanie, her children, and their families . . . all gathered around her, all gathered in love. "Mmm mmm mmm," she said, shaking her head. "Give the boy a name that means something. A name has to have meaning."

Those were the last words she spoke to me. She died a short time later. Auntie never weighed you down with words, as much as she loved them. Maybe she was just more comfortable with them written rather than spoken—unlike her sister, my mother, who so often heaped her words of advice. No, she was a woman of few words, and I guess that is why when Auntie said something, her words carried tremendous weight.

I decided to name my new son William and call him Billy, after the man my mother had loved most of all. Though I never knew him, I loved him too. I couldn't begin to count the number of times my mother had recounted how much she loved Uncle Billy and considered him the standard for all men. Whenever I was skeptical about men, my mother would always cite Uncle Billy as the epitome of everything good, and so I chose his name for my second son.

Buddy and Billy! My golden baby with the deep-set dimples joined our happy duo so that we became the indivisible trio, effortlessly. It was a perfect fit. I knew for a fact that God was awesome. I simply knew that God was with me, watching over me, caring for me, transforming me, restoring me, and I was going to let Him make me into what He intended me to be. After all, I had the evidence of His love. When Billy came into Buddy's life and mine, I realized that God had in fact been with me all along, every step of the way, during my painful journey home to Him.

There was a time when my life seemed so out of control, a time when it was simply a mess. Through no strength of my own, what had been a mess now felt like a mansion. And this mansion has a garden that is always like springtime, because, as the Talmud says, "Every blade of grass has its angel that bends over it and whispers, 'grow.'" I am that blade of grass, and my children are my angels. For them, I live and grow.

Chapter Thirty-One

If there was anything that gave me greater clarity about all that I had been given, the richness of my life and the grace that abounds in it, it was losing my grandmother. I was in London with the boys when I got the call that Nanny had gone to heaven. She wasn't sick; she just sat down in her favorite chair, leaned her head back, folded her hands in her lap, and took her last breath. My Uncle Mike was at home with her at the time. He said she had the most peaceful look on her face when he came in from the other room. He would not have suspected a thing because she looked so at peace, but then he noticed that she was not breathing.

This was the only selfish thing I can recall Nanny doing—leaving us like that with no warning and no way to tell her just one last time how much we loved her, leaving us in the cold cruel world without the protection of her prayers. But she was prepared to go home. I guess we were being selfish by wanting to keep her here. I boarded a flight to New York with the kids, who promptly went to sleep. I basically sobbed for the entire six-hour flight.

I stared out into the black sky and the blinking lights on the wings, and I thought about a conversation I'd had with her years before. I apol-

ogized to her if I'd brought embarrassment to the family. Her response
was so simple, so true. "Robin, people are always going to talk. That's
what people do. You can trust one thing, baby. You are going to be better for this, we are all going to be better for this." I wondered at the time
how she could ever be better. Although I listened to her words, I hadn't
really heard them until that very moment . . . maybe because I hadn't
really believed them until now. I agonized about seeing my mother and
what I would say to her about this tremendous loss.

As usual, I need not have worried about Mom. She had gone into
another gear, planning a celebration of her mother's life. There
would be one in New York, and then we would fly to Lexington for
yet another, where we would give her back to the great mother earth
and to the Father from whom this magnificent matriarch came. Family and friends who had not seen her in years, maybe even decades,
came to see her once again.

Our celebration in Lexington of this wonderful woman's life was
all that my mother had hoped for; it seemed like a miracle in and of
itself. Father Norman held a funeral mass far beyond anything we
could have imagined. Nan wore her favorite dress, the one she'd worn
to my wedding reception, a black dress with a black and white sash.
She had her diamond cross around her neck and her rosary beads in
her hand. On one finger she wore a glittering diamond ring that
Michael had given her, one that she cherished despite everything that
happened later. "Happy Mother's Day, Nan," he'd said, with that endearing smile. She loved the ring because he gave it to her out of love,
and she cherished it because she'd cherished that sweet, generous
spirit in him.

The organ began to play, and a beautiful voice rose up into song—
"Amazing Grace."

We will all be better for this, Robin. Once again, I heard Nan's words
of assurance, and at this moment I was beginning to agree. I held on
to her words as I struggled to let her go. Nan looked absolutely beautiful. She was the last of the fifteen children to be born and the last to

go to heaven. At eighty she had lived longer than any of her five brothers and nine sisters. I hoped we had taken good care of her, because
she sure took good care of us.

*Amazing Grace, how sweet the sound that saved a wretch
like me. I once was lost but now I'm found was blind but now
I see . . .*

We began the long walk from the back of the church to the front
where we would sit near her.

*T'was grace that taught my heart to fear and grace my fears
relieved . . .*

My mother went first, the oldest of Nanny's children now since
my Aunt Peggy's return home the year before. I don't think Nanny
could ever really accept losing her daughter. Then we all followed.

*We've no less days to sing God's praise than when we first
begun.*

And we each took a seat in the pew and faced Nanny.

*Thro' many dangers, toils and snares, I have already come.
'Tis grace hath bro't me safe thus far.*

The priest slowly rose and took his place at the pulpit.

My eyes were fixed on Nanny, and for the first time I realized that
Nanny would be gone from my sight, but not from my spirit. I knew
at that moment she would live on. Nanny once told me, "The greatest gift we can give our children is our walk with God." I looked down
at my little children nestled into me, and I understood exactly what she
meant. And Nanny herself walked so close to God you could almost

see His loving arms around her. Then came the last, sweet notes of Nanny's favorite hymn:

And Grace will lead me Home.

The priest's eulogy captured my grandmother's spirit with uncanny accuracy.

> *Grace is evidence of God reaching out to man. It is nothing we can earn and certainly nothing we deserve. Grace is only God's to give. Then it only stands to reason that it is His to take. Now your mother, your grandmother, your great-grandmother served her time on earth doing His will, fulfilling His purpose for her. You are evidence of that. She deserves to rest and she deserves to sit back and watch you fulfill your destiny, your God-given purpose, and she deserves to realize all of the hard work and, most of all, the prayers that she has put into you. I would say to you on behalf of Grace: Be humbled by the world but not discouraged, for every stumbling block can become a stepping-stone, and when the world asks from you more than you believe you have to give, give it anyway, and you will discover more than you knew and all that you truly have.*"

Then we all got up and took turns thanking her for all that she had given us. It was a fitting tribute to her.

It is amazing how your life can be coming apart, when in reality it is coming together. As we sorted through some of Nan's things, I opened her Bible to Psalm 139, which was her favorite. Nanny always said you had to be a lot of woman to read that psalm and to live it, because it demands of us the courage to invite God into our lives to clean it up—as the psalm asks, "Search me, O God, and know my heart; test me and know my anxious thoughts."

There was a piece of paper marking this psalm. I unfolded it and

began to read it—it was in my mother's handwriting and dated
October 21, 1966.

> *Mama,*
> *I hope that you can forgive me and I hope that I haven't*
> *disappointed you too much. I know you tried to tell me and I*
> *know I didn't listen. But, if you'll forgive me I promise I will*
> *make you proud. I love you so much. And in your prayers,*
> *please ask God to forgive me too.*
> *Your Loving Daughter*
> *Ruth*

I could only guess that this one had something to do with my
mother's broken marriage to my father, because it was written soon after my sister was born. In the midst of all that my mother was going
through, it was her own mother's faith in her that meant the most, because that would give her the strength she would need to go on. I understood completely.

Being a mother became my complete focus. And I felt relieved to
think about emotions and needs other than my own. My days became
like those of every mother. My house was noisy and alive and happy
with laughter and a few tears, the sounds of playing and boys brawl-
ing—I loved every minute of it.

All of my life is about my sons. They consume it and I offer
more. I bow at the throne of motherhood and should a single mother
sit on the throne I lay prostrate at her feet. If being a mother shows
one the many possibilities, being a single mother shows you that anything is possible.

No one can prepare you for motherhood. There are no words for
the joy we feel when our children are happy or the agony we feel when

they hurt. This is God's greatest gift to me, and I will do all that I can to give these two young men to the world whole, healthy, and loving. Because I know that a man who loves God can with all his heart love the woman God chooses for him. When that time comes, I just hope I can stay out of the way. I hope I don't second-guess the boys—or God, for that matter.

I want to do for my children what my mother did for me. As it turns out, my older son developed a passion for tennis—understandable since my sister played professionally and I play enthusiastically and we are very close to the tennis community. He has a gift for tennis. And my younger son followed in his footsteps, both because his brother is the coolest thing on the planet and because he loves it. We live in Florida so they can take advantage of incredible tennis training, and I spend much of my time driving—driving, driving—across the country for my sons to compete. I also spend my time pacing, with my heart in my mouth. And running for PowerBars and Gatorade and everything else they might need.

The life that I have now is greater, more full, more rich, more loving than anything I might have dared to dream. My love and passion for acting returned. Acting was what I had always loved to do. I had no real agenda, no overwhelming ambition really: I just loved acting, and I acted because I loved it. In general I've been able to work and be the mother I want to be.

Sometimes it gets a little complicated, like the day when I had to get fitted for a full-body cast for a movie I was doing with Chris Rock at the same time Buddy was playing the finals of a tournament. The cast was made and I was sawed out quickly so that I could run to sit in the grass and watch my Buddy while keeping another eye on Billy, who always seemed to get slightly bored watching his brother play. So we made a castle out of rocks and we dug for worms or one of the other tricks I had devised to keep him busy. I could always come up with something. And then I rushed back to the set to shoot a scene. Life was good again.

And it still is. I can juggle my acting with their tennis. And when I have to be away, Mom—every bit the loving, caring grandmother that she was a mother to Stephanie and me—fills in. I feel blessed to have her, and for her to experience raising two little boys after rearing two dutiful daughters. And Stephanie is a fun, dynamic auntie who can still show them a thing or two on the court, which they plead for her to do all the time.

⸎

When in New York, I still see the good doctor on occasion. And this was such an occasion. The doorman asked if I would need a taxi as I was leaving the apartment, but I just shook my head, smiling in thanks. I decided to take the walk to the good doctor's office to prepare myself for the visit. It wasn't a long walk, perhaps a dozen blocks or so; I've always enjoyed walking, and walking gave me more time to mull things over.

This was the man whom I'd first met with Michael and because of Michael. I never dreamed then I would be seeing him for myself.

I knocked on his door.

"Good morning," he said, in that way that always relaxed me the moment I stepped through the door. I smiled at him.

"Good morning. Mom will be here soon." Today, my mother would join us for the second half-hour of our session.

I eased back into the big, brown leather chair that had come to feel that it was a perfect fit for me.

The session began as it always had, with me talking about what was on my mind and him asking just the right questions to draw out the meaning of things seemingly so insignificant. The first half-hour must have gone very quickly. Just as he asked, "Have you had any dreams lately?" there was a knock on the door. Mom came in, smiled at us both, and took a seat next to me.

My first response was, "No, no dreams" . . . but then I remembered a dream that had repeated itself over the last few nights.

> *The wind howls, beating against the trees, and the trees all sway in unison, bending to the wind's ferocity. Some struggle more than others to stand erect.*

As I recalled my dream, my grandmother took a seat beside me and though she went unnoticed to the doctor, even to my mother, her spirit was obvious and very much alive and present to me. I placed a hand on hers and continued describing my dream.

> *I am amazed by the strength and resilience of those trees, battered by the wind but still standing. Then I notice one tree in particular. It appears she can struggle no longer and will soon break, be snapped from her roots. But just as it appears this tree can no longer bear the pressure, the wind subsides a bit. There's a moment of peace, and this fragile tree eases back into place.*

I gazed into my grandmother's face, still describing my dream. Oh, how beautiful she was! I think I had almost forgotten that beautiful could be filled with such beauty . . . delicate like the most beautiful flower, yet its scent could last beyond a lifetime, with beauty strong enough for its petals to endure the most menacing storm. I never stopped recounting my dream . . .

> *I watched her—the tree—for what felt like a very long time, before I must have drifted off to sleep. I opened my eyes, grateful that the children had slept through the storm. The morning sky was blue, the waters quiet, and the tree I had watched with such fear, such compassion, was still standing, more erect than I had recalled.*

I took a deep breath and I was relieved to still see her, sense her presence near me, this woman who had given me strength . . . given me love . . . given life to one who had given it to me.

Though my relationship with Michael was the catalyst that began the healing process, it was just one of the relationships from which we had to heal. This was a burden that had not begun with him, but was one that had been generations in the making. It was a cross we had borne for generations . . . but as it is said, "no cross, no crown." It was the same cross that had brought Nanny such a deep sense of faith, given her such victory . . . convinced her beyond any shadow of a doubt that God is real.

Nanny kissed my mother lovingly, and then turned to me. She leaned close and kissed me, whispered loving words in my ear. And as she vanished, her words echoed in my ear: "Baby, I told you, you would be better for this . . . we are *all* better for this."

Chapter Thirty-Two

Some confetti blew past my bench, and the gentle movement brought me out of my thoughts, back to the present. The croissants were no longer hot. And I realized I'd been gone too long. I took in a deep breath of cool, refreshing air. I simply loved the taste of New York, the feel of New York, its brand of warmth on the coldest days and its people like no other. The crisp air only added to the freshness of this New Year's Day and this new, exhilarating time in my life.

I was practically running back home now, trying to make up for the time I had been sitting and daydreaming. Suddenly, I remembered the gifts that I'd had made especially for my boys, gifts that I wanted to give them today. It's never too soon to begin journaling, to write your thoughts and your feelings, and so I had leather-bound journals made just for them with their names embossed on the cover. But I'd been so tired at the last rehearsal that I'd left them at the theater. I wanted to give them their journals along with the chocolate croissants.

I hailed a cab to the theater and—telling the driver, "Please wait, I'll be right back out!"—I ran straight to my dressing room. I grabbed the journals and leaped back into the waiting taxi. I hoped my little ones were still asleep, so I could have the pleasure of their first, sleepy waking moments. As we pulled away, I permitted my-self to look back. This was something I had promised myself I would never do again . . . look back in an attempt to fix the past . . . look back and reexperience the pain. No, I would only look forward with the assurance that the past had brought me to the here and now I loved.

But this time, when I looked back I saw the marquee reading: "*Chicago,* starring Robin Givens." I would be the first black woman to play Roxie on Broadway. Nanny would be proud, my mother was proud, and my children were too. *I am so blessed,* I thought, as I headed home to my greatest blessings of all.

Nanny would indeed be pleased. I hope she would think that my shoulders were growing just a little stronger so that they would be ready for yet another generation. It is all by Grace, I am here by Grace. I have been comforted in the arms of Grace. I have been disciplined by Grace. It is by her actions, her example, and most of all her calloused knees that I have made this long journey home.

I opened the door, excited to see them, but before I could say a word, both of the boys ran to me and threw their arms around me. "Mom, what took you so long?" I handed them their chocolate crois-sants and their beautiful journals. I said, with a smile, "I've been ask-ing myself the same thing."

Acknowledgements

I would like to thank all of my friends . . . who made it possible to put my experiences into words

First and foremost I'd like to thank the only father I've ever had . . . The father I've always had. And though it has taken me a while to know Him and to rely on Him and to trust that He is there and has always been there, even during my most difficult and darkest days . . . This book will lend testament to that. And it has in fact been in the darkness where I first laid my eyes on Him. Where I first felt my hand in His . . . it was because of the darkness that I laid my head on His shoulder and placed all my worries and confusion in His arms. All my hope for redemption in His heart, I thank you . . . My God . . . My Father . . . My Friend for plucking me from the world and placing me in the fire where you could mold and shape me into all you intended me to be. I thank you for sticking with me in my darkest days and shining your light on me . . . I pray that light shines so bright that wherever I go it shines through me and reaches others.

How can I put love and gratitude in words that are enough to fill up the universe? Because that is what I want to give you and still it would be just a small fraction of what you deserve. Through your new consciousness, new awareness, and new birth, I filtered every experience, every thought and every feeling and if my words should have any healing power for anyone it is because of you. How can I say "I appreciate and adore you" in a way you haven't heard it before? My heart and soul aches and longs for the "perfect" way to say these things to you. But time has taught me that I am far from perfect and I'm learning that's ok. So me as your imperfect humble daughter simply says, I love and appreciate you. Our bond has been one that's stronger and sweeter than words can possibly describe. It began before I was on this earth and will last long after we have gone. We've learned together, we've grown together as women, and our souls have nurtured one another. I'm so deeply grateful to God for giving me you. My mother, my protector, my critic, my friend, I love you.

Making a new friend is a natural thing done with such ease when we are young. As we get older we become a bit less trusting and as we go through some of life's crises something as natural and as necessary as making a friend can become even more "un" easy. JillEllyn Riley you are not only my editor, you are my friend. I feel so blessed to know you and so blessed that you have come to know me. Thank you for trusting me to write this book and thank you for making me comfortable enough to accept a friendship that I will have for a lifetime. You are patient yet relentless, encouraging yet critical—all of the things I suppose that make a good editor . . . and that I know make a good friend.

Rob Weisbach, I have you to thank for your wisdom and your vision. It was you who said, "Robin, with a good editor I believe you can write this book." You found me a wonderful editor and I thank you. And I have you to thank for the gentle prodding that permitted me to go on when I faced hills that seemed too steep to climb and the ghosts from the past that seemed too frightening to conquer. Thank you for trusting me to write this book.

Harvey Weinstein, your friendship brought me here . . . you made me feel safe enough to say yes, I can share my life's journey . . . it is time for me to share. Thank you, Harvey, it has without a doubt been the most healing experience of my life.

Oprah . . . the miracle of writing this book began with you . . . your encouragement and your phone call . . . God working in and through you . . . thank you.

Thank you, David Vigliano, my agent . . . you are so smart and so exciting every moment spent in your company is a moment of renewed hope. Greg Gorman, you are an artist of extraordinary gift. Thank you for capturing the spirit of the transcended woman . . . the spirit that is mine. I simply love working with you . . . I always have.

Olga Rosario, no one can do what you do, though I cannot put into words what it is you do because you do everything and once again with this book you did it . . . thank you . . . I love you. Lori McNeil, everyone should be so blessed to have a best friend like you. Thank you for keeping me laughing through it all. And thank you to my baby sister, Stephanie Lynn Givens, for just being my sister . . . you're all grown up and what a woman you are. I love you so. And thank you, Nanny, for all that you have given us and I hope this book makes you proud. And finally . . . Michael Gerard Tyson, may the grace of God abound in you, warming you with friendship, filling you with peace, and may your heart rest assured you are truly loved.